Don't Fence Me In

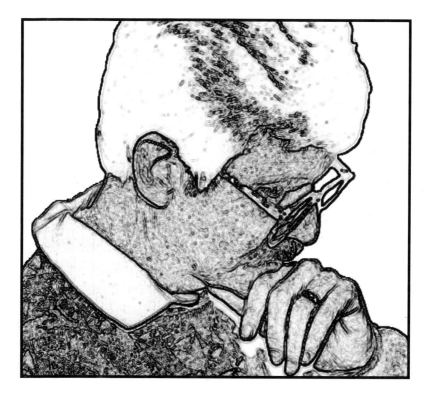

An Anecdotal Biography of
Lewis Grizzard
by those who knew him best

Don't Fence Me In

An Anecdotal Biography of
Lewis Grizzard

edited by
Chuck Perry

LONGSTREET PRESS
Atlanta, Georgia

Published by LONGSTREET PRESS, INC.,
a subsidiary of Cox Newspapers,
a division of Cox Enterprises, Inc.
2140 Newmarket Parkway
Suite 118
Marietta, Georgia 30067

Printed in the United States of America

1st printing 1995

Library of Congress Catalog Card Number 95-77248

ISBN: 1-56352-250-0

This book was printed in the U.S.A.

Book design by Jill Dible

Film Preparation by Holland Graphics, Inc., Mableton, GA

The town of Moreland, Georgia, has established The Lewis Grizzard Memorial Trust to preserve the memories of their favorite son. A museum and scholarship fund has been created in his honor. The Trust is funded solely by donations and museum sales. If you would like to help, write to The Lewis Grizzard Memorial Trust, P.O. Box 67, Moreland, GA 30259, or phone 404-304-1490.

TABLE OF CONTENTS

DEDICATED TO
THE AUTHORS

Introduction

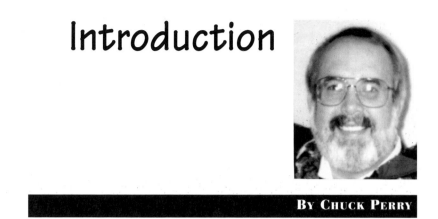

BY CHUCK PERRY

Chuck Perry is president and editor of Longstreet Press. He worked for fifteen years in the newspaper business before entering publishing. In both professions he worked closely with Lewis Grizzard.

It was the winter of 1967-68. I was the sports staff — all of it — for the fledgling *Athens* (GA) *Daily News*. I was also a sophomore studying journalism at the University of Georgia.

My boss, sports editor Lewis Grizzard, was a senior in the Henry Grady School of Journalism. We took classes in the mornings, sometimes together, occasionally hacked at a golf ball in the early afternoon, and then worked from 4 p.m. till midnight producing the sports section. Afterward we would both go home for a few hours of sleep — me to my family home, Lewis to his new wife, former high school sweetheart Nancy Carroll — before getting up and doing it all over again.

It was quite a grind, even for energetic young men willingly obsessed with journalism.

Some nights, when the tension and Cokes and cigarettes wouldn't turn off at midnight, we would sit outside the newspaper in Lewis' baby blue Volkswagen Bug, vaguely listen to a west coast baseball game, and talk about our lives. It was on those pensive nights that I first encountered one of the raging conflicts that tormented Lewis — he was driven to succeed, to please, and to be recognized for his achievements, but he also hated the attendant pressure. Even at nineteen years old, he longed for a simpler existence.

On numerous occasions Lewis would turn to me and say, "You know, Pal, we could leave right now and drive to Miami. We'd be there before noon tomorrow. Then we could sell this car and use the money to buy passage to Jamaica. I hear they've got pretty good newspapers in Jamaica — the British tabloid influence. We could get jobs there. Take naps on the beach during the day and put out the paper at night. Nobody would ever know what happened to us. We would be free!"

Several years later, when he was executive sports editor of the *Atlanta Journal* and I was again his assistant, the "get away" dream setting changed to a bait shop. "I just want to own a bait shop in a small town," Lewis would say. "I won't sell anything but bait and cold drinks — beer and Cokes iced down in a big open cooler. The most complicated question anybody will ask me all day is, 'Do you have any red wigglers?' And the answer will always be yes or no. Nothing else."

But his talent and drive always betrayed him. One more step toward respectability, toward celebrity, toward success, and one more set of pressures.

"If I could just take a whole year to write a book, without having to produce 150 newspaper columns and make thirty speeches at the same time, I think I could write something really good," he said to me. At that very moment, his humor column was syndicated in more than 400 newspapers across the nation, and he had another book on the *New York Times* best-seller list. But it wasn't enough. "You're only as good as your last column or your last book," he often said in frustration.

Like so many creative geniuses, Lewis Grizzard was hammered by self-doubt and insecurities. He carried the additional personal burdens of alcohol abuse, which had subdued his father and often lured Lewis beyond his limit, and by the time bomb in his chest — a genetically defective heart that resisted repair. Even without these additional complications, he was one of the most complex people I've ever known.

In 1983, with Lewis' encouragement, I left the newspaper business and entered book publishing. I was fortunate enough to edit seven of his books, including *Shoot Low, Boys — They're Ridin' Shetland Ponies*, which was dedicated "To Chuck Perry, the editor's editor." Today I am president and editor of Longstreet Press, which Lewis' investment helped to found in 1988.

After his death on March 20, 1994, I was approached by no fewer than six people who wanted to write biographies of Lewis Grizzard. I resisted them all. Since none of them had been close to Lewis through the many different stages of his life, I didn't believe any of them had enough firsthand information to produce a good book. There was certainly no shortage of second- and third-hand information about Lewis (mostly truth, partly fiction), but I felt a good deal of that was better left to a future biographer — one without any personal agenda — and a future publisher — one less protective of a friend's reputation.

A year later, however, fans were still hungry for information about Lewis. They just didn't want to let him go. So I had an idea: How about an anecdotal biography of Lewis — great stories, warm memories, and a few good-humored warts — by those who knew him best at various times of his life?

Dudley Stamps, Lewis' childhood buddy in Moreland, Georgia, and a lifelong friend; Glenn Vaughn, our first editor at the *Athens Daily News*; Jim Minter, Lewis' mentor and father figure at the *Atlanta Journal-Constitution* and the man who made him a columnist; Ron Hudspeth, who tutored Lewis on "street life" and partying in Atlanta; Tim Jarvis, who was Lewis' tennis partner and friend during the lonely years in Chicago; Tony Privett, his manager for seven years as Lewis became a national figure; Loran Smith, a University of Georgia loyalist and friend; Ludlow Porch, humorist and Lewis' beloved step-brother; Bob Steed, Atlanta lawyer and friend; Steve Enoch, Lewis' manager for the last three years; Dr. Randolph Martin, his attending physician and friend; and Dedra Kyle Grizzard, his companion and finally his wife (the fourth Mrs. Grizzard).

In the pages that follow, each of these people shares intimate memories of life with Lewis. The perspectives may be different, memories may sometimes conflict with the facts, but one thing is the same in each of our stories — like you, his fans, we all loved Lewis. And we miss him.

Early Lessons Of Life

By Dudley Stamps

Dudley Stamps, a real estate developer and construction equipment salesman, lives in Moreland, Georgia, with his wife Elaine. He is the chairman of the Lewis Grizzard Memorial Trust.

From the day he walked into Mrs. Bowers' second-grade classroom in Moreland, Georgia, in 1953, Lewis Grizzard was different. Like any kid in a new school, he was a bit timid and shy, and like most of the boys in that era, his ears stuck out too far from his shaved head. But that's where the similarities ended. For one thing, his mother was a teacher at our school. For another, his grandfather was the custodian. And for another — which, frankly, few of us noticed but was a big issue with Lewis — he didn't have a father at home.

Seven-year-old Lewis

Lewis' father was a decorated hero during World War II and in Korea. As a combat captain in Korea, his entire company was wiped out and he was left for dead. He survived not only that ordeal but also a stint as a prisoner of war before finally escaping. Lewis Sr. was never able to escape those harrowing memories, however, and after his discharge he began to drink and vanish for days at a time. When Lewis Sr. and the money ran out once too often in 1953, Christine Word Grizzard took her seven-year-old son, Lewis Jr., and went to live in Moreland with her parents and sisters.

Years later Lewis confided in me that he was always embarrassed that his father was never around for any school functions and never came to any of our baseball games. The rest of us didn't notice, but Lewis was haunted by his missing father.

In a different way, he was also haunted by his mother and by Mrs. Bowers; being a teacher's son always put Lewis in the spotlight at school. One of Mrs. Bowers' favorite things was to catch kids not paying attention when she was reading to us. One day Lewis and I were caught whispering to each other. Mrs. Bowers came directly to my desk and said, "Dudley, point to where we are in the text." I had no earthly idea where we were, but I put my finger on a paragraph and sheepishly looked up at her for the verdict. By a stroke of sheer luck, I had pointed to the exact place she had stopped. She frowned at me, knowing I was not paying attention, and immediately moved on to Lewis. He was not as lucky. "Lewis, hold out your hand," said Mrs. Bowers. She grabbed his four protruding fingers, bent them down, and hit the palm of his hand three times with a wooden ruler. Needless to say, she had the attention of the entire class for weeks to come. And Miss Christine had Lewis' undivided attention that night at home.

Lewis soon became a regular member of our gang — me, Bobby Entrekin, Mike Murphy, and Danny Thompson, all of whom you've read about in Lewis' books and columns over the years, all of whom became lifelong friends. Our leisure time was spent like any boy in a small, rural town in the early 1950s. We played basketball on a dirt court with a net-less hoop; we pitched horseshoes; we shot marbles on hardpan; and we went to the baseball field and pretended to be our favorite players — DiMaggio, Musial, Mantle, Williams, Ford, Feller, and Bob

Montag of the minor-league Atlanta Crackers.

Bobby Entrekin got a new football helmet for Christmas in 1954. When the holidays were over, he brought it to school. We had never seen a real football helmet up close and were completely awed by this fantastic gift. Bobby, of course, was very proud and milked this majestic moment to the fullest. He passed the helmet around and explained how it protected you from on-rushing opponents. He even let some of us wear it for a few moments.

Lewis, always the cynic, said, "Bobby, just how good is that helmet?"

Bobby immediately replied, "Why, it's so strong I can run into that wall at the back of the room and it won't hurt me."

"I'd like to see that!" challenged Lewis.

Bobby said, "I'll do it, but there needs to be some sort of bet on this, because I might scratch my helmet." Lewis promptly put up his sack of marbles against Bobby's — a big wager in those days.

Now remember, this is a very old building and the walls are constructed of one-inch by four-inch tongue and groove wood. Bobby assumed a three-point position at the front of the class room, took several deep breaths, and charged full bore at the wall twenty-five to thirty feet away. As he crashed into the wall, there was a loud thump; dazed, he staggered around the room but never went down. We all looked on in absolute amazement that he hadn't broken his neck. Bobby wobbled over to Lewis and said, "I'll have that sack of marbles now."

Lewis handed them over and, with a little smirk on his face, said, "I wish I had some more marbles. I'd like to see that again!"

We all got new desks for the 1954 school year. The metal legs were supposed to have rubber pads on the bottoms, but somehow they had been left off. Those desks would slide on the old waxed wooden floors like a puck on ice. In fact, you had to be careful when you sat down or your desk would scoot away from you. And, of course, every time the teacher went out of the room, we had races and played "bumper desk demolition derby."

We always stationed a lookout at the door, but one day the lookout was laughing so hard she didn't see the teacher coming. Lewis, with a wicked smile on his face, had Bobby Hosmer trapped in a corner; every time Bobby tried to slide his desk out, Lewis would ram him back into the corner. When our teacher, Mrs. Summers, came into the room, she went into shock. Minutes later, we were all standing outside the principal's office listening to the sound of a paddle on a backside, followed by yells and moans.

Lewis was ahead of me in line. When he came out with watering eyes and holding his butt, I asked, "How bad was it?"

He said, "Not near as bad as the one I'm about to get. I have to report to my mother in the first-grade room!"

We had to remain in the classroom during every recess period for a week and write five hundred times "I will not misbehave in the classroom." Lewis figured out how to use two pencils to write two lines at a time. When the teacher discovered his trick, she said, "You're so very good at this, let's see how quickly you can do a thousand lines!"

Lewis' grandfather, "Daddy Bunn," soon was sent to our room and nailed all the desks to the floor. He didn't say much, just shook his head a bit and smiled.

In 1955 a terrible thing happened to me and Lewis: Our mothers decided we should take piano lessons. Every mother wants her son to play the piano, but no self-respecting fourth-grade boy would willingly submit to such a "sissy" thing. We would be the laughing stock of the whole school!

Of course, all our pleading was in vain. On Wednesday after school we were to meet Mrs. Laura Bailey, who would journey the six miles from Newnan to Moreland just to teach us piano in the upstairs school auditorium, where there was one of those big old high-back pianos that had last been tuned just before VE Day. Lewis and I began scheming to keep our secret from the rest of the school.

When the first Wednesday came, we still had no plan. Mrs.

Bailey taught school in Newnan, so we had thirty minutes to kill before she arrived. As soon as school was out, we headed to Steve Bohannon's Service Station only a few hundred yards away. Drinks, candy bars, and chips were only a nickel back then. For a dime you could have a great snack; for a quarter you could get sick. We got our dime's worth and continued talking about what we were going to do.

Mr. Steve overheard our conversation and asked what was the matter. We had told absolutely no one about the piano lessons and were reluctant to tell Mr. Steve, but Lewis said, "Hey, we need help quick!" So we told him the whole story. He listened with great concern and fully understood our predicament. Mr. Steve said, "Let me think a few minutes on this." We all stood there finishing off our Cokes and peanuts while he devised a plan. The key was for no one to see us going up the stairs to the auditorium. That would have led to all sorts of embarrassing questions.

After a few minutes, Mr. Steve finally spoke. "Boys, I think I've got it. You know there's a fire escape on the side of the building. Now, if one of you watches till the coast is clear, the other can run up the fire escape and get into the auditorium without being seen." Of course, the fire escape was off limits to everyone except in an emergency, but this was an emergency!

We casually drifted toward the fire escape when no one was around. Lewis' lesson was first, so he began to climb the metal stairs. Suddenly I saw a seventh grader coming around the corner. I whistled and Lewis fell to his stomach on the second-story landing until the guy was out of sight. Then he eased in the window and went unnoticed down to the auditorium. Each lesson lasted thirty minutes, so I waited below hitting rocks with a stick. When Lewis came out the window, I had to hurry in; there was no time to ask him how it went, but there would be plenty of time for talking afterward. Mrs. Bailey was a very nice lady and made me feel at ease. I'm sure she knew that most boys our age were not taking lessons by choice. My thirty minutes went by quickly.

I hurried to the window and looked out for Lewis, but he was nowhere in sight. I climbed down and looked for him around the building; still no Lewis. I figured something awful had happened, like he'd been caught by a teacher. As soon as I got home I phoned and asked what had happened. "If I had waited for you to finish your lesson," he said, "I would have missed 'Superman' on TV. Anyway, what was I supposed to say if anyone asked what I was doing there?"

A couple of weeks later Mrs. Bailey caught us going in and out of the window. When we explained, she agreed not to tell the principal if we promised not to do it anymore. A deal was struck. And after about six months, when neither Lewis nor I could play two notes back-to-back, our mothers finally realized they were wasting what little money they had and let us quit.

To my knowledge, this is the first time either of us ever told about taking piano lessons. Lewis never even told any of his wives. But if you go to the Lewis Grizzard Museum in Moreland, Georgia, under glass in a display case you'll see sheet music for "Tomahawk Trail" with Lewis' name written in pencil across the top.

About the time we reached sixth grade, we started noticing girls. Something very interesting was going on inside their sweaters. They didn't seem to be much impressed by shooting marbles or baskets, but fighting always seemed to get their attention.

Lewis was skinny and had no muscles, but there was one kid in class — Elmo — who was even smaller. Elmo, however, was fiesty like a bantam hen, always going around scratching the ground and kicking up dust. One day he and Lewis got into an argument, and Lewis thought this was his chance to impress the girls (some of whom had probably whipped Elmo themselves).

They tore into each other like two tom cats in an alley, rolling in the red dirt of the basketball court. As they slung each other around, they disappeared behind the big well house. Before we could get around there to see what was happening, Elmo came walking out dusting his hands. Lewis had been defeated.

Years later I was commending Lewis for his grand accomplishments and told him how proud we all were of him. Lewis was really a humble person, and praise usually embarrassed him. He responded, "You know, Dudley, I learned at a very early age, with a little help from Elmo, that my strength was with words and not muscle. If I can't talk my way out of a bad situation, then I ought to walk away. And if that doesn't work, then I'm going to run like hell!"

I first witnessed Lewis' ability to talk his way out of trouble in the sixth grade, when he accidentally shot one of our female classmates in the chest with an air rifle. Bobby Entrekin had somehow persuaded our teacher to let him bring his new Daisy pump air rifle to school. She checked very carefully to make sure there were no BBs in it and that Bobby wasn't hiding any in his pockets.

Later that morning when she was called to the principal's office, all the boys wanted to hold this beautiful new air rifle. Everyone who touched it had to cock and shoot it. When Lewis finally got his hands on the gun, one of our petite classmates — who had been out all morning — walked into the room. Lewis drew a bead on her and said, "I'm going to shoot you." The girl was terrified. She had no way of knowing that the gun was supposed to be empty.

Lewis walked toward her holding the BB gun to his shoulder. She backed against the wall and pleaded with Lewis not to shoot her. He said, "Sorry, but your time is up," and he pulled the trigger. She immediately grabbed her chest and let out a scream. Lewis thought she was kidding and just turning the joke on him. But the other girls in class gathered around her and opened the appropriate button of her blouse. There was the BB stuck in her skin.

We all stood there with our mouths open wide. How could this have happened? Bobby Entrekin was thinking, "Oh, no! They're going to confiscate my air rifle and chop it into little pieces." Meanwhile, Lewis' whole young life ran before his eyes. Here he was trying to impress the girls, but instead he had shot this poor little thing. He ran to her apologizing in every way he could think of, but the more he apologized, the louder she cried.

Lewis dropped to his knees. "Oh, *please* don't tell the teacher this happened. I swear I didn't know there was anything in the gun. If you won't tell, I'll help you with your math," which he knew was a difficult subject for her. But she just looked at him and let out another loud wail. An offer to carry her books netted the same response. Not one to give up easily, Lewis then said, "I'll carry you to the church picnic!" Well, that went over like a ton of bricks.

She screamed, "You just shot me with a BB gun and now you want to take me to the church picnic? No thanks!"

Time was running out. The teacher would be returning to the room any minute. So Lewis made the ultimate sacrifice: "If you won't tell, I'll give you my ice cream money for a month!" For anyone who doesn't remember, most schools would let students buy ice cream during the last recess of the day. Many parents used this as a ten-cents-a-day incentive for their kids to do well in school.

Slowly the girl's expression changed from a sob to a surly grin, and she said, "OK, but I want that money every day!"

Lewis kept his word, and she never told. That may have been his first alimony payment. I know for a fact that it scared Lewis so much he was afraid ever to handle a gun for the rest of his life.

The spring of 1958 brought us one of the greatest thrills of our lives: Mr. Pete Moore of the Baptist Church helped form the Western Baptist Baseball League. Until then all we had ever been able to do was pretend on the school play ground with a stupid softball. Softball was a girl's game, we thought. When you hit a softball as hard as you can, it sounds like two overweight nuns bumping into each other, and it goes nowhere. It's so big you can't get a decent grip on it, but you need a bread basket to catch it. Softball can make even a good athlete look bad.

But finally we had someone to teach us how to play the game of baseball. We would travel to far off, exotic places like Macedonia, Sargent, Mills Chapel, Corinth, Warm Springs, and Hogansville to match skills with their best. But Lewis was a Methodist. Would they let him play on the Baptist team? "All my relatives are Baptists," argued Lewis. Mr. Pete set his mind at ease. "Fact is," he said, "we don't have enough boys in this age group just in the Baptist church. You can play, but once a month you will have to come to church here." No problem; Lewis would have converted for the chance to play baseball.

We practiced every day after school, and soon Mr. Pete, drummed us into a pretty good outfit. I played third base. Lewis wanted to be a pitcher. Since he wasn't all that strong, he relied on control and tried to develop a curve ball.

Week after week we became more experienced and confident. We were having the time of our lives. Lewis' curve ball continued to improve, and he became a good hitter and fielder, playing several different positions. It was early in that season that Lewis surprised us all — not with his baseball talent, but by telling us that one day he was going to be a sportswriter. We were worried about graduating to the next grade, and Lewis was choosing a career!

Some thirty years later we were reminiscing, and Lewis recounted this story exactly. I couldn't believe how vividly and accurately he remembered details from so many years ago. I asked, "Lewis, how do you remember all that stuff so well?"

He explained that he had talked to his mother about his desire to be a sportswriter. She was very proud he had made up his mind at such a young age. She advised him to keep a journal and to write in it every day about the things that stood out in his mind. Lewis said he did this through high school, college, and even into his married years. He said that after he became a newspaper columnist, any time he couldn't think of a subject for his next column, he would go back to those journal notes and very shortly would have an idea. "They saved me many a time," he said.

Not long after Lewis announced his goal in life, the local paper, the *Newnan Times-Herald*, called Mr. Pete and asked if he could arrange for someone to report to them on a weekly basis the results and highlights of our league. Lewis immediately volunteered, and although Mr. Pete was a bit skeptical, he finally gave in and let Lewis try it. This was the actual start of a great journalism career.

It just so happened that Lewis was scheduled to pitch his first game that week. We beat the pants off them, and Lewis' first article appeared the following Thursday. It read,

By LEWIS GRIZZARD

Brilliant Moreland righthander Lewis Grizzard, in his first start in organized baseball, baffled the visiting Macedonia Baptist nine 6-0 Saturday afternoon with a no-hitter. His teammates, in a lesser role, hit four home runs.

The next two years were among the happiest times of our lives. Lewis became our star pitcher and I was his catcher. He had mastered the art of control, and at age thirteen he had an impressive slider and curve ball. In fact, he had developed a pitch that no one else used. He gripped the ball with his index finger curled back so that only the knuckle was touching; the other three fingers controlled the ball. He delivered the pitch with a sort of side-arm motion and twist. A couple of years later Sandy Koufax of the Dodgers was using this very same pitch and calling it the knuckle curve ball. Lewis could never under-stand how Koufax found out about the pitch he had invented.

That baseball team was the best thing that ever happened to us. It gave us confidence and self-esteem, traits that were in short supply in the rural South. We had a good coach in Mr. Pete Moore, who taught us that if you don't win fair, you haven't won anything at all. Years later, every time Lewis and I were together our conversation would drift back to those won-derfully happy days. They just didn't last long enough.

Lewis Sr.: Loving But Flawed Father

BY LUDLOW PORCH

Ludlow Porch is one of America's most popular radio talk-show hosts and the author of twelve books. He and Lewis Grizzard were stepbrothers. Ludlow lives and works in the Atlanta area.

My Uncle Frank's brother, Lewis Grizzard, Sr., was one of the people in my life that I loved and admired most. He was a war hero, a coach, a teacher, a loving father, a musician, and a singer with a voice you could hear in the next county. He was a religious man who, all his life, enjoyed a one-on-one relationship with his Maker. He was a humorist whose stories could reduce any audience to howls and tears. He was, without any doubt, the funniest man I ever knew.

Lewis Sr. was also an alcoholic, a con man, and a scalawag without peer. He fought bravely in WWII and in Korea, where he was captured and held prisoner by the Chinese. Some people say that Lewis was forever scarred by his combat days, but according to his boyhood friends, he was a rounder long before he put on the uniform of his country. Like every other Grizzard male I have ever known, he had great charm and a great thirst.

I don't know much about the disease of alcoholism, but I do know that Lewis Sr. had very strange drinking habits. While he was never able to win his battle with the bottle, he fought it every day of his life. I don't mean he resisted drinking; I mean he fought it harder than he had ever fought the Germans or the Chinese. He would go for as long as six months without a drink, but once he took that first one, he was on a long road that only went downhill.

He would do almost anything to keep a binge going. He would borrow, beg, tell any lie, or work any con to get one more drink. But even during his escapes into the bottle, his charm, personality, and humor would never leave him. He kept his face shaven, his shoes shined, and his clothes fresh. His full gray head of that thick Grizzard hair was always neatly cut, and he was the last man on earth you would ever suspect of any impropriety, let alone of being the world's foremost flimflam man looking to get his hands on your pocketbook.

But the truth is, no coffers were safe when Lewis Sr. was ready to tie one on.

As a young man, Lewis Sr. was very active in his church. He was there every time they opened the door, and his rich voice filled that little country chapel. Every member of the congregation was convinced that the Lord had sent him especially to their choir. He was also one of the members who took up the offering at Sunday worship service.

It had to happen — some church money came up missing at about the same time Lewis came up missing. Everybody in the church was sure they knew where the money was, but

The charming Lewis Sr.

they had no proof. They held a meeting to decide what steps, if any, should be taken. One dear lady pointed out that none of them knew for certain that Lewis had taken the money, and even if they did, they should have Christian forgiveness in their hearts. So they all agreed to pray for whoever took the money.

In a few weeks, Lewis returned to town from his unexpected absence. He was back in the choir on Sunday morning, and when the pastor said it was time to collect the offering, Lewis got out of his chair and passed the plate. Christian charity probably enjoyed its finest hour that day.

I first met Lewis Sr. while he was still in the Army. We were both at my Uncle Frank's house, and Lewis was holding the hand of an eight- or nine-year-old boy he called Skipper — it was his son, Lewis McDonald Grizzard, Jr. I was a teen-ager then and could never have guessed that one day Skipper and I would be closer than blood brothers, nor that the tall soldier would one day be my stepfather.

I didn't see either of them again for several years. In fact, the next time I saw Lewis Sr. was at Uncle Frank's funeral in 1958. Like all Southern funerals, Uncle Frank's did not end at the cemetery. We all met afterwards for dinner and shared our grief. Lewis had been divorced for quite some time, and my mother was a widow. It was easy to see that they enjoyed each other's company.

One thing led to another, and in a few months they were married. Lewis was working at Rich's department store in Atlanta, and there was no clue that he was not a pillar of the community. I was a young married man, and since my mother had always been my best friend, the four of us spent a lot of time together. For the first six months of their marriage, I had never seen my mother happier.

One night at dinner Lewis announced that he had landed a teaching job at a nearby private school. We knew he loved teaching and were pleased at his good fortune. A while later I needed to talk to Lewis about some weekend plans we had made, so I called him at the school. They had never heard of him. It was a preview of things to come.

A wise man once wrote, "In the South there are three kinds of drunks: lovin' drunks, fightin' drunks, and travelin' drunks." I happen to believe that is true, but Lewis Grizzard Sr. rarely traveled drunk. He was usually coming off one or on his way to another. He could cover more ground without a dime in his pocket than anyone since Christopher Columbus.

It took me a few years to get used to the fact that almost every time I heard from him, he was in a different city. There was no particular pattern to his travels, except that he always stayed in the South. When he was ready to stop for a few days or take a job for awhile, he usually chose a small town. He knew that small-town people spoke his language, and given just a few hours, he could either find work or talk someone out of money.

If it were at all practical, he would try to take Lewis Jr. along with him, much to the chagrin of young Skip's mother. You would think that a man broke or semi-broke and on the road, if not on the lam, would not want the responsibility of a small boy. Not so with Lewis. He loved Skip so much that he would do almost anything to be with him.

Once, when Skip was about eight-or nine-years old, Lewis picked him up for the weekend. His mother was not to see him again for more than thirty days. Lewis Sr. talked with her every few days so she wouldn't go out of her mind with worry, and every time they spoke he promised to bring Skip home in a day or two. She knew better, but like the rest of the world she was under his spell. She knew that even though Lewis was the world's foremost rounder, he would never let any harm come to Skipper.

On that particular trip, the two of them wound up in Albany, Georgia, absolutely broke. Lewis Sr. noticed a sign in a store window announcing a minor league baseball game in town that night; Albany was playing Waycross in the old Georgia-Florida league. Never one to allow a temporary lack of funds get in his way, he steered Skip straight to the ballpark and talked their way inside. They were watching batting practice when, the first thing Skip knew, his father was down on the field talking to one of the coaches.

The record will never show how it happened, but for the next month Lewis and Skip traveled with the Waycross Braves. They rode the bus with the team and stayed with them on the road. Needless to say, Skip loved it. The team even gave him a little

Waycross uniform. During that month-long odyssey, Lewis Sr. borrowed money from the manager and the entire left side of the infield.

When it came time for the start of Skip's school year, Lewis finally returned him to his worried mother.

Once when Lewis Jr. was in high school, about six months went by when he didn't hear from his father. That was highly unusual, because no matter how good or bad things were going for Lewis Sr., he always managed to stay in touch with his son.

Skip was on the Newnan high school basketball team, and one night the team was in Atlanta playing a game. Skip was taking the ball down court when he heard a familiar voice cheering him on from the stands — it was his daddy.

When the game was over, Skip ran up and asked, "Daddy, what on earth are you doing here?"

"I teach here," Lewis announced.

"What do you teach?" asked Skip.

"I teach mechanical drawing."

"But, Dad," Skip pointed out, "you don't know anything about mechanical drawing."

"That's true, son," Lewis said, "but neither do the students."

Of course, not all of Lewis' and Skip's reunions were ideal. Once when I was living in Birmingham, Alabama, we invited Lewis Sr. to come stay with us awhile to see if the change might help him get his act together. He was in one of his non-drinking periods and seemed to be trying hard to stay dry. My kids enjoyed having him around, and he kept us all laughing.

After a week or so he found a job at a small country club on the edge of town. It was perfect for him; he was an excellent manager, and the staff and members soon fell under the spell of his great charm. He came home every night and told us hilarious stories about his day.

The club closed for the month of August every summer, but Lewis went in every day just to make sure all was in order. When he didn't come home for three days, we began to worry. I didn't want him to think I was checking up on him, but I did want to know what was going on.

I called the club and let the phone ring about twenty times. I was about to hang up when an obviously scared young voice said, "Hello?"

I said, "May I speak to Mr. Grizzard, please?"

"He can't come to the phone now."

I said that I would call again later and was about to hang up when the voice said, "Bob?" (That's my given name.)

It hit me all at once. "Skip! What in the world are you doing in Birmingham?"

He said, "Boy, am I glad to hear from you!" And he told me the whole story.

Lewis had called Skip's mother and asked her to let him catch a bus to Birmingham for a visit. He told her about his new job and said that he and Skip could swim in the country club pool and have a great time together. He assured her he would meet his twelve-year-old son at the bus station. With Lewis Sr. on one end of the line begging and Lewis Jr. on the other end pleading, she never had a chance.

When Skip arrived at the Birmingham bus station, his dad was nowhere to be found. He looked everywhere for him and was near tears when he heard his name being called over the public address system. He had a telephone call from his father, explaining that he had been delayed and that Skip should take a taxi to the country club.

When Skip arrived at the club, he found his dad in bad shape. He was *really* drunk. Lewis had unlocked the country club's liquor room and was playing the part of Br'er Rabbit in the briar patch. By the time I talked with Skip on the phone, he had been in Birmingham for three days and his daddy had been in a semi-drunken stupor most of the time. Whenever he would begin to sober up, he would crawl right back into another bottle. Skip was pretty upset.

"Where is your dad now?" I asked.

"He's passed out on the sofa in the lobby," said Skip.

"Don't worry," I said. "I'm on my way."

Driving to the country club, I was furious. How could he possibly bring that kid all the way over here and pull a stunt like that? When I arrived, Skip gave me the kind of hug you get only from a frightened youngster. He had been living off packaged food from the kitchen but had not had a full meal or a shower since he got there.

I took Skip to our house and just left Lewis Sr. asleep on the club sofa. We got Skip fed, showered, and calmed down. A little while later my conscience started bothering me, so I said, "Let's go back and see about your daddy."

When we arrived at the club, Lewis was gone. On a hunch, I called the nearest motel — figuring that if he had called a cab, that's where he would go. I guessed right. The operator confirmed that Mr. Grizzard was registered. We got in my car and headed for the motel.

The motel manager insisted that we get "that drunk" out of his establishment, and I explained that was exactly what we were trying to do. When we opened the door to Lewis' room, we saw him comatose on the bed, an empty whiskey bottle on the table beside him. We shook him and tried to talk to him, but nothing helped. Then we soaked a towel in ice water and placed it in the middle of Lewis' ample stomach, but he didn't even twitch. I finally decided that our only option was to carry all 260 pounds of him to the car. Somehow we managed.

With Lewis snoring in the back seat, I decided to drive him and Skip back toward Atlanta. I hoped we could sober him up before we arrived in Moreland to drop off Skip. As we crossed the state line, Skip said he was hungry, so I pulled off the road and sent him inside a restaurant for food. While he was gone, a deep voice sounded from the back seat:

"Robert? Robert? Are you there?"

"Yes, Lewis, I'm here."

"Robert, don't hate me."

"I don't hate you, Lewis."

"Are you mad at me, Robert?"

"Yes, Lewis, I'm mad at you."

"But you don't hate me?"

"No, Lewis, I don't hate you."

"Do you hate me just a little?"

"No, Lewis, I don't even hate you a little. Are you hungry, Lewis?"

"No, I may never eat again. Gully dirt doesn't get hungry, and I'm just as sorry as gully dirt. I don't deserve anything to eat."

"What do you want to eat, Lewis?"

"Two cheeseburgers and an order of fries."

I couldn't do anything but laugh when I realized that, as drunk as he was, he had just turned on that Grizzard charm.

When Lewis Jr. returned with the food, Lewis Sr. was sitting up for the first time all day. He said, "Skipper, don't hate me."

"I don't hate you, Daddy."

"Do you hate me a little?"

"Lewis," I interrupted, "we don't hate you, but if you don't hush and eat, we're going to make you *walk* to Atlanta."

"*Walk* to Atlanta?" Lewis replied. "In the name of Gawd, Robert, I'd do good to get the car door open!"

We all cracked up.

Lewis Sr. wouldn't let me take him to my mother's house but insisted that I take him to his sister's. When he got out of the car, we gave each other a hug. "Lewis, Lewis, Lewis," I said. "What is going to become of you?"

"Oh, you know me, Robert," he said. "I'll be all right."

God rest his soul, he never was.

On August 12, 1970, Lewis McDonald Grizzard, Sr., died in the hospital of the tiny Georgia town of Claxton. A stroke had stopped that huge heart one week shy of his fifty-eighth birthday. Lewis Jr. was at his bedside, holding his hand, when he took his last breath. Lewis Sr.'s sole possessions on that hot Georgia night were a watch, a ring, and a Georgia driver's license.

Stepbrothers Ludlow Porch and Lewis Grizzard often shared memories of "the Marvelous Major."

A Moment 'On Top Of The World'

BY DUDLEY STAMPS

Dudley Stamps, a real estate developer and construction equipment salesman, lives in Moreland, Georgia, with his wife Elaine. He is the chairman of the Lewis Grizzard Memorial Trust.

One of Lewis' best-selling books that struck close to home for me was *I Haven't Understood Anything Since 1962.* I distinctly remember a conversation which helped inspire that book.

"You know, Dudley," Lewis said, "when we graduated in 1964, no one had ever heard of marijuana, LSD or cocaine. The strongest things around were Budweiser and MD20/20 wine, and it was hard to get your hands on either one of those. Today they catch ten-year-old kids selling drugs at school. I just don't understand it. Our heroes were always on the side of good; they weren't punk rock singers who look like they've been through the rinse cycle, or drug-using athletes. What are today's kids going to grow up like with those kinds of heroes? If I had a choice, I would go back to 1960 and stay there forever."

I agreed with him — 1960 was the best of them all. It was the year we became teen-agers; the year we left grammar school and entered high school; the year we got our first kiss from a girl; the year I got a motor scooter and we finally had wheels that would carry us over the endless miles of dirt roads to new adventures and sometimes into trouble. We explored the world around us, riding up to fifteen miles away to find a new swimming hole, or to wander through an old abandoned house or barn. Although gas was only twenty cents a gallon, we were using fifty cents to a dollar's worth each day. How could we keep up such an expensive habit?

The answer came to us one day on Moccasin Road just south of Moreland. The county had left a big grader there after scraping the road. We, of course, had to stop and climb on it, sit in the seat and pretend we were driving it. These old motorgraders used diesel fuel, which would not work in the scooter, but on closer examination we found that they had what was called a "pony motor" on them. The diesels back then wouldn't start very well by themselves, so a small gas engine was used to spin the diesel over. These little engines held several gallons of gas. We dashed back to Moreland to find a hose.

I was raised on a farm, so I was quite experienced at the art of siphoning gas; you just had to make sure that what you were drawing it out of was higher than what you were putting it into, and most importantly you had to be careful not to suck too hard, or else gas would flood your mouth, your nose, and your ears. It burns and tastes awful.

Lewis never mastered the art of siphoning gas. After one aborted attempt, he started looking a little green, so I took him back home. His mother wanted to know what was the matter and why he smelled like gas. Lewis said that we had stopped at the service station for a drink, he had gotten a ginger ale and walked over to where Steve Bohannon was working on a car. "Mr. Bohannon had poured some gas in a ginger ale bottle to put in the carburetor, and I sat mine down and picked his up by mistake and drank it." When I left she was wiping his face with a wet rag and telling him he must be much more careful in the future.

There were a lot of dirt roads to be scraped in our area, so we began to search out those motor graders. We spread the word and any other kid that spotted one parked would let us know where it was. We carried a hose and gallon can with us at all times. If the scooter wouldn't hold all the gas, we would fill the can and save it for later. I have often wondered if the county ever figured out why their little pony motors used so much gas; we never drained the tanks dry, but we didn't leave much in them either. I believe I have paid enough property taxes to the county over the last twenty-five years to make up for the gas we borrowed back, but Lewis and I both appreciated the loan.

In 1960 our baseball team was almost unbeatable. We won the first thirteen games before a loss. And, like the team, Lewis' writing for the newspaper had become very good. He was always throwing some big, sophisticated, hard-to-pronounce word into his article, causing me to have to go to the dictionary to see what he was saying about us. The girls wanted to be around us now that we were winners, so the stands were filled at every home game.

One morning in school I was bragging about how we were going to beat the socks off the team coming to play us that afternoon. One of the girls said, "You guys think you're some-thing, don't you?" As a matter of fact, we did, and to prove my point, I bet her that I would hit a home run that afternoon. She replied, "I'll bet you a kiss that you don't!"

Needless to say, every time I came to bat I was trying my best to hit that home run. And I did — a fat fastball right down the middle did the trick. I felt the bat whip in my hands; the ball took off like it was shot from a cannon. As I rounded third base I saw the girl in the stands holding her hands over her mouth and smiling.

After the game I went to collect on the bet, but the girl was embarrassed and wouldn't pay off. Luckily she was sitting with a friend named Nancy Carroll, who stepped forward and said, "Well, if you won't, I will!" and she put a big kiss right on my lips. I was instantly in love — my first girlfriend.

That summer she went to every game at home and away. She sat in the stands and I could hear her cheering above all the oth-ers. She inspired me with a kiss before the game and another one afterward. I could tell Lewis was a little jealous, because he didn't have a girlfriend yet. Besides that, she often took his place on the back of my scooter.

The months went by so very fast that year. A few weeks before we entered high school, one of the churches in town held a hay ride. For some reason I couldn't go, so Nancy went without me. I found out much later that Lewis was also on that hay ride, and he sat beside Nancy and stole a kiss from my girlfriend. He began to call her at home and ask her to go to the movies. Nancy liked that because I had never taken her to a movie. They kept everything a secret for almost a month. But Lewis was afraid I would find out and kill him, so finally he and Nancy both came to me and confessed what had happened. He was prepared to stand up and fight for her, even though he knew I'd lick him a lot worse than Elmo had in the fourth grade. I probably would have been fighting mad if I had found out earlier, but by that time we were in the first couple of weeks of high school, and I had never seen so many pretty girls! I played the field, and we all remained friends. Lewis and Nancy dated on through high school and were married in 1966. Of course, she later became plaintiff No. 1 and took Plato, the bassett hound, with her. They didn't divorce for lack of love, however; their love was always there. Lewis just got more and more popular as a sportswriter, went to too many parties, and forgot where he lived too many times.

Going from the eighth grade at Moreland to the high school in nearby Newnan was one of the biggest steps of our lives. At that time, Newnan, Georgia, (nicknamed "The City of Homes" and populated largely by well-paid employees of Atlanta's growing airline industry) was the richest town per capita in the whole United States, and its high school was rated one of the best in the Southeast. We had heard stories of how hard Newnan High School was and how the rich kids there looked down on everyone else. Absolutely no one in Moreland had any money. Most parents either worked on a farm or in a textile mill, where top pay was $1.50 to $2 per hour. Everyone lived in modest homes and had to budget themselves very carefully. The term "going to town" for us meant going to Newnan, and this was done only

Lifelong friends: (L-R) Lewis, Dudley Stamps, Bobby Entrekin, and Danny Thompson

on Saturday. Newnan may have been only six miles away, but in reality it was much further than that.

On a warm September morning in 1960, we boarded the bus for our first trip into that new world. In the next few weeks we met and made many new friends — a lot of them the rich kids we had heard so much about. Lewis became very popular and joined a variety of clubs and organizations: He was in the Beta Club, a member of the student council, a homeroom representative, and a member of the Key Club. He also made the varsity baseball and basketball teams. He even went out for football his freshman year but soon decided that was not the sport for him.

Getting around in high school was tough the first two years without driver's licenses, but we had a friend named Anthony Yeager who helped. Anthony had failed a couple of grades and we had caught up with him in the eighth grade at Moreland, so when we entered high school, Anthony already had a driver's license. We chipped in on the gas, and Anthony took Lewis and me and our dates to ball games, dances, and even to Atlanta — forty miles and several decades away. He was our saviour with wheels for two years.

One time Anthony was not there to help us, and the result was not good. Lewis and I had gotten very friendly with two girls who lived about twenty miles from us. One Saturday night Lewis called and said these girls wanted us to come see them.

"How are we supposed to get there? Anthony's gone off for the weekend," I said. I was fifteen years old and had a learner's license; Lewis was still fourteen. He knew my parents were gone and would not be back till late.

"Why don't you get your Dad's old pick-up truck," he said. (This may be where Lewis' love of pickups came from — he learned to drive in that old truck.) "We can go see them and be back before your folks get home."

I knew this was trouble, but Lewis was persuasive even at four-teen. He talked me into taking the old '49 GMC. Minutes later I picked him up outside the Baptist Church, and we headed out.

We made it through Newnan, which we thought would be our most likely place to be caught, but about six miles from our des-tination we rounded a curve and saw headlights everywhere. "What in the world is that?" I said.

Lewis, anxious to see the girls, said, "Don't pay any attention to it. It's only the Goat Man." The Goat Man was a peculiar fel-low who traveled throughout Georgia, Alabama, and Tennessee with a giant wagon pulled by forty or fifty goats. The wagon had pots and pans hanging all over it, and the goats had bells around their necks. People came from miles around just to see this man who lived with and smelled like goats. The commotion in the road in front of us on this particular Saturday night, how-ever, was *not* the Goat Man.

There had been an accident, and before I could bring the old GMC to a wobbly stop, I almost ran down the State Patrolman who was standing in the middle of the road with a flashlight. He hurried over to the truck and demanded to see my license. I fumbled around, hoping something would distract him and maybe he would let us go, but it was no use. I handed him all I had and prepared for the worst.

"Hell, this is only a learner's license!" he yelled. He shined his flashlight in Lewis' face and said, "What about you, boy, what are you doing with him?"

Lewis quickly replied, "I don't even know him. He picked me up hitchhiking back down the road."

When the patrolman went to radio the Sheriff to come pick me up, I turned to Lewis and said, "Why'd you tell him you didn't know me?"

He said, "There's no use in both of us getting in trouble. Besides, I'm going to help you get out of this." Yeah, the same way you helped me get into it, I thought.

Later that night my Daddy came to the county jail and picked me up. Lewis had gotten a ride back home, and I don't think his mother ever found out. The next week Lewis went all around school taking up a collection to pay my $20 fine. Shortly after that he gave up on the out-of-town girl and went back to Nancy, who lived only a half mile away.

In the summer and fall of 1962 our lives changed dramatically: We turned sixteen years old and got our driver's licenses. The ball and chain was taken off our legs, and we were set loose on the world. Of course, a few of us were set loose sooner than the others. My birthday was in July, but Lewis didn't turn sixteen until October 20. He was a little embarrassed to still be bumming rides for the first two months of the new school year.

I had been saving my money for more than a year and begging my parents to get me a car for my sixteenth birthday. I promised to get a part-time job and pay for it. One week before my birthday, I spotted the car of my dreams — a 1959 Thunderbird. It was white with red interior and had 140 MPH on the speedometer. The front end looked like a shark with its mouth open, and the rear end had more tail lights than I had ever seen. It had enough chrome inside and out to dress up forty-two of today's Hondas.

My dad bought it, and I slept in it for the next week awaiting my birthday. Lewis came over every day, and we would sit and play the radio till we ran the battery down, talking about the places we could go and the things we could do. I promised I would drive him around until he got his license.

My day finally came. I picked up Lewis and two other friends and we rode all day long. We picked up our girlfriends and circled the Dairy Queen and Tastee Freeze so many times the girls were beginning to get dizzy. The next day I again picked up Lewis, Bobby Entrekin and Mike Murphy, and we headed off not knowing where we were going or what we were going to do. What fun this was! We rode for several hours before we decided to go back to Moreland.

As we rounded the curve onto what was known as the Moreland Straight in those days — a stretch of road two and a half miles long and level as a board — a 1958 Chevrolet was bouncing up and down a few feet off our bumper. I said, "I think this guy wants to race." As we came out of the curve into the straight, I looked in the rearview mirror and saw him go into the left lane to come around. I could not stop myself; I floored it.

At 110, the Chevy was still right beside us. Everyone in the car was laughing and urging me on — everyone, that is, except Lewis, who had begun to pray. "Oh, my God! Oh, my God! We're going to die!" he moaned above the roar of the engine. At 125 we began to pull away and topped out at 130; the Chevy was still in my rearview mirror. As we slowed down coming into the Moreland city limits, red lights and a siren penetrated the air. In those days the police had red lights, not blue. Although we had slowed down when we passed him (hidden in my Aunt's driveway), he still nailed us for speeding. As the patrolman walked toward the car, Lewis said, "Damn, I'm going to be walking again. But I think I'll prefer it to what I've just been through."

Lewis finally got his driver's license that fall, but he never got a car of his own. His mother always lent him her old Pontiac. I don't think he ever drove it over 50 MPH, and I know that Lewis drove like an old man for the rest of his life. After our little race, he never wanted to go fast again.

1963-64 was our senior year. The Cuban missile crisis had alerted us to the threat of nuclear war, President Kennedy had been assassinated the previous fall, and we were beginning to hear about a war in Southeast Asia. Life was starting to get a little more complicated as we prepared to leave the security of our parents' homes. But the last few months in school were great. The teachers were much more lenient, because they knew we would soon be gone and out of their hair.

Late one afternoon in the winter of our senior year, Lewis called and asked if I would come get him and just ride around for awhile. He was down in the dumps because a guy named Frankie was taking Nancy, Lewis' girl, to a junior varsity basketball game that night. As we rode, Lewis got madder and madder. He wanted to do *something* to Frankie, but he couldn't figure out what. He certainly didn't want to fight him; Frankie outweighed him by forty pounds. It was getting dark and Lewis was getting madder. "What if she lets Frankie kiss her?" Suddenly a possum ran across the road ahead of us, and Lewis yelled, "Stop the car! Stop the car! Let's catch that possum!"

"What the hell are you going to do with it?" I asked. "And besides, I don't want that nasty thing in my car." If you've never seen a possum up close, they are one of the ugliest, smelliest things in the world. They can't run fast, so they're easy to catch, but when you get close they will hiss and show their long, sharp teeth. We picked this one up by his tail and put him in the trunk.

"I've got a great idea," Lewis said. "Let's put this possum in Frankie's car while they're watching the game." He smiled for the first time all evening.

We went down to the trash container at Steve's Truck Stop and found an old onion sack; we didn't want this thing to bite anyone. We put the possum in the sack and headed for the school. Lewis spotted Frankie's car. There was no one in sight. We stopped right behind his car, and Lewis put the possum in the floorboard on the driver's side. We parked across the road where it was dark but where we still had a good view and waited for the game to end. By the time the game was over, I'm sure that car was smelling pretty bad.

As Frankie and Nancy approached the car, we realized there was another couple with them. They got in the back seat while Frankie, like a gentleman, opened the door for Nancy. Frankie went around, jumped in behind the wheel, and put his feet right on top of the possum. He couldn't figure out what it was, so he leaned down and felt the sack. That's when the possum started hissing and wiggling around. Frankie let out a scream you could hear for a mile, and all four doors flew open at the same time. I have never seen an automobile vacated more quickly!

Lewis and I were laughing so hard we had to hold our hands over our mouths so they wouldn't hear us. Everyone had backed off about thirty feet from the car and was yelling, "What is it? What is it?" The noise had scared the possum, too. It was wiggling so hard trying to get out of the onion sack that it fell out of the open car door. Frankie finally found a stick and cautiously approached the bouncing bag. Every time the sack jumped, so did Frankie.

The principal, who had witnessed the whole event, walked over to the sack and started laughing like crazy. "Hey, it's only a possum," he yelled between laughs. "Does anyone here claim it?" Of course, no one did, so he let it loose.

Frankie was quite embarrassed. We could hear him pleading with Nancy to get in the car, but she was stomping her foot and saying, "I'm not getting in that smelly car! And besides, there's no telling what else might come out from under the seat!" She headed down the road on foot, preferring to walk the couple of blocks to her house.

As we drove past Frankie, with Lewis slouched down in the seat, he was swearing that he would find out "who put that damn possum in my car and beat the hell out of him!" Well, he never found out, and Nancy never dated him again. In fact, when the word got out about what had happened, Frankie had to trade cars before he could get a date with any girl again.

Graduation finally came the first week of June 1964. What a proud bunch we were as we left Newnan High School and went off to make our mark in the world. Lewis most certainly made his — one that will last for years to come. His success resulted from hard work, determination, and his natural gift for having a way with words. He could make you mad, make you laugh, or make you cry, but you always wanted to read him again to see what he was going to say next. He made everyone feel like they knew him personally because he shared himself so completely with his readers — the good times and the bad, from his marriages to his divorces, and all the things he saw right and wrong in a changing world.

Lewis was different. He was special. He was extraordinarily talented. But to those of us who were fortunate enough to grow up with him, he was always just Lewis.

Many years have passed since a couple of boys had such wonderful times. When I remember them, it seems like only yesterday. I can see Lewis and Nancy dancing close to "In the Still of the Night" at the country club after a Friday night ball game. He gives me a wink over her shoulder, as if to say, "I'm on top of the world!" And for that moment in time, we were.

With A Little Help From A Friend

BY LORAN SMITH

Loran Smith lives in Athens, Georgia, where he serves as executive secretary of the Georgia Bulldog Club. He is the author of numerous books and articles.

In the summer of 1964, an old college track teammate of mine, Charlie Harris, called for a favor.

I had just joined the Georgia Bulldogs as assistant sports information director, working with Dan Magill, the man who has meant so much to so many at the University of Georgia.

Charlie called to tell me about Lewis Grizzard, a skinny high school student from Moreland, Georgia, who was nuts about sports, wanted to be a sportswriter, and needed financial help to get through college.

"Would you help him?" Charlie asked.

Charlie, who later died of leukemia, was a wonderful friend, one of those men who saw sports as an opportunity to help young kids. He coached with the old-fashioned view that you put the kids above personal goals and ambition; he was not in coaching for financial reward.

Charlie said that Lewis had played basketball and baseball at Newnan High School and wasn't a bad high school player, but he obviously had no future as an athlete. He did have one, as we all now know, as a writer. It is doubtful that Charlie Harris ever wrote much more than a few letters and a theme or two when he was a student at Georgia, but he sensed that there was something special about Lewis as a journalist. He felt Lewis had promise.

"He's a deserving boy," Charlie said, "and I want to see him get an education." Charlie was drawn to Lewis' clever ways of doing things and liked his enthusiasm and eagerness. He saw something creative about Lewis. He saw enterprise in his make up.

It didn't matter at that point, however, whether Charlie's assessment of Lewis was right or not. When an old friend calls in that situation, you do what you can to assist.

This was a transitional time in the state of Georgia. The Supreme Court had ruled ten years earlier that segregation was unconstitutional. LBJ presented his Civil Rights Act to Congress in 1964, and there had been demonstrations and sit-ins throughout the South. In Atlanta, the *Journal and Constitution*, led by the *Constitution's* Pulitzer prize winning editor Ralph McGill, took far too liberal a stance on these and other issues to suit many in the state. You could hear far and wide throughout Georgia that "something ought to be done about them lyin' Atlanta newspapers."

A group of Atlanta businessmen decided to do something. Or at least they decided to try. They started the *Atlanta Times* and poured big money into an ambitious attempt to compete with the *Atlanta Journal-Constitution* on the established papers' level from the beginning.

In Athens, over dinner with Dan Magill at Harry's Restaurant in Five Points, the consensus was that it would be good if the Times made it. But not for the reason that most Times supporters cited, which was "to see a conservative-run paper whip up on one that's run by a bunch of ungrateful liberals."

What Magill wanted was competition for the *Journal-Constitution's* sports pages. He thought that would bode well for the University of Georgia, which he felt had gotten the back of the hand from the Atlanta newspapers during the heyday of

Bobby Dodd and Georgia Tech. The *Times* might take a liking to Athens and Georgia, he suggested.

With Al Thomy (a long-time sports writer for the *Constitution*) joining the *Times* sports staff after the *Houston Press* folded, we felt that things might be looking up in Athens. Al spent a lot of time covering Bulldog events and was quite excited about Georgia's young, new football coach, Vince Dooley.

Al had told me on a recent trip to the Classic City that he would be looking for a campus correspondent for the *Times*. "Somebody like you," he grinned, making me feel proud that he appreciated the job I had done as campus correspondent for the *Journal* when I was a student at Georgia. Even though the *Journal* and *Constitution* operated under joint ownership, the sports staffs were highly competitive. News and scoops were a big thing with them, and because I was well connected in Athens with the coaches and, of course, Magill, I had stumbled onto some news features that got me a few "attaboys" from Journal sports editor Furman Bisher and his associate Jim Minter. Al knew exactly what he was looking for.

When Charlie Harris' call came in shortly after that, I decided to recommend this Lewis Grizzard, sight unseen, to Al Thomy.

"Look, Al," I said, "my friend says this boy is really good. We'll train him and work with him. He can use my office for whatever he needs, and Dan and I will look at his copy and make suggestions before he sends it in." Al thought that was a good plan, but what Magill thought was better was that we would know if Al's man in Athens was snooping around and sending in tips and tidbits of information detrimental to the best public relations interests of the University of Georgia. It was a win/win situation.

Lewis Grizzard already had a job when he walked into my office in late summer of 1964. I didn't know it, but he already was a member of the Bulldog family.

He certainly didn't lack for enterprise, then or at any point in his career. Of his own initiative, he had called the late Ed Thilenius, then Georgia's play-by-play football announcer, and talked himself into a job as a spotter for the Bulldog radio broadcasts.

When the Dooley era officially began with Georgia playing Alabama in Tuscaloosa on September 19, 1964, I was in the press box, glum and depressed that Joe Namath and Bear Bryant were treating the Bulldogs with no respect, eventually winning easily 31-3. Lewis was down the hall in the cramped Georgia radio booth, having the time of his life. He would later become a great and emotional Bulldog fan, but at that time he was so enraptured with his good fortune, to be where he was and doing what he was doing, that he had no time to worry about Alabama's dominance in that particular game. Life had taken a big and favorable upturn for Lewis. This was big stuff.

Soon Lewis was coming by my office every day with his story before sending it to Al Thomy at the *Atlanta Times*. I started out giving him suggestions on grammar, content and the like. After I had made a few corrections, he would nod and head out the door to Western Union to file his story. It wasn't long before I realized that he had imagination and a writing style that was special. Al Thomy realized it, too.

Unfortunately, the ambitious *Times* soon folded, still owing Lewis money. That was something he never let me forget, although we always had great fun reminiscing about those early days of his freshman year.

In Athens soon after that, there developed a newspaper opportunity ripe for plucking. The old *Athens Banner-Herald*, operated from a trust by the Phinizy estate, was aging, tired and lifeless. To give you an idea of what the *Banner-Herald* was like, long-time Georgia coach Bill Hartman once said, "When I want to go to bed with nothing on my mind, I always read the Banner-Herald."

A lot of people in town, especially those on the University of Georgia campus, felt that the community deserved a better newspaper. As if on cue, here came a group putting together a paper on a small scale, seeking a niche. It worked.

It worked because the *Banner-Herald* lacked competence, and because the competing ownership had the good sense to hire an editor like Glenn Vaughn and a young sportswriter like Lewis Grizzard.

The competing paper, the *Athens Daily News*, faced serious financial challenges, but it hung on with savvy, creativity and good sense journalism. (Eventually the *Banner-Herald*, owned by Southeastern Newspapers in Augusta, bought the *Daily News*.) Georgia was rebounding in football, and it was not uncommon to see Lewis' byline about a certain Bulldog game or development on the front page of the paper.

One thing the new paper gave priority to was layouts. It was a small-town publication, but it looked good. Lewis has always gotten high marks from his old *Atlanta Journal* buddies for his abilities as an editor, including an uncanny way of coming up with the perfect picture caption or headline, but another of his talents that has often gone unrecognized was his great instinct for layout. He wanted his sports pages to read well but also to look good.

In those days, Lewis had his heart set on becoming a career newspaperman. He was a natural-born, ink-stained wretch. And he was off to a good start, understanding from the *Times* experience that it is a tough business but learning from his *Athens Daily News* experience that it can be fun, too.

'Details,
Page 2':
Journalism 101

BY GLENN VAUGHN

Glenn Vaughn is the retired publisher and chairman of the board of directors of the Columbus (GA) Ledger-Enquirer. He was also the founding editor of the Athens (GA) Daily News.

Lewis Grizzard packed several lifetimes of remarkable success into his too-short life, but in his mind he never topped the thousand-day stretch that started his newspaper career.

Those were his days, thirty years ago, as a minimum-wage staffer following the launching of the *Athens* (GA) *Daily News* in 1965. Lewis called it "a perfect newspaperman's dream." All of us who were there still savor, as did Lewis, those memories and share a special bond. We called it "The People Paper," and so it was. We called them the morning newspaper's glory days, and so they were.

For years original staffers have told and retold stories of this great, fun time of our lives. On the newspaper's twentieth anniversary in 1985, a remarkable turnout of People Paper people gathered for a reunion in Athens. Master of ceremonies, of course, was Lewis Grizzard. That night we talked ourselves into exhaustion, and Lewis slept on a day bed in my hotel room.

What was it that made the newly-started *Daily News* such a special place for Lewis and all of us? Why has it stayed fresh in the memory of so many original staffers for so long? Mostly, it was the coming together — largely by happenstance — of an extraordinary group of people, primarily college students. As a group they seemed to create a kind of chemistry that made things happen. Lewis said we were charmed. Veteran reporter Larry Young said it was due to "The Man Upstairs."

Converted from a feature weekly called the *Athens Advertiser*, the new morning daily went up against the then 130-year-old *Athens Banner-Herald*, an afternoon paper. First issue was June 16, 1965. It published every morning except Monday. Claude Williams, who had owned the *Advertiser* as well as Georgia Outdoor Advertising, Inc., was president and general manager of the new venture, and I had come up from Columbus, Georgia, to become editor and publisher. We, along with a third partner, Charles A. (Chuck) McClure, who headed a Columbus-head-quartered radio group, were the "...crazy people who had an idea to start a competing morning newspaper" that Lewis wrote about in his best-selling book about his newspaper career, *If I Ever Get Back to Georgia, I'm Gonna Nail My Feet to the Ground.*

Lewis Grizzard was actually the third person hired for the morning paper staff. Wade Saye, my second hire, whom we had grabbed away from his sports editor's job at the *Athens Banner-Herald*, wisely lined up Lewis to work in the *Daily News* sports department in the fall. It was, as I recall, the first Sunday in June, 1965, when I met Lewis. He was nineteen and a rising sophomore at the University of Georgia. It was at the *Advertiser* offices in an old home on Milledge Avenue. Wade wanted my OK to hire Lewis, and the three of us talked under a tree in the backyard.

Wade was an Athens native who had served four years as a U.S. Air Force officer after graduating from the University. On leaving the service he had taken a $50-a-week sports editor's job at the *Banner-Herald* because he wanted to stay in Athens. Lewis had done some part-time work for Wade the year before.

Our backyard conversation didn't take very long; Wade, who at times has been too shy for his own good, was never one to waste words. The crew cut and unshaven Lewis had not expected to come my way that Sunday afternoon and was apologetic about his appearance. Here, in what was to be the fermenting decade of the 1960s, was a very well-mannered young man who obviously knew and loved sports and whose conversation was peppered with quick "yes sirs" and "no sirs." It was easy to agree with Wade's choice, and Lewis said he could join the staff in about two months.

Even into the 1960s, most newspapers still had not conceded to the electronic media the immediacy advantage the latter had on news and sports. Sunday morning headlines, even in college towns, focused on scores as if readers had not heard a word about the Saturday games. We took a different approach. While we thoroughly reported game particulars, we sought to portray game day as a huge event. We wanted our readers to sense the excitement in the city and in the stands and to *hear* the traditional University Chapel bell ring. Typifying our headlines was one we used after a Georgia-Georgia Tech game:

OH, HOT DIGGITY DOG, MR. DOOLEY, YOU HAVE WRECKED OLE TECH AGAIN!

Wade was a good sports editor, and his young assistant was notably professional from the start. Both were hard workers and their results made the *Daily News* shine. When Wade was moved up the newspaper's management ladder, Lewis, young as he was, stepped into the sports editor's slot without missing a beat.

My wife Nancy and I were a kind of workplace mama and papa for Lewis and the other wonderfully talented students who joined the *Daily News* staff. Nancy's enormous ability and people skills made her a perfect People Paper fit both in terms of our readers and our young staff.

During that first year Lewis didn't have any romantic entanglements that we knew about. He did have a date with the lovely Colleen Kelly, also a journalism student on our staff. Their date set tongues to wagging in our plant because some had already decided they would be a good match. For a time no one had a clue on how things were with them. Lewis later grumbled quietly to Nancy that his date with Colleen was so expensive he was left flat broke with several more days to go until payday.

In his book *If I Ever Get Back to Georgia...*, Lewis, bless his soul, put me on too high a pedestal. But he also nailed me good. He wrote that I often seemed to be in the "Newsroom Out Yonder," referring to my absentmindedness and describing me as "given to forgetting what the conversation is about." Unfortunately, my wife Nancy and others will confirm that. And here I am, at sixty-six, getting worse.

Of Lewis' many tales about me, one or two always got a good laugh from his speaking-circuit audiences. One was the time, after getting married and setting up housekeeping, he asked for a raise and got five cents an hour added to his paycheck. That's true, but a five percent hike is not bad, folks.

Also, he often told about my "plan" for newspaper coverage of the Second Coming. The story, I confess, was pretty much true. But I must say, being the great storyteller he was, Lewis embroidered my little leg-pulling act quite a lot. At the time it did occur to me that when the Lord returns, an appropriate headline might very well read, "HE'S BACK!" Below that would be a full-page photo of the event and the refer-line that said, "Details, Page 2." It was great fun watching the intense eyes of a nineteen-year-old Lewis Grizzard contemplating every word of my suggestion, in some detail, about how such an event from On High might be covered. After all, dreaming too is serious business, and when one dreams of a big story....

We all laughed a lot at the *Daily News* and we wanted our newspaper to have the kind of personality that said, "Loosen up." A People Paper credo could well have been, "Yes, there are problems and let's address them, but let's enjoy and respect each other in the process." I like to think our fun kind of work environment helped to point Lewis in the direction of humor.

For example, a kind of mystery once developed at the *Daily News* when rolls of toilet paper kept disappearing from the men's room. Lewis sounded off about it in the newsroom. A day or two later, it was also Lewis who got to the bottom of the problem. He happened to look into the office of seventy-nine-year-old Earl Braswell, whom we had also hired away from the *Banner-Herald*, and saw maybe a dozen rolls of toilet paper in assorted sizes. For reasons none of us ever knew, Mr. Braswell had been squirreling away toilet paper in his office. Most likely, Mr. Braswell, a grand old man who could barely see, simply picked up the rolls absentmindedly.

Mr. Braswell came our way not long after the *Banner-Herald* he headed for forty-four years was sold. Claude Williams learned he was unhappy about what he felt was rude treatment from the new management. We offered him the post of executive editor of the *Daily News* at a modest salary ($50 per week). He delightedly came with us and even wrote a column.

Another example: Lewis joked in one of his books about our front page obituary following the death in Athens of a well-known madam named Effie Matthews. The headline below the fold proclaimed, "Prominent Business Woman Dies." She was indeed widely known. For decades she had presided over houses of ill repute in Athens and was so often whispered about, it was impossible to get through the University without knowing about Effie. The city was not proud of the fact, but she was easily the town's best known woman.

Looking back, Lewis could not have had a better foundation for what was to be his remarkably successful career. The hours were long and the work was hard, but that magic time turned out to be an amazing kaleidoscope of the real world. In one of a series of ads featuring our employees, Lewis was spotlighted along with his wife Nancy and their dog, Plato. The ad read, "... while Lewis' specialty is sports, he is hardly limited to one field, having written such notable stories as the exposé of fortune-telling in Athens, speed trap controversies, stories from the Georgia Legislature on the election of Governor Maddox, and in-depth stories on the tax structure and teacher salaries."

At the *Daily News*, one did what needed to be done, even if it was sweeping the floor. It was not uncommon for major stories to involve the whole staff. Everyone, including Lewis, pitched in when we devoted the entire front page to the brutal murder of an elderly woman. Same thing for a spectacular Athens bank robbery. The lessons of work and of the craft stuck. After all, Lewis never forgot his experience with the burly and outspoken police chief of a tiny town north of Athens.

When he went into the one-room police department to inquire of the chief about reports of a speed trap, Lewis was advised with clarity to remove him-

'People Paper People': Nancy, Lewis and Plato in 1967

Twenty-five years later: Nancy and Lewis at the reunion

self from the community without delay, or there might be consequences. Though frightened, Lewis soon realized that this probably made for a better story than if the chief had simply denied that his town was a speed trap. The next day's front page headline, **DAILY NEWS REPORTER THREATENED**, was so sweet.

Another good scare that Lewis had also served our new newspaper. In a sports column, Lewis made fun of legendary Clemson University coach Frank Howard's thick drawl, and he mocked Howard's weekly television show. Coach Howard, who didn't hide his feelings, called Lewis at home raising the devil and threatening legal action. Lewis clearly remembered the coach's words: "I'm going to sue your butt!" Still only nineteen, Lewis was really worried when he came to me. I was delighted. Getting that kind of attention from one as well known as Frank Howard was a clear message to our readers and advertisers of just how important our newspaper was. And what a great headline it made at the top of our front page the next day.

CLEMSON COACH THREATENS
SUIT AGAINST DAILY NEWS

Of course, Coach Howard had no intention of suing. He knew, or would soon find out, that pockets around the *Daily News* were not very deep.

What a delight it is to work with bright, fun-loving young people. It keeps the focus from locking onto the dark side of life. It was fun getting ahead of the competition. Also, there seemed to be a lot of fun stories to print. Take the catfish story we ran one April Fools' Day.

We borrowed a set of false teeth from a dentist's office. Larry Young and photographer Browny Stephens took the teeth to a lake near Athens, where they acquired a good-size catfish and inserted the teeth into its mouth. Browny photographed a fisherman holding the strange looking catch. Wade Saye wrote a very fine tongue-in-cheek story about how a fish with human-like teeth had been caught and speculating how it might be some kind of ancient species. We ran the picture on the front page along with Wade's story, and at the very end were the words, "APRIL FOOL." Reaction was very good.

Inextricably linked to savored remembrances of Lewis in the Athens workplace are those of his life with Nancy, the tall and lovely blonde who was Lewis' first wife and his deepest love. Lewis started his second year with the *Daily News*, in August, 1966, with her as his new bride. Their love for each other was to outlast their short marriage. Nancy, who became "Paula" in Lewis' book *If Love Were Oil, I'd Be About a Quart Low*, joined the newspaper as a receptionist. This made their People Paper years also their honeymoon years. Lewis once confided that things were not going smoothly at home. He said Nancy was often frustrated with him because of the long and late hours he was working. He said it especially upset her that all their friends were doing things on Friday and Saturday nights and the Grizzards never could because of his work schedule. Lewis asked my Nancy to have a talk with his Nancy about things, particularly about what it is like to be the wife of a newspaperman.

It had to be an incredible strain on the young married couple. He was working no telling how many hours per week, every night except one. She had a daytime job and did household chores at night. He went to class at the University during the day and was back on the job at the paper in the afternoon.

And, believe it or not, Lewis was making the dean's list nearly every quarter. There was a high price to pay, for sure, but it was very clear by then that Lewis Grizzard had the brains and the work ethic to achieve whatever goals he set.

Lewis joked at the twentieth reunion of People Paper people about how, after working sixty hours, he would sign a time sheet listing only forty. While my recollection would be a bit fuzzy regarding that particular, there is a remarkable story here involving a formal charge to the Wage and Hour Division of the U.S. Department of Labor alleging unpaid overtime.

The charge was levied by a young man who worked in our press plate developing area at night and hung around the proximity of a lovely classified clerk during the day. When we fired him for stealing a radio out of the darkroom, he went to the Wage and Hour folks and charged he was owed wages he had not received. Those who worked in the back shop punched time clocks, but he claimed to have done some work off the clock during the day.

So a federal investigator came and asked to talk with our employees. One by one, he questioned every *Daily News* employee and, one by one, they insisted they were not owed any back wages and, without exception, signed waivers to that effect. The loyalty of People Paper people was unbelievable.

While Lewis was later to control what had to be huge travel expense budgets as executive sports editor, first at the *Atlanta Journal* and later at the *Chicago Sun-Times*, he was well-grounded at the *Daily News* on ways to get by without spending much money covering games.

One knows he is working for a low-budget newspaper when he has to stay with his editor's brother-in-law while covering an out-of-state football game. That was Lewis' lot. Once he and Nancy rode to Lexington, Kentucky, with my Nancy and me where he was to cover the Georgia-Kentucky game. On the way up, we stopped near Ellijay, Georgia, and enjoyed fried chicken with my wife's parents (another budget item savings). We arrived Friday evening, in plenty of time for the Saturday night game, where the two Nancys and I just about froze to death in the stands. Accommodations and more free, good eating were provided by my Nancy's brother and his wife.

Lewis' many fans were aware of his fear of flying. He often said he understood why the word for an airport building was "terminal." Claude Williams believes the fears had to do with a flight to Jackson, Mississippi, where Lewis went to cover a Georgia-Ole Miss game. Claude, the *Daily News'* president and general manager, hitched a ride to the game for Lewis and himself aboard a four-seat, single-engine Mooney. The plane was owned by a plumbing supply wholesaler who brought along a flight instructor.

After making the tight squeeze with Claude into the back seat, Lewis learned that the flight was to be a training session on instrument flying for the pilot. Lewis didn't say anything.

Well into the flight, Claude noticed that the aircraft was flying about twenty knots slower than it should have been. Turned out that so much attention had been paid to instrument flying,

48

the student pilot had forgotten to raise the landing gear at take-off. Lewis was taking in all this conversation, about the wheels being left down, still without saying a word.

Next came the revelation that the plane was on course to the wrong airport. It took a few minutes to determine that the radio was somehow on a different frequency. Finally, contact was made with air controllers at the Memphis Airport and a new course to the correct Jackson Airport was established.

Noticing that Lewis seemed quite tense, Claude asked if he was OK and how he was liking the flight. "Not good at all," Lewis replied. "This is my first flight."

"You mean this is your first flight in a small plane?" asked Claude.

"No," said Lewis, "I mean it's my first flight in *any* kind of plane."

A major disappointment in Lewis Grizzard's young work life came, ironically, at what was one of the most ecstatic moments at the People Paper. That's when the excellence awards came. The first time our newly-established newspaper was eligible to participate in the Georgia Press Association awards competition for journalism excellence, the *Daily News* cleaned up.

That year our newspaper received more awards (five) for journalism excellence than any other daily newspaper, large or small, in the state and was the only daily to win first place in two categories, which were Community Service and Local Photography.

One of the great strengths of the *Athens Daily News* was our sports section, under Lewis' direction. Our game coverage, which always got top play on our front page, along with our unique headlines, were by then the talk of the state. But this was one time the luck of the draw was not with us.

The 1967 awards were based on material published in 1966. One drawback to these competitions, which are judged by out-of-state editors, is that rules require entries to be submitted from mandated dates. In one case, the day selected was not one we would have picked.

The *Daily News* won third place in the Local Sports Coverage category, and, of all newspapers, the *Athens Banner-Herald*, then so fiercely hated by our young staffers, got second place. That was a real downer for us all, and Lewis, especially, was crushed. But he quickly put it behind him and we all basked in our glory. A full-page ad touting our awards read:

EVEN PAPER PEOPLE PICK THE PEOPLE PAPER!

Groundwork for the first-place Community Service award had been laid early in 1966 with an editorial inspired by a drive to a beautiful old covered bridge northeast of Athens, between the small communities of Colbert and Comer. "What a perfect place for a park....," our editorial began. The rash of community activity that followed soon involved political leaders and the State Parks Department, all fully covered by the *Daily News*, of course, and Watson Mill Bridge State Park was born.

Considerable support for our state park campaign came from neighboring Oglethorpe County where the managing editor of the weekly *Oglethorpe Echo* was one Frank Frosch. Frank also wrote a gripping, widely-read, three-times-a-week column in the *Daily News*. And he taught freshman English at the University, was band director at the high school, and a volunteer coach. Football prowess as a star quarterback in his Speedway, Indiana, hometown had earned Frank a scholarship to Virginia Military Institute, from which he graduated, although an injury had cut short his playing days.

Frank's easy-going manner belied his unbelievable crush of activity. He was a People Paper person we all cherished. Lewis often wrote about the basset hound, Plato, that he and Nancy kept for the Frosches when Frank left for the Army. Frank's fantastic career, as an intelligence officer in Vietnam and later as a Pentagon reporter and foreign correspondent for United Press International, ended with his and a photographer's senseless execution at the hands of Communists in a remote area of Cambodia. Lewis and Nancy adopted Plato.

As for our second top prize, there was simply no way we

could *not* win the Local Photography first-place excellence award. Browny Stephens, a University of Georgia journalism graduate, could do it all, but what he did best was take really outstanding, unusual photos. He never even considered taking what Lewis called "firing squad" pictures, where the photographer "just lines 'em up and shoots 'em."

Browny was certainly the most unusual newspaperman I have ever known. Once when we were relaxing at a local restaurant after work, I asked Browny to write down on a napkin all of the newspapers for which he had worked over the years. He listed fifty-seven. He also was an avid outdoorsman and frequently took Lewis fishing and whitewater rafting. Browny Stephens died of cancer a few years ago, the very day Lewis conducted a benefit on his behalf.

To be sure, it was largely the engine of youth that made the *Daily News* go, but Larry Young proved that being young was not altogether a matter of years. At age forty-four when the newspaper started, Larry must have seemed like a senior citizen to the student staffers. Along with experience, Larry brought electricity and excitement to the paper, and when it came to cultivating news sources, he was unbeatable. Larry got the story and he didn't waste time doing it — a lesson that young Lewis Grizzard learned well by watching him daily. Larry had a distinguished career with the Athens Newspapers, serving many years as an editor of the *Daily News*. He died in late 1984.

While Lewis, as well as Larry and Browny, have now passed on, it may be well to remember a few of the others, primarily news staffers in this case, who worked closely in a grand effort to do what many people said couldn't be done. These people remained close personal and professional friends of Lewis' throughout his life.

Among the fine young staffers was Gerald Rutberg, a talented Auburn University student who had inquired about a summer internship at the Columbus *Ledger*, but whom I persuaded to come along with me to Athens. After completing his final year at Auburn, the lure of the People Paper brought Gerald back to Athens where he attended the University's Lumpkin Law School. He is now a highly-regarded attorney in Orlando.

Lewis often wrote about Gerald's remarkable talent for getting into any event, no matter how exclusive, no matter how secure. They met at various times at the Masters Golf Tournament, the Super Bowl, and the Kentucky Derby — none of which Gerald had credentials for. And photos of Jimmy Carter's swearing-in as President of the United States show Gerald in the background standing beside a Supreme Court justice. He was amazing.

Chuck Perry started in the *Daily News* mail room during his high school days. While a student at the University's Henry W. Grady School of Journalism, he worked in the sports department under Lewis and became sports editor when Lewis left Athens. Chuck went on to become a managing editor at the *Atlanta Journal-Constitution* and now is president and editor of Longstreet Press, which published many of Lewis' books.

Peter Trigg also worked as a reporter for the *Daily News* while a journalism student at the University. He now is director of art/graphics for the *New York Times* News Service.

Colleen Kelly, who was to break our hearts when she later married the competition's sports editor, went on to work her way into a management position with Atlanta Newspapers before moving to advertising/promotion work.

Jim Wooten, also a fine reporter on the People Paper as a University journalism student, is having a distinguished career with Atlanta Newspapers and currently is editorial page editor of the *Atlanta Journal*.

Wade Saye, who later served well in editor positions in Columbus, is an assistant managing editor with the Knoxville (TN) *News-Sentinel.*.

John Futch, who worked with Lewis and Chuck Perry on the sports staff before he was sent to Vietnam, is now managing editor of the *Boca Raton* (FL) *News*.

Mark Smith, a third-generation newspaper professional who was on the *Daily News* advertising staff, went on to become a long-time publisher of Athens Newspapers before being promoted to a corporate executive position with Morris Communications.

Christmas Eve, 1967, was a very sad day for the entire People Paper staff. That's when the sale of the *Daily News* to the Morris group in Augusta was announced. That meant the two Athens newspapers would be merged under one management umbrella.

When we moved to our new quarters in February, it was even sadder. The night we moved, *Banner-Herald* Publisher Buddy Hayden walked into my old office and found me crying almost uncontrollably. Looking back, I often wished I had tried to arrange some kind of special reward for those young staffers who worked their hearts out. At the time Gerald Rutberg made an eloquent appeal for me to try. However, I was a minority stockholder and mostly what we were being paid was over a ten-year period, and I was reluctant to open what I feared might be a can of worms.

In an effort to keep the *Daily News* independent, I had in those final weeks quietly talked with several Athens businessmen. There was some interest, but I did not then have the expertise to follow through. Claude Williams, who in recent years helped organize a new bank in Athens, told me not long ago that he has since learned how we could have kept the original People Paper going despite our fragile financial position.
Lewis once wrote, "I've said it a thousand times in my life: 'If I could go back, I'd go back to Athens and do it all over again.'"

If only we could have a resurgence of youth and rally the old gang. If only we could have Lewis back, and Larry, and Browny and Frank, and....

Lewis Grizzard:
The Ultimate
Newspaperman

By Jim Minter

Jim Minter, former editor of the Atlanta Journal & Constitution, is one of the country's most respected newsmen. He writes a weekly column from his home in Fayetteville, Georgia.

The first time I laid eyes on Lewis Grizzard, he was covering a University of Georgia baseball game for the *Athens Daily News*. I was on a scouting mission for the *Atlanta Journal* sports department, looking for a rookie who would start at the bottom on a small salary.

Earlier in the day, I had met with Vince Dooley, the Georgia football coach. I asked Vince if he knew of a young sportswriter who did his homework, asked good questions, got the facts straight, and didn't think he was necessarily God's greatest gift to journalism. He said he had been impressed by a kid named Lewis Grizzard, a journalism major who worked for the Athens newspaper. I put the same questions to Joel Eaves, the athletic director. He gave the same answer.

I went looking for the young man. When I located him in the baseball press box, I introduced myself and tried to size him up. He had a round baby face and seemed on the shy side. He knew how to keep a baseball scorebook while carrying on a conversation. He said he had been reading the *Journal* sports pages in

Moreland as long as he could remember. I was impressed.

Before I offered him a job, I had to ask the critical question: "What's your draft status?" This was during the Vietnam war and it made no sense to hire somebody who would be at Fort Jackson, South Carolina, before he learned headline counts at the newspaper.

"I'm okay with the draft," he answered. "The army won't take me because the doctors say I have a slight heart murmur. Something I was born with. Nothing to worry about, just some sort of medical technicality."

How many times in future years did we wish that had been true!

Lewis was not happy to be turned down in the draft. He was a patriot, impressed by his father's war record. He wondered if he could have done the things Capt. Lewis M. Grizzard, Sr., did in Europe and in Korea. Lewis' admiration for his father, being born into a military family at Ft. Benning, Georgia, shaped much of his thinking as an editor and columnist. He was of, but not among, a generation of young Americans (not all of them) who burned the flag, bugged out on the draft, marched on ROTC buildings, went to Woodstock, and through a fog of marijuana smoke thought they saw all the answers.

Lewis, Sr., who wasn't an army captain anymore, occasionally dropped by the office to hit his son for a loan. He had been forced to leave the army for reasons unknown to Lewis. He drank too much, and whenever he landed a good job he soon lost it.

One afternoon the hospital in Metter, a small town in South Georgia, called Lewis on the telephone. His father had suffered a stroke. He was unconscious, not likely to recover. He owed the hospital $400. Lewis immediately emptied his and Nancy's savings account and left for Metter.

He got his father moved to a veterans hospital in Augusta, where he died, after running up a hefty bill the VA wouldn't pay because Capt. Grizzard's discharge from the army was less than satisfactory. Lewis was making barely enough to survive at the paper, but he paid the hospital in monthly installments.

He was deeply troubled about his dad's having been kicked

out of the army after a battlefield commission in Europe, being wounded in Korea, captured by Communists, escaping, being carried piggy-back by one of his men to friendly lines. Several times Lewis asked me to have the newspapers' lawyers use the Freedom of Information Act to get his father's military records. I always told him I would. I never did.

The newspaper business is a seductive mistress. It is hard on wives, especially young wives. Newspapers don't pay very well, or at least they didn't when Lewis was breaking in. After rent, utilities, car note and groceries, there's precious little left for nights on the town.

Since events that make news don't necessarily follow a clock, newspapers demand long and irregular hours. Newspaper husbands are seldom home when they're supposed to be. Whatever is happening in the news takes precedent over all else, including birthdays, anniversaries, even babies being born. Newspaper wives spend a lot of time warming over dinners, waiting in stadium parking lots, and answering the telephone to hear how he needs another hour at the office.

To make matters worse, newspaper husbands aren't among the world's most sensitive, caring people. They have large egos and think whatever they are doing is the most important thing in the universe. The result is they have trouble keeping wives. They certainly have trouble keeping wives happy.

In his first marriage, maybe in all of them, Lewis was a typical newspaper husband. He was a workaholic. He thought about, dreamed about, his job twenty-four hours a day. If anyone had been keeping score it would have been: Newspaper 10, Wife 2.

The way it looked to me, Lewis had one love that overshadowed all others. She was Nancy, his first wife, his childhood sweetheart from Moreland. They played together, went to school together, went to church together. They married soon after he enrolled at the University of Georgia, where he also worked a full-time newspaper job. They married too young, without ever exploring other relationships. It might have worked out if

Nancy had been a school teacher and Lewis a CPA.

When Lewis left the University and the *Daily News*, moving from Athens to Atlanta, he brought Nancy, their dog, Plato, and an elderly Volkswagen. They bought a nice little house in the suburbs. Plato romped in the backyard. Lewis, when he was home, cooked hamburgers on the patio. Nancy got a job at a printing company.

They would have children, grow old together, and move to St. Simons Island or a place in the North Georgia mountains when he retired from the newspaper. I'd like to blame the newspaper for their divorce. I'm afraid I did more to cause it than the newspaper.

Not long after Lewis came to work, we lost our slotman in the *Journal* sports department. The slotman was so named because he sat in the mouth of a large horseshoe-shaped desk, surrounded by five or six lesser editors who under his supervision wrote headlines, captions for pictures, fixed grammar and corrected spelling for reporters who had gone to journalism school at the University of Georgia. Because of computers and other questionable inventions, newspapers don't have slotmen anymore. That's one thing wrong with newspapers.

The slotman (we never had a slotwoman, or a slotperson) was the most important editor in precomputer newsrooms. While writers traveled around the country on expense accounts, to the Kentucky Derby, the Super Bowl, the World Series, the Final Four, any event justifying an expense account, the slotman stayed home and did the heavy lifting. He was in charge of everything, including avoiding libel suits, putting out fires when careless reporters threw lighted cigarettes into trash cans, fending off the managing editors who thought the front sports page was as important as the front page, supplying crotchety union printers with free baseball tickets, bailing reporters out of jail whenever they got DUIs or skipped alimony payments. He also got blamed for everything that went wrong.

His was a horrible job, made worse on an afternoon paper, which is mostly produced in the wee hours of the morning so it can be printed before noon, to keep from paying overtime in the circulation and mechanical departments. The slotman had to be at work by 4:30 in the morning. If he stayed on his feet until time to go home, he had to go to bed hours before his wife got through watching television. He also had to work from two o'clock on Saturday afternoons until three o'clock Sunday mornings, wrestling the big Sunday paper. If he took his lady to dinner, it had to be a quick trip to McDonald's.

So, as I said, we lost our slotman a few months after Lewis came to Atlanta. I can't recall if it was suicide or nervous breakdown. We lost a lot of slotmen. This time, the job fell to me. After several years of artful dodging, I became the slotman. My wife was badly out of sorts and my children thought I was deceased.

One Sunday afternoon, when I finally staggered out of bed, my wife suggested we have a heart-to-heart talk. We did. She told me to get a slotman or get a divorce.

The next day, I called Lewis to my desk. "Lewis," I said, "how would you like to be the slotman?" I could tell he wasn't thrilled, but Lewis was a loyal soldier. He had trouble saying no. He became our slotman, with a $5 a week raise. Several months later he and Nancy got a divorce. I'm still happily married.

With his long hours and early wakeups, they couldn't have had an ideal married life. Lewis complicated it when he developed a habit of going for an afternoon beer, or two, or three, with Frank Hyland and Jim Hunter, two of the *Journal*'s whiz kids, but the main culprit was the job. Many wives can't tolerate newspaper husbands. I don't blame them.

I don't know details. I do know Nancy and Lewis parted reluctantly, regretfully, and sadly. I don't think Lewis ever recovered.

On Friday afternoons, we shared the exercise of planning the big Sunday sports sections. This was something Lewis really enjoyed. He was at his creative best putting all the pieces together for the enjoyment of several hundred thousand readers. I don't think he ever did anything else that gave him the satisfaction he got from his Sunday sports sections.

On this particular Friday, as we faced each other across my desk and began our work, he seemed distracted and disinterested. He had a far-away look. He appeared to be on another planet.

"Dammit," I snapped, "if you don't want to help, go on and I'll do the Sunday paper myself." That's when I saw the tears, rivulets trickling down his cheeks. "Nancy left this morning," he said. Maybe those tears never really stopped.

Odds are that was the moment when he began his journey to fame, to a different lifestyle, to a column in more than 450 newspapers, to twenty-five books, to a regional and national reputation. His old life came apart. It would never again be the same. He lost something, gained something. An ordinary husband who went home after work to walk the dog and cook hamburgers on the patio could never have written the columns he wrote. But he could have been one helluva editor — not just of the sports section, but of an entire newspaper. He almost was.

A couple of years after he landed in the *Journal* sports department, a rookie from the University of Georgia, top management at the *Journal-Constitution* moved me, the *Journal's* executive sports editor, to the morning paper, the *Constitution*, as managing editor. Furman Bisher, *Journal* sports editor who stayed busy with his daily column, and the other bosses installed Lewis in my old job of running the day-to-day operation.

With Lewis in charge, the *Journal's* sports pages instantly became better, brighter, more interesting, more creative. Many of the innovations in *USA Today*, grudgingly copied by stodgy newspapers around the country, basically are innovations Lewis thought up all by himself in *Journal* sports. There's no proof, but I've suspected that Al Neuharth, founder of *USA Today* and an old sports hand himself, noticed the *Journal's* sports pages when he was passing through the Atlanta airport and appropriated some of Lewis' ideas. If so, I wish he'd read more closely. Grizzard-edited newspapers, in addition to being sprightly and entertaining, plowed deep and hit hard.

Lewis had an uncanny talent of knowing what people wanted to read. Glenn Vaughn, his editor at the *Daily News* in Athens, had been a great teacher. A rarity in newspapering who didn't follow the crowd, Glenn thought working for a newspapers ought to be fun, and that readers ought to enjoy reading them. He told Lewis a story about what's wrong with newspapers, now and then. Lewis listened and learned. The story:

Four or five editors are sitting around selecting stories to put into the paper. One tears an item off the Associated Press wire, reads it, chuckles, and passes it on to the next editor, who reads it and passes it on to the next. The last editor reads it, chuckles, and tosses the story into the trash. Readers never saw it. The reason they didn't was because the story wasn't about politics in Washington, a bombing in Beirut, or a debate in the United Nations. Nor was it likely to be used by the *New York Times*. Never mind that it was probably the most interesting story of the day.

Furman Bisher taught Lewis why newspapers are called NEWSpapers rather than pamphlets or magazines. They are supposed to report NEWS. Get it first, get it right, or get out of town.

In the 1950s and 60s many aspiring journalists were attracted to the *Atlanta Journal* because of the sports department's historic reputation for excellence, and by Bisher, one of the nation's premier columnists.

Among the bright young men who sat at Bisher's feet were Bill Robinson, who wrote auto racing like it had never been written before: "Richard Petty...running flat out, belly to the ground, chasing a hurrying sundown," is a sample; John Logue, later managing editor of *Southern Living* magazine, editor-in-chief of Oxmoor House, author of mystery novels; Kim Chapin, who moved to *Sports Illustrated* and wrote books; Pritt Vesiland, a star staffer for *National Geographic*; Chuck Perry, founder of Longstreet Press; Gregory Favre, executive editor of the *Sacramento Bee* and vice president of the McClachey newspaper chain; Terry Kay, nationally known author and playwright; Lee Walburn, editor of *Atlanta Magazine*; and Ron Hudspeth, who founded his own weekly newspaper covering Atlanta's night life. All are graduates of the Bisher School of Journalism.

Lewis, like others who labored in Bisher's vineyard, found that sitting at his feet often led to a blistered behind, if there

1990 AJC sports reunion: (front row, L-R) Jim Minter, Lee Walburn, Furman Bisher, John Logue, Tom McCollister, Wilt Browning, (back row, L-R) Bill Whitley, David Davidson, Chuck Perry, Frank Hyland, Lewis Grizzard, Norman Arey, Don Boykin, Ron Hudspeth, Darrell Simmons.

was one left to blister. Furman is a perfectionist, a taskmaster, a fierce competitor who thinks that any newspaper, TV or radio station that beats his newspaper to a story has committed a criminal act.

Before he mellowed and turned the day-to-day operations over to a series of executive sports editors, Bisher was — to be honest — hell to work for. It was like playing football for Vince Lombardi: you wouldn't take anything for the experience but it's not much fun while you're getting it.

Furman traveled a lot, but he didn't hesitate to keep tabs on the office by telephone. Lewis hated to answer the telephone, fearing Furman was on the other end of the line ready to point out some news story the *Journal* had missed, or a mistake in a box score. An executive sports editor could more easily sneak a sunrise past the proverbial rooster than a goof-up past Bisher. When I was the *Journal*'s executive sports editor, he taught me the most valuable lesson of my career...over the telephone.

He was in Thomasville, Georgia, covering a semi-important golf tournament. The morning after the first round, my telephone rang. "Isn't anybody watching the shop?" he demanded. "We didn't have results of this tournament in the papers that came to Thomasville. The local paper had results. The Tallahassee paper had results. We didn't. What the hell went wrong?"

What went wrong was that Thomasville is on the Florida border, about three hundred miles from Atlanta, over two-lane roads with twenty-five or thirty small towns to navigate. The golfers were still on the course when our delivery truck had to load in Atlanta. There was no way under the sun to get up-to-date results in our papers that went to Thomasville. I explained all this to Furman.

"Well," he said, "that's your problem. You figure it out and get the scores in the paper."

I couldn't think of any way to do it, but I didn't like to think about what would happen if I failed. I went to the managing editor and begged him into an extra thirty minutes before going to press. Then I went to the composing room, and using our free baseball tickets (free tickets weren't against the law at that time) I bribed the composing room foreman out of another half hour. In a pinch, composing room foremen who like baseball can fake mechanical delays.

Using the remainder of our free baseball tickets, I persuaded the driver of the Thomasville truck to discover an engine problem before pulling into the loading dock. Miraculously, the Thomasville golf results got in our paper, just like Bisher had commanded. If newspapers had more Bishers, they wouldn't have to worry so much about losing readers.

Lewis later dedicated one of his books to Furman. It was Furman who called Jim Kennedy, chairman of Cox Enterprises, and got him to send the company jet to Orlando to fetch Lewis home to Emory University Hospital for the last operation that almost saved his life.

Shortly after Lewis took over the daily operation in *Journal* sports, publisher Jack Tarver, a veteran newsman at least as demanding as Bisher, noticed the fuzzy-faced youngster sitting in the slot.

"How old is that kid?" Tarver asked, not bothering to hide his skepticism.

"Mr. Tarver," I said, "he's older than he looks. He's going on thirty." He was. He was twenty-three, the youngest executive sports editor in the newspaper's history, perhaps in the history of big-city journalism.

Lewis had judgment beyond his years. The *Journal* and *Constitution*, in the same building and both owned by the Cox family, nevertheless were sworn enemies. I had defected to the enemy. We weren't supposed to speak to each other. But I, almost twenty years his senior, often sneaked into his office late at night to solicit advice on a story the *Constitution* was working on.

Most newspaper editors get "new" ideas by stealing from other newspapers and other editors. Lewis thought up his own. He made pages more sprightly, devised ways to encourage readers to interact with writers. He squeezed in stories other editors threw in the trash, as Glenn Vaughn had warned him they would. He persuaded a hot college football prospect to keep a diary on the pressures and excesses of recruiting season. He engineered thoughtful, hard-hitting stories. He raised caption and headline writing from a chore into an art form.

The best journalism textbook on headlines and captions is a chapter in one of Lewis' books I lent to a reporter and never got back. I can't recall word for word, but here's an example of the Grizzard touch: Under a picture of Jack Nicklaus hitting out of a sand trap, the average editor will write, "Jack Nicklaus hits out of sand trap," which is obvious to even the most obtuse reader. Lewis would spice it up with something like, "ON THE BEACH: Nicklaus lifts off enroute to a birdie and a Masters' record." See the difference?

He out-thought other people. When Henry Aaron was about to break Babe Ruth's homerun record, Lewis positioned his *Journal* team to cover all angles. He even sent a reporter to the men's room, to record the reaction of the unlucky fan who missed the historic moment because he drank a couple of beers and had to seek relief.

When Woody Hayes, the controversial Ohio State football coach, was fired for hitting a Clemson player on the sideline in the Gator Bowl, every major newspaper in the country tried to arrange an interview with him. Hayes was secluded at his home in Columbus, Ohio, refusing to talk to reporters.

Lewis didn't telephone. He had his man fly up to Columbus, go to the Hayes' home, and knock on the door. Mrs. Hayes invited the reporter into her living room. Woody came in and talked for an hour. The result was an exclusive story picked up by other papers and published all over the country.

Lewis' reputation was making the newspaper rounds. Other sports sections were copying his. He was on top of his world. Trouble was, the *Journal* was an afternoon paper and, like all afternoon papers in the television age, was losing circulation at an alarming rate. The big bosses at the newspaper had an idea: Move Lewis out of the sports department and let him do to the entire newspaper what he had done to the sports section.

They moved him, but they made a mistake, one that newspaper management often makes. They put him only partly in charge of what he was supposed to do. People in other departments, news and features, were baffled by Lewis.

They didn't know about eighteen hour days. They didn't know about spending half a night getting page layouts, pictures, captions, stories and headlines just right. They didn't get sick to their stomachs, or pound desks with their fists, when somebody else got the story about a city councilman sticking his hand in the cookie jar. They didn't understand why Lewis threw fits when editors passed a story among themselves, chuckled, and then threw it into the trash because it wasn't "important" and probably wouldn't make the *New York Times*.

The straw that broke his spirit fell the day President Jimmy Carter pardoned Vietnam draft-dodgers living in exile in Canada. Frank Hyland, one of the talented old hands in the sports department, happened to be in Toronto with the Atlanta Braves. Lewis immediately picked up the telephone, woke Frank in his hotel room, and told him to find some of the exiles and get their reaction to Carter's pardon. Frank did, and the *Journal* had an exclusive on an important story. They put it on page sixteen.

Soon afterward Lewis left the newspaper. He took a job with a new publication that never got off the ground. He was trying to figure out what to do with the rest of his life. I persuaded him to come back as special assignments editor for the *Constitution*, a new and not well-defined position. Although he didn't have the absolute power he had enjoyed in *Journal* sports, he helped make Atlanta and Georgia take new notice of the *Constitution*. He coached writers into turning out personality sketches that were meaty and entertaining beyond. He spotted front page stories we had been missing. He pumped ideas into all departments. He stepped on a few toes, inside and outside the building. He also helped engineer a remarkable series of stories about Atlanta.

In the mid 1970s, Atlanta was a city in transition, moving from a mid-sized southern city, tended by old-line blue bloods and business leaders, into a fractious multi-colored metropolis. White flight to the suburbs was epidemic. Maynard Jackson, the city's first black mayor, came in with a chip on his shoulder. The old power structure met his animosity half way. The police department, under its first black chief, one of the mayor's college buddies, was consumed by infighting and a test-cheating scandal.

Working with city editor Bill Shipp, Lewis planned and produced a sensational series called "City in Crisis." The city editor bosses reporters who cover local and state news. Shipp was the finest city editor Atlanta's newspapers have had, before or since. Grizzard and Shipp gave the *Constitution* a one-two punch reminiscent of Blanchard and Davis, the legendary Touchdown Twins of Army football fame.

Perhaps the title of their series was too strong. The *Constitution* was accused of pouring gasoline on fire, and, inevitably, of racism. The Chamber of Commerce types weren't happy. Neither were emerging black politicians. The series made Atlanta face up to issues many would have preferred to sweep under the rug.

Atlanta soon got a new police chief, a professional who eventually went on to head the New York City police department. The former police chief eventually went to prison for taking bribes when he was a county commissioner. Lewis understood hard-hitting journalism.

The Atlanta Falcons in football and the Braves in baseball

were perpetual losers when Lewis was in charge of special assignments. He fathered a controversial series that labeled Atlanta as "Losersville," so far as professional sports were concerned. Boosters who preferred puffery to truth didn't like it either. Happily, the *Constitution*'s detractors didn't include average readers. Circulation kept going up.

The two biggest news events occurring while Lewis was special assignments editor were the end of the Vietnam war and a devastating tornado that heavily damaged much of the elite North Atlanta residential section, including the Governor's Mansion. On both, Lewis stepped in and took charge of the newsroom, which, in the traditional pecking order, he wasn't supposed to do.

The front pages and the special sections he turned out were sensational. They eclipsed the other paper's efforts and stand today as examples of how to cover, coordinate, and present news of major events.

When he was hot on a story, Lewis, quicker than any person I've ever known, thought of all the angles. He selected the pictures himself, wrote the captions, wrote the headlines, and made it all mesh. He wasn't always diplomatic. He was resented by some of his colleagues. They grumbled when he never took the trouble to learn how to operate the newspaper's new computers.

He would hammer out headlines, captions and editor's notes on his typewriter, then hand them to other editors and reporters to be punched into computer terminals. Lewis said if he'd wanted to be a mechanic he'd have gone to Georgia Tech.

Once again he became disillusioned with the newspaper business. He was impatient, perhaps ahead of his time. He quit. He was offered the top editing job on a mid-size South Carolina paper. He turned it down. He talked about buying a little country store down around Moreland, his hometown. He'd sell Vienna sausage and pickled pigs feet, have a coal stove with a sandbox where old men could sit around and spit tobacco juice. He would close every day at noon and go fishing. Some days he might even put bait on his hook. Lewis had been newspapering eighteen hours a day, seven days a week, since he was sixteen years old. He was under thirty and burned out.

Then he got an offer he couldn't resist from Jim Hoge, editor and publisher of the *Chicago Sun-Times*. Hoge is one of the nation's top newspaper executives, a prize-winning foreign correspondent, Washington bureau chief; hard-nosed, sophisticated, decisive, the kind of editor a newspaper warhorse wants to work for.

The *Sun-Times* was in a heated battle with the *Chicago Tribune*. Sport sections are essential weapons in any newspaper war, especially so in Chicago, a big sports town. Hoge's sports department at the *Sun-Times* had grown old, lazy, out of touch. He offered Lewis *carte blanche* to come to Chicago and turn it around.

Lewis did, in record time. He also made an acquaintance with the American Newspaper Guild. *Journal-Constitution* newsrooms were not union shops. Union rules were new to Lewis, silly and unprofessional. If the baseball writer's forty-hour week ended in Houston, a replacement flew out and continued with the Cubs to San Francisco.

If Lewis wanted to switch a Chicago writer from baseball to football, he had to consult the Supreme Court. In Atlanta, you point a finger, say a few words to the parties involved, or post a one-sentence memo. Lewis' work ethic — stay until you get the job done, do what the boss tells you to do — was foreign to the Guild.

Being a white male from Georgia, he was suspected of being a racist. The *Sun-Times'* pro basketball writer was a black man, a part-time preacher who worked his particular brand of religion into his basketball stories. Lewis was appalled. Apparently, nobody on the *Sun-Times*, fearing the Guild, had ever told the writer to keep his church stuff out of his basketball stories.

Reading one of his epics, Lewis decided the story didn't belong in his newspaper. He threw it into the trash, which was where editors in Atlanta put unacceptable stories. The writer filed a grievance with the Guild, accusing Lewis of being a racist. Jesse Jackson put his PUSH lawyers on the case.

Lewis asked me to come to Chicago and tell them he wasn't

a racist. I flew up on a cold, dark, rainy day. I grabbed a cab to a downtown office tower, where I was ushered into a plush waiting room. An expensively dressed black man carrying a briefcase came in and took a seat. A few minutes later, the receptionist nodded to him and said, "They're ready for you." He disappeared into a doorway.

Lewis told me later the *Sun-Times* lawyer defending him was ecstatic when this gentleman appeared in the hearing room, where they were expecting Jim Minter, managing editor of the *Atlanta Constitution*. "Lewis!" exclaimed the lawyer. "Why didn't you tell us Jim Minter is black? He will certainly help our case." The receptionist had called the wrong witness.

When they got that straightened out, I walked in to face five lawyers, three from the Guild and two from Jesse. I had to admit to being born in Georgia, being white, having gone to segregated schools, and not being able to immediately identify the presidents of all of Georgia's predominately black colleges. Honestly!

"What does Mr. Grizzard call Hank Aaron?" one of the lawyers asked.

"I think he calls him Henry," I said. "Most people who know Henry Aaron pretty well don't call him Hank."

"Have you ever heard Mr. Grizzard refer to Mr. Aaron as a nigra — n-i-g-r-a?" I hadn't.

"Have you ever heard Mr. Grizzard refer to Mr. Aaron as a nigger — n-i-g-g-e-r?" Of course I hadn't. I wondered how in hell Henry Aaron got dumped into a Chicago basketball writers' grievance. When we broke for lunch, Lewis led me out to a sandwich shop. We actually had to hold onto a rope to keep from blowing away while we crossed the street.

"Lewis," I said, "you better get the hell out of Dodge."

He had other troubles. The food, the cold, the wind, living alone. His second wife, a pretty young woman from Mississippi who had worked for the newspapers in Atlanta, had moved out to pursue a singing career.

The telephone rang at my office or home almost every night. Lewis wanted to come home. He flew to Atlanta, accepted our offer to edit the new Weekend sections we were launching, and then flew back to Chicago to give notice.

Hoge, who had supported him in his battles with the Guild and Jesse Jackson's lawyers, wouldn't hear of it. He had plans for Lewis beyond the sports department. Lewis called, explained that he had unfilled obligations in Chicago, and resigned from the Weekend job he had just accepted. Technically, he now had left the Atlanta papers three times. He was right. He owed Hoge. Not long afterward, he was invited to Austin, Texas, where Cox had bought the newspaper and publisher Jim Fain was shopping for a new editor. Lewis almost went to Austin, but Austin wasn't home. He decided to stick it out in Chicago for a few years. He could do that. His daddy had spent six years fighting wars.

Like management at the *Atlanta Journal* had done a few years earlier, Hoge decided Lewis' talents shouldn't be confined to the sports department. He asked Lewis to become night managing editor of the *Sun-Times*, one of the country's biggest, best, and most respected newspapers. Night managing editor is the hotseat. The brass has gone home, or to the club for cocktails. The night managing editor makes the decisions. Hoge was putting Lewis on track to become the top editor at the *Sun-Times*.

Lewis had to make the biggest decision of his career. Accept Hoge's offer and he'd be committed to the *Sun-Times* for a long time, possibly a lifetime. He might never get home, might never taste Sprayberry's barbecue again, might never sit in Sanford Stadium in Athens, cheering his beloved Georgia Bulldogs.

He decided to come home. The problem was how to get there. The *Journal-Constitution* had an unwritten rule: Quit once and you might not get a second chance; quit twice and you're history. Counting the Weekend editorship he passed up, Lewis had quit three times. How could I explain hiring him for a fourth time?

If the truth be known, Lewis Grizzard got to be a famous newspaper columnist because of barbecue. Pork pig barbecue, slow-roasted and smoked over hickory coals, the way God intended. I was sitting in my office at the *Constitution* on a pleasant spring afternoon. Lewis was in Chicago, sitting in his office at the *Sun-Times*, wishing he wasn't. The elevator opened on the eighth floor of the *Journal-Constitution* building, into our newsroom. Out stepped one of the most beautiful young women I had ever seen.

She was dressed all in white, a stylish sun hat atop long dark tresses. Olive skin. Liquid eyes. Terrific figure. She looked like she had walked off the page of a glamour magazine.

Every eye in the newsroom followed her progress to the assistant managing editor's desk. She took a seat, talked with the AME for a few minutes, got out of her chair, and headed back toward the elevator, sweeping across the floor like a breeze from some exotic Pacific island. I strolled over to the AME's desk.

"Who was that?" I asked. "What did she want?"

"Can you believe it?" he guffawed. "She wants to be a copyboy!"

"Copyboy" is a pre-politically correct, pre-sensitivity committee term for an employee who in pre-computer newsrooms ran pieces of paper from one editor to another, down to the composing room, and got sent out for coffee. The job paid minimum wage and was filled by high school dropouts or an occasional journalism student trying to get a foot in the door. The *Constitution* had never had a female copyboy.

"Did you hire her?" I asked.

"Of course I didn't!" he replied.

"Then catch her before she gets on the elevator!" I ordered. "We can't discriminate against females."

That's how Liz became the *Constitution*'s first female copyboy.

She was more than beautiful. She had a great personality and cheerfully performed all the mundane chores that fell to copyboys, traditionally the lowest form of life in a newsroom. She was twenty-one, enrolled in journalism school, anxious to become a reporter.

Liz had been on the job several weeks when Lewis came back to Atlanta for a weekend visit. Somebody introduced them. The next Wednesday, he called from Chicago, collect, as usual.

"I need a favor," he said. "Your new copyboy has agreed to fly up to Chicago this weekend and bring me some barbecue and Brunswick stew. I'm starving to death eating this stuff the natives call food. I've sent her a round-trip ticket on Delta. She needs to be at the airport by three on Friday afternoon, after she's picked up my barbecue and stew. Could you arrange for her to have Friday afternoon off from work?"

Around lunchtime on Friday, Liz walked into my office and asked me to sign her out in a company car. Company cars are always in short supply at a newspaper, reserved for reporters and photographers chasing fires, convenience store killings, wrecks and robberies.

"Why do you need a company car?" I asked. "I thought you were making a mercy flight to Chicago."

"I am," she replied, "but first I've got to drive down to Sprayberry's in Newnan to get Lewis' barbecue and stew."

Sprayberry's is a historic barbecue place about thirty miles south of Atlanta, near Lewis' hometown of Moreland. Natives will rob, steal, and possibly kill for a Sprayberry sandwich, chopped, outside brown, medium hot sauce. Lewis grew up on Sprayberry's barbecue.

"How are you going to drive down to Newnan, bring the company car back here, and make your three o'clock flight to Chicago?" I asked.

"Lewis said I could park the car at the airport," she explained. Nobody, not even a Pulitzer Prize-winning reporter, is allowed to park a company car at the airport over a weekend.

"We might need the car before you get back from Chicago," I said. "Besides, do you have any idea how much it costs to park at the Atlanta airport?"

"Lewis said the paper would pay for it."

"Did he specify his paper or ours?" I asked.

"He didn't say. He just said give you the bill and you'd take care of it."

I don't know how she paid for the barbecue. Odds are the tab from Sprayberry's went through our business office as six dozen legal pads and a gross of pencils for the newsroom.

Liz made her flight to Chicago with her CARE packages. Sunday night I got a call from Lewis at my home. He explained that Liz had never seen the Sears Tower. Could I arrange for her to have Monday off so she could go see the Sears Tower?

Her Friday afternoon trips to Sprayberry's, followed by the mercy flight to Chicago, became regular events. With the onset of winter and Lewis' worsening homesickness, his Sunday night calls requesting extensions for Liz went into Mondays and Tuesdays.

Our business office began to ask questions: Where was the company car? Why was a lowly copyboy spending $60.50 cents every week on airport parking? Why was the copyboy away from the office three or four days a week?

I told the bean counters I'd look into it. I called Lewis in Chicago. "Lewis," I said, "you'll have to learn to eat bratwurst, or boiled cabbage, or whatever they use for food up there. I'm about to get fired because of Liz's weekly barbecue trips."

"Managing editors have been fired for causes less noble," he replied.

"If I get fired," I said, "you'll really be out of luck. Who else would sign Liz's phony expense accounts and time slips?"

"Then the only thing you can do to save your job is hire me and get me back to Atlanta," he said.

"Lewis, you've already quit three times. Jack Tarver told me if you ever get back in this building you'll have to be driving a tank. Besides, we don't have any job openings."

"You told me you were looking for somebody to write a column for the local news section," he said.

"So?"

"So hire me!"

Lewis had never written more than a handful of columns for a major newspaper, none outside the sports section. Great columnists aren't discovered. They happen. I knew Lewis wouldn't write a *bad* column, but I didn't think he'd turn into a sensation. Although he had a keen wit and rare powers of observation, I'd never seen either greatly reflected in the handful of columns he had written. He was a superb, no nonsense editor, committed to the complete newspaper process. I didn't think he'd be happy writing a column. I worried that he wouldn't be good at one-liners. He seemed more the essay type, which if you aren't Furman Bisher or Red Smith comes out d-u-l-l.

But I figured, what the hell? We can let him come back for the column and then, first chance we get, we'll move him into a desk job where he belongs. Put him in charge of one of our sections that needs help. To cover my rear, I asked him to write several sample columns and ship them to Atlanta before we closed the deal (at a salary substantially less than he was making in Chicago). Two days later, six columns arrived in the mail. They were a little long and not in the format that he would later perfect, but they were terrific. One of them, promising "If I ever get back to Georgia, I'm gonna nail my feet to the ground," later became the title of one of his books. Lewis had bought his ticket back to Atlanta, one way.

He poured all his newspaper savvy and his own sensitivities into the column. He mined childhood memories and wrote about growing up in a small town. He wrote intimately and honestly about himself, his alcoholic war-hero father, his struggling grade-school teacher mother, his school janitor grandfather, his marriages. He defended traditional values. He wrote about the singles scene in Atlanta. He could be outrageous, going right up to, but never over, the line of good taste. He was in touch. He was timely. He made personal contact with readers; he knew what they wanted to say, needed to say, didn't know how to say, and were sometimes afraid to say. He said it for them. Made them laugh and cry. Fan letters and requests for personal appearances began to pour in.

One way or the other, he would have expanded his audience beyond readers of the *Journal-Constitution*. He was too good and too universal for that not to happen. Tom Wood, our publisher at the time, and Eddie Sears, who had taken over as managing editor of the *Constitution*, encouraged him to syndicate the column in other newspapers. I wanted him to write exclusively for Atlanta and Georgia, as Mike Royko does in Chicago. Fortunately, my wishes didn't prevail.

Eventually, his column was carried by more than 450 newspapers. He wrote twenty-five books, made countless speeches for fees up to $20,000, appeared on "Larry King Live," "The Tonight Show With Johnny Carson," and had a fling on the hit TV sitcom "Designing Women." Sometimes he traveled in his own tour bus, like the entertainment star he became.

So that's the story, or close to it, of how Lewis became one of the best-loved columnists in the history of newspapers, compared by some to Will Rogers and Mark Twain.

Sprayberry's barbecue, Delta, and Liz deserve a lot of the credit. For a while I thought he might take her on one of his trips to the altar, but it never happened. It should have, and the same goes for Miss C., a beautiful, talented and attentive Savannah lass who came later. For the most part, Lewis was lucky with hearts, except his own. He didn't hate any of his ex-wives or ex-girlfriends as some of his more sensitive female readers concluded. The barbs he tossed their way were exaggerated. They made good reading.

When he was unconscious and not expected to live after his next-to-last surgery, there was a gathering at Emory University Hospital not duplicated since a funeral in Alabama more than a century ago. Major John Pelham, a youthful Confederate officer, a favorite of Robert E. Lee, was killed in Virginia and brought home for burial. Five women showed up in mourning clothes. By my count in the Emory waiting room, Lewis topped him by two. Nancy drove all the way from her home in Charlotte, North Carolina, in a blinding rainstorm, in the middle of the night, to be at his bedside.

The summer after Lewis died, Dudley Stamps and other childhood friends and neighbors in Moreland staged a Story-Telling Day in his memory. Hundreds came, including at least two wives and several girlfriends. They had a new book on sale at the Moreland Story-Telling, proceeds going to the Lewis Grizzard Scholarship Fund. Title of the book: *Memories of Lewis Grizzard: Recollections of Hometown Friends and Family*. The book had been published by Plato Communications, 233 S. Sharon Amity Road, Charlotte, North Carolina. A collection of pictures from Lewis' childhood, plus recipes for Aunt Jessie's cream corn and Aunt Una's buttermilk pie, it was authored by Nancy Grizzard Jones, his first wife, and by Camilla Stamps Stevens, Dudley's first wife.

Ed Jones, Nancy's husband, owns the printing company in Charlotte that published the book. The Plato imprint comes from Lewis' and Nancy's dog, the one Nancy got in their divorce settlement. Appropriately, the preface was written by Kathy Snead, a professor in the University of Georgia's School of Social and Family Affairs. Her explanation of relationships can't be improved:

"There is Dudley Stamps, Lewis' best male life friend, who still lives in Moreland today. They were in Moreland School together, along with Nancy, and shared many tales of adventures throughout their forty-seven years. Dudley, Lewis and Nancy met up with Camilla when they had to go from Moreland to Newnan High. Dudley was friends with Nancy and Camilla, was eventually married to, then divorced from, Camilla. Then there is Nancy. She was first Lewis' and Dudley's friend, Camilla's best friend, Dudley's girlfriend, then Lewis' first wife. Lastly is Camilla. She was Nancy's best friend, Lewis' buddy, then Dudley's girlfriend, and eventually Dudley's wife. They fondly refer to themselves as the 'Four Ex's.'" Whew!

Among the acknowledgments in the front of the book, the authors make special mention of two: "Elaine Stamps, for kindly letting her ex-husband help with a book authored by his ex-wife." And, "Edward Jones, for kindly letting his wife author a book about her ex-husband."

Jimmy Carter thinks he's good at conflict resolution. Compared to Lewis, he's a piker.

I asked Ed Jones if he didn't get a little miffed over Lewis' continuing friendship with Nancy, and hers with him.

"Miffed with Lewis!" he exclaimed. "How could I be? Because of him I've had Nancy for fourteen years!"

Many of Lewis' fans remember Dorsey Hill, the University of Georgia superfan he sometimes wrote about. Dorsey Hill is really Gary Hill, a college chum. In 1985, when Gary married

Charlotte Irwin in the chapel at the Big Canoe resort community in the North Georgia mountains, he asked Lewis to address the wedding party. This is what Lewis said:

"Several weeks ago, when Gary and Charlotte were planning their wedding, Gary asked if I would say a few words on this occasion. I suppose he thought someone with as much experience in weddings as I have might have something to say of some interest.

"What we are doing today is celebrating love, the love that Charlotte and Gary have for each other. All I can say is that I wish for them a very special sort of love; one that is rare, and one that many of us will never know. It is a love that is unconditional.

"It is easy to say I love you IF...and I love you WHEN. But what is difficult is to love without boundaries, and without limits. The two best examples of unconditional love I know are a mother's love for her child, and God's love for all of us. Those are loves with no ifs and whens whatsoever. Gary and Charlotte, that is what we all want for you.

"When one falters, may the other carry. When one of you is weak, may the other be strong. May you be able to hold back each other's storms, to ease each other's pain, and above all, to always be able to forgive. If together you can build this kind of love, an unconditional love, then you will have forged a bond nothing under Heaven can break."

Lewis had one foot in the old-fashioned values of his mother and grandparents, and in the teachings of the little Methodist church he attended in Moreland. He had his other foot in the lifestyle of a liberated generation in a new age. That's one reason his columns were so popular with a wide assortment of readers, and successful beyond his wildest dreams. That's why he so deeply touched my mother-in-law, the proper wife of a Methodist preacher; a young black man in Jacksonville, Florida; swinging singles in Atlanta; rednecks in Alabama; and widow women in Kansas. That's why when he was fighting his desperate battles in Emory University Hospital prayer groups sprouted in churches around the country, why they bought billboards to wish him luck, why so many letters came in the mail, and why, all alone, they got down on their knees and prayed for his recovery.

Life On The Streets Of 'Hot-lanta'

BY RON HUDSPETH

Ron Hudspeth is publisher of <u>The Hudspeth Report</u>, a month-ly metro Atlanta publication chronicling restaurants, nightlife, and lifestyle. He is also the author of two books.

I met Lewis Grizzard in the press box at Atlanta / Fulton County Stadium on a warm night in the summer of 1969. We were both twentysomethings, naive and nursing common insecurities.

Jim Minter, who would turn out to be both Lewis' and my newspaper hero, had hired me only hours earlier. I had arrived from the *Miami Herald*, as wet behind the ears as a boy from a rural South Florida swamp town named Belle Glade (population ten thousand, not counting alligators) could be.

Lewis, whom Minter had recruited from Athens to the *Atlanta Journal* sports staff six months earlier, was just as small town, a product of a whistle stop south of Atlanta called Moreland.

That was one reason Lewis and I struck an immediate bond. We were both small town boys, Southern to the core. I hadn't even seen snow when I hit Atlanta at age twenty-six. We had spent most of our young lives dreaming about being sports writers on a big newspaper, and now it was happening. We were pinching ourselves.

"One day someone is gonna walk up and tap me on the shoulder and say, 'Aren't you little Louie Grizzard from Moreland, Georgia, son?'" Lewis would always say, "Well, son, I don't think you belong here. Now run on home to your mama."

I felt the same way, totally insecure that someone was paying me money to go to games and write about them. Lewis and I laughed about that a lot for the next twenty-four years.

We both loved the *Journal* sports department. It was, as much as anything, why our relationships with women never lasted. We loved the newspaper too much.

What a place it was to work. The old *Journal-Constitution* on Forsyth Street in Atlanta was a real newspaper building — cigarette burns and initials carved on the desks, paper strewn everywhere, old Royal typewriters, the rattle of teletype machines.

The sports staff was a cast of characters. Take Frank Hyland, as crusty, brilliant and offbeat an old school newspaper man as you'll ever meet. Once Hyland co-hosted Skip Caray's 11 p.m. sportscast on Channel 11. Only problem was that Caray (now voice of the Atlanta Braves) and Hyland had prepped for the show by drinking at the Brave-Falcon lounge for five hours. They giggled and stumbled their way through it, maybe the first totally intoxicated sportscast in Atlanta history. Channel 11 executives were not amused. Caray was fired the next day.

Not many people recall, but Hyland, Caray and Grizzard were roommates in the early 1970s. A friend of mine from the Florida swamps, Doug Sands, lived with them. He was the only sane one.

The house was decorated in a style I would term "early underwear." The others took pride in dumping trash in Lewis' room, which would have scared a homeless person. Lewis literally once had to use a rake to find his bed.

Technically, as executive sports editor of the *Journal*, Grizzard was Hyland's boss, but that mattered little. There was no taming Frank.

One night — or morning, I should say — Hyland, Caray and Sands arrived back at the apartment at 5:30 a.m. with three painted ladies in tow. Lewis, who had just arisen and was due at work in thirty minutes, was in the shower. Suddenly the shower curtain was ripped open and there stood all six, the three guys pointing at Grizzard and saying in unison, "See, we told you he had a little pee pee."

Lewis didn't write in those days. "I'm a line drawer," he would groan. "On Saturday night at 2 a.m., when you guys have finished your stories and are in a Bourbon Street bar or a Peachtree nightclub, I'm in the press room fighting with some printer who hates my guts." Grizzard's duties as executive sports editor meant he mostly laid out the paper, choosing which stories and photos would go where. It also meant arriving at the newspaper office downtown between 5:30 and 6 a.m.

One night Lewis and I began at Manuel's Tavern, and before long the party had expanded to a motel lounge. There Lewis, as he was prone to do, fell in love, this time with a young nurse.

I departed bleary-eyed with the car at 1 a.m., but Lewis wound up in a room where he later awoke from his romantic interlude in a sudden cold sweat of "Where am I?" and, more importantly, "What time is it?"

He peered at his watch; it was 5:45 a.m. "Oh, my God," he moaned, "Minter will kill me!" We not only respected Minter as the finest newspaperman we'd ever known, but we on the *Journal* staff also were totally terrified of him. One cross word from Minter could humble any man.

Grizzard leaped up, hopping to get his legs in his trousers, and bolted out the door in desperate pursuit of a cab. He found one, but when he reached into his pocket he discovered only two dollars and some change.

"Take me as far as that will get me," demanded Lewis, crawling into the back seat.

The cabbie sped up Ponce de Leon as Lewis' heart pounded in panic. Suddenly the cabbie came to stop near the intersection of Peachtree and Ponce de Leon streets.

"What is it?" cried Lewis.

"Sorry, pal," said the cabbie, "but that's as far as $2.34 takes you."

Lewis climbed out of the cab and began to run, past Crawford Long Hospital, past the old Imperial Hotel, past the Hyatt Regency and Peachtree Center, on to Forsyth Street and, finally, into the *Journal-Constitution* building. Probably two miles.

It was only 6:15. He got the paper out on time. Lewis had a stronger heart back then.

While the rest of Lewis' life was at loose ends in those days (he and first wife Nancy had broken up), he was totally dedicated to his work.

One Thanksgiving he spent all night at the newspaper putting out what he hoped would be another near perfect sports section. What he didn't recall was that he had parked his car on the curb in front of the newspaper; that's no big deal on Thanksgiving, but the day after Thanksgiving signaled the biggest sale of the year at nearby Rich's, where maybe one million ladies were backed up trying to get into the parking lot.

The problem? Lewis' car.

As it was towed off, a crusty policeman noted, "In twenty years I thought I'd seen everything, but I never saw any fool park his car here the day after Thanksgiving."

Actually, Lewis and cars never agreed. Once he emerged from a date's apartment at daybreak, late for work as usual, only to find his car sitting on its rims. Someone had stolen all four tires. This time, however, he had full cab fare.

Although we had to rise early to put out the afternoon newspaper, doing so meant that many days we were finished with work shortly after noon. And that meant Underground Atlanta, newly opened and truly a wonderful place — unlike the imitation new one — beckoned as our lunchtime destination.

We almost always wound up at The Bucket Shop, where lunch turned into a marathon of cold beers. We often stayed for happy hour and last call. The best part was that the regular barkeeps always charged us the same.

"What'd you guys have?" one of them would say when we

started to close out our tab.

"A burger and quite a few beers," we'd say.

"Does $5 sound OK?"

"OK."

Going to Underground after work built *esprit de corps* for the *Journal* sports staff, but it did little for home life. We measured it at about seven divorces. Lewis was to be a major contributor to that record.

Lewis and I shared an apartment in the early '70s after he and Nancy split. Our apartment was decorated in early divorce. In fact, Lewis acquired his bedroom furniture from Aaron Rents. We had no living room furniture, save for a few beanbag pillows.

Lewis always hated to be alone. One weekend I went off to cover a NASCAR race at Darlington, South Carolina, and left him there by himself. When I returned late Sunday evening, he was sitting on the floor, looking depressed while flipping his cigarette ashes into a cookie pan.

"I'm going back," he said.

"Going back where?" I asked.

"Back to Nancy," he said. "Don't try to stop me or you'll have to fight me."

And he was out the door like a flash. Later he confessed to me that he expected to roar up to his former home, dash to the door and find Nancy there smiling, wearing a skimpy negligee, ready to sweep him into her arms, all warmth and sexiness.

That was the fantasy. The reality was something different. Lewis arrived and pounded on the door until Nancy answered, wearing an old robe, hair curlers and her face covered with cold cream.

"What do you want, Lewis," she said in a tone colder than the cream.

Lewis came limping back to our apartment, his tail and ego between his legs.

Lewis was forever "going back to Nancy." Somehow, I think, he always wanted to rediscover the innocence of his youth. Nancy, in a sense, was family, almost as much as the father he loved more than anyone and his sweet mother, who loved Lewis so much she spoiled him rotten.

One of Lewis' "returns to Nancy" we called the "Tire Tool Syndrome." We laughed about it for years. Actually, it is a sobering lesson to any guy who has loved and lost.

Lewis had gone on a road trip with the Atlanta Braves and wound up falling in love in Montreal. "She was so wonderful," he cooed. "There we were in this restaurant overlooking the lights of Montreal and she was speaking French and...."

That went on for a couple months until Lewis got a week's vacation and decided to drive to Montreal to see his new love. Yes, drive. For some strange reason, Lewis loved to drive. He could go down a two-lane blacktop for hours on end and never think anything about it. It didn't hurt either that he was scared to death to fly.

Lewis arrived in Montreal, knocked on his new love's door, and — as so often happens — a semi-stranger answered. She was not as pretty or as friendly as he had remembered.

Immediately, Lewis knew the truth: He didn't want to be in Montreal. He wanted to be with Nancy.

He began to drive south and the hours rolled into the night. Nancy was living in a northwest Atlanta apartment complex at the time and had a new boyfriend. After driving around the clock, Lewis arrived at Nancy's apartment at 2:30 in the morning. He immediately recognized her new boyfriend's car and anger welled inside. He went to the trunk of his car and took out a tire tool and waited.

And waited and waited and waited.

When the sun came up, Lewis was still sitting there in his car holding the tire tool. Fortunately, neither the boyfriend nor Nancy ever emerged.

Tired and embarrassed, Lewis drove home. It was a good lesson for any man who has made a fool out of himself over a woman.

I sort of divorced Lewis to get married. Lewis and I had been working the Atlanta neon lights and sampling the array of attractive women for quite some time, but now I had a steady girl, and my travels with Lewis weren't doing much good for my steady relationship.

"You've found the one you were looking for." Lewis would say, "but you're like me. You ain't finished looking."

One night Lewis and I had been out nightclubbing up and down Peachtree and ran back to the apartment to pick up some more cash. My intended was supposed to be spending the night with a girlfriend. I left Lewis sitting in the front seat of the car and said I'd be right back. I charged through the apartment door to find her standing there with anything but a happy look on her face. After an hour-long chat and an extended apology by me, we went to bed.

I forgot all about Lewis.

Next morning I awoke early and peered out the window. There was Lewis right where I left him, sound asleep, his head hanging halfway out of the car window. The boy could sleep and snore anywhere.

Lewis and I had more than our share of wild times in those days, and someone was surely looking out for us. Covering the Braves, I got to be friends with Denny McLain, the former pitching great who was winding down his career but not his fondness for a good time.

Denny invited me to a party at his apartment complex starting at midnight. Yep, midnight. That ought to tell you something. Lewis went with me and all was well until about 4 a.m. when some guy punched out Mike McQueen, another Braves pitcher, for dancing with his girlfriend.

As luck would have it, McLain, who had not had a lick of sleep, was the starting pitcher the next day, a Sunday afternoon game at Atlanta Stadium. It was July and the temperature was a muggy one hundred degrees on the playing field.

McLain, massively hung over, walked the first four hitters he faced. Fortunately, manager Luman Harris yanked him from the game before he threw up or passed out on the mound, but, unfortunately, he called upon McQueen in relief.

McQueen, who had been in the bullpen sipping soup from a straw because of his swollen jaw, was just as bad. He gave up a double and then a triple.

When the dust had cleared, the Braves were down 7-0 in the first inning.

Grizzard and I decided not to mention the party in my game story, since we had been a part of it. In fact, Lewis had met a girl that night he fell in love with. Yes, for the umpteenth time, Lewis had fallen in love and the Braves had lost another game.

Neither event was startling news in those days.

That was probably the only time we ever "covered up" a story. In fact, Lewis and I spent endless hours over cold beers trying to think up new ways to write about sports.

We created a controversial column called "Perspective," in which we tackled subjects and waited for the reaction. We got it. I wrote a column saying it was silly to play the national anthem before sporting events, since most people were talking or trying to buy a beer while it was going on and used it only for a starter's gun.

The letters came flying in, calling me everything from a traitor to a "Commie pinko," but when a crude looking box wrapped in brown paper arrived with nasty notes on the outside, we all scattered to the other side of the newspaper office while a postal inspector opened it. Fortunately, there was no bomb.

What Lewis and I didn't realize was that we were both feeling the first pangs of being pigeon-holed as sports writers. We wanted to write about the sport of life, and at that moment, little did we know how that would eventually evolve for both of us.

Things changed rapidly in the mid 1970s. Minter left the *Journal* sports staff to become managing editor of the *Constitution*, and Lewis eventually left to try editing on the news side. He hated it. Before long he quit, and then Chicago called.

Lewis moved to Chicago and became executive sports editor of the *Chicago Sun-Times*.

In later years, Lewis lambasted his time in Chicago, saying he hated the place and couldn't wait to get back south. A little of that was for show, I believe.

I visited Lewis in Chicago one winter — en route to cover the Falcons against the Packers in cold, cold Green Bay. I found him as happy as I ever remember.

He had a cozy apartment on Chicago's northside, an adoring wife named Faye (his second) and was in love with the fact that Chicago was a big league, two newspaper city. His *Sun-Times* staff and the *Tribune* battled for a plethora of stories daily. I listened to his stories and envied him.

"This is a real newspaper town," beamed Lewis, as we sat over cold beers at the infamous Butch McGuire's on Division Street. "Life's not bad here except for the cold. I've got everything I need right in my neighborhood — tavern, grocery, laundry. You don't even need a car. I like it, but when I see you or anyone else from the South, I get homesick."

In my opinion, Faye was the sweetest of Lewis' wives. They had met while she worked in public relations at the *Journal-Constitution*. The thing that probably kept them together was that they both liked to perform. A party at Lewis' Atlanta apartment in those days always wound up with a group in the kitchen listening to a slightly smashed Lewis and Faye sing their rendition of "The City of New Orleans."

That was the first inclination I got that there was a ham, an entertainer, a frustrated comedian, trying to climb from Lewis Grizzard's body.

It was a rather funny happening when Lewis and Faye got married. He stood me up.

I was waiting for him to play tennis at Bitsy Grant Tennis Center on a beautiful spring afternoon. We were going to play three sets, then head to Harrison's on Peachtree to chase beautiful Southern girls.

Lewis never showed.

Instead, he got in one of those "I'm going back to Nancy" moods, but this time when Nancy wasn't around, sweet young Faye was. Lewis quickly arranged for a preacher, got married at half-brother Ludlow Porch's house, and then caught a train to Florida for his honeymoon.

Looking back, I think Lewis was more excited about the train ride than marriage.

When I saw him a few days later in the office, he hung his head, grinned weakly, and said, "I'm sorry I didn't make it for tennis."

I actually taught Lewis how to play tennis. It's one of the things I remember most about Lewis that made him an extraordinary person.

First time on the tennis court, he was the worst I ever saw. Debutantes with no hand-eye coordination could hit the ball better. But when Lewis Grizzard put his mind to something, he was relentless.

For several years we hit tennis balls three or four times a week for two and three hours a session. Before long, Lewis was wearing me out on the tennis court, and he eventually became an A level player before he gave it up because of his health . problems.

Lewis was nothing if he wasn't determined. If it was something he loved, he went at it full force. If he wasn't interested, forget it. He was the same way with people. Some of his friends were strange, terribly strange. But he didn't care what anyone else thought. He picked 'em and they were his friends.

Lewis and I both loved dogs. The country music song, "My wife ran off with my best friend, and I miss him," was one of our favorites.

Lewis' first dog was Plato, a huge bassett hound with big sad eyes and a roaring bark like a lion. He got joint custody of Plato when he split with Nancy. "I think I miss Plato more than Nancy sometimes," Lewis joked. I wasn't sure he was kidding.

When Plato came to stay with us in our apartment, he was a terror. His bark frightened everyone in the building and he quickly chewed up our prized bean bag furniture, not to mention the carpet. Sometimes I couldn't figure out who had the sadder look — Plato or Lewis.

Catfish, of course, was Lewis' most famous dog. He, too, had a ferocious bark when someone entered Lewis' home, but as soon as he smelled the scent of my two Golden Retrievers on my clothes, Catfish and I were tight as thieves.

Lewis loved that dog and it's easy to see why. For all the celebrity, Lewis was essentially a loner, and you'd be surprised, even at the height of his popularity, how much time he spent alone — except for Catfish, who was always there at his feet, sharing cheeseburgers and pizzas with Lewis. "He eats what I eat," said Lewis. He called me shortly after Catfish died. He didn't say much, but I could tell it hurt him terribly.

One way or other, Lewis and I seemed to connect when marriage or the dissolving of same was contemplated by either of us. He had moved in with me after breaking up with Nancy. He stood me up on our tennis date and married Faye. Then one day the phone rang and it was Lewis.

"I've got to decide whether or not I'm gonna marry Kathy (his eventual third wife)," he said, his voice sounding worried. "I've thought and thought about it and I got to make a decision. I'm depending on you. Tell me what to do. Should I marry her?"

I gulped. Here was a wedding and relationship hanging in the balance, and a friend was asking me — of all persons — whether or not he should go through with it.

Until this day, I'm not completely sure why I answered — maybe because I liked Kathy, or maybe because I figured Lewis was lost on the streets and needed someone to take care of him — but I remember saying, "Yeah, if you love her, marry her."

A few days later, Lewis married Kathy. Their marriage didn't last all that long, but I think it provided Lewis with some of his happiest moments. He respected her, which I found astounding. Lewis' basic view of women was that they should remain barefooted in the kitchen cooking country fried steak and mashed potatoes before cleaning up after him.

And, I almost forgot, they should be redheaded. Lewis loved redheads. Kathy was a blonde.

Kathy later married a cowboy and moved to Montana to get back to the basics. I hear life there can be hard, especially during the long cold winters. But Kathy will probably be the first to tell you a cold Montana blizzard isn't half as tough as taking care of Lewis Grizzard.

Jimmy Carter invited the Southern press, NASCAR stock car drivers (of which Jimmy was a fan) and assorted hangers-on to a barbecue on the south lawn of the White House on a beautiful October night in the late 1970s.

There was a gorgeous full moon, and there Lewis and I stood, in the White House, in the same space trod by Lincoln, Roosevelt, Kennedy, and others. Yep, the two Southern boys had come a long way. Nonetheless, we both did get drunk as Cooter Brown that evening. It seemed like the Southern thing to do.

Waiters were always a favorite target of Lewis', and one of the classic Lewis vs. The Waiter stories happened in New Orleans. My date and I and Lewis and Kathy were having one of those classic, Sunday morning, New Orleans courtyard brunches.

The waiter was slightly less than masculine and that was Lewis' trigger. "Sir," said Lewis, "I'd like my eggs over medium well. That means that I don't want the yellow to run, I want it to crawl ever so slowly."

The waiter was not impressed with Lewis' humor. As we continued to order, Lewis continued to pepper the waiter with requests and demands. "I'd like my bacon crisp around the edges but not burned, and my toast...." I could see the waiter beginning to steam.

"I usually get up and go to the ladies' room when he orders," admitted Kathy. "I'm too embarrassed to stick around."

It was, oddly, a confrontation Lewis provoked and loved immensely. I should mention this was the same Lewis who always refused to pick up the paper wrappers after eating a hamburger because "they need to hire someone to do it. I'm not here to do a job. I'm here to eat."

That morning in New Orleans we waited quite a while for our main courses to arrive. We waited and waited. Finally, a man appeared and identified himself as the manager.

"I'm sorry," he said, "but we will have to assign you another waiter. Your waiter has become so frustrated he's quit." Lewis howled.

We finished our meal and were about to pay our tab when four complimentary Bloody Marys arrived at the table. Shortly afterward, the manager reappeared. "Excuse me," he said politely, "but these are from your former waiter. He has reconsidered quitting his job and sends you over these drinks to let you know he's sorry." Lewis howled again. As far as I know, there were no waiters at Lewis' funeral.

In 1982 Lewis found out he had to have heart surgery. We decided to have one last big bash before he went under the knife. "I might not come out," he said bluntly. We rented a beach house in Destin, Florida, and a Winnebago to get us there. We also invited along our two favorite bartenders from Harrison's on Peachtree. Lewis and I determined that no one should take such an extended vacation without his own bartender.

Running buddies: Ron Hudspeth and Lewis Grizzard cut a wide swath through Atlanta.

We also invited several pretty and rather wild Atlanta ladies. It was, putting it mildly, a blowout to end all blowouts. Again, Lewis' heart proved to be stronger than anyone had imagined.

Lewis had true grit when he needed it, more than most of us, and that made him special. I recall the day in the late 1970s when he had just begun writing a column for the *Atlanta Constitution*. He called me and said, "I'm dry, I ain't got nuthin' to write about. I'm getting out of here."

He also told *Constitution* editors the same thing and walked out of the newsroom into the newspaper parking lot before it hit him: "I can't quit. They're liable to say, 'Aren't you little Louie Grizzard from Moreland? Now go on home to your mama.'"

It was a fateful moment in Lewis Grizzard's life.

He went back in and wrote a column. "It was awful," he said, not even recalling what it was about. The important thing was that he wouldn't let it whip him. We always agreed that writing a daily column was like being married to a nymphomaniac — it's fun for about two weeks.

Like tennis, I introduced Lewis Grizzard to snow skiing. It was the only sport that Lewis, a fair country high school baseball and basketball player, never mastered. But that doesn't mean he didn't try. He'd fall and get up, fall and get up. Finally he developed a little proficiency and began to ski some of the easier slopes without falling. By that time Lewis had begun to make money, so he looked good on the slopes with all the best equipment and ski clothes.

It was also about that time that he met Beth, a young aspiring journalist who was a bit wild and totally fearless, especially about ski slopes and Lewis Grizzard.

"I do think she is the sexiest woman I've ever known," Lewis once told me.

Lewis and Beth and my date and I shared a condominium for a week that ski season in Winter Park, Colorado. It was Beth's first venture on snow skiis. Lewis, ever the romantic, envisioned helping this poor little Southern girl learn how to ski, followed

91

by steamy nights in front of a roaring fire.

But that wasn't Beth. By the second day, she was whizzing down the black slopes for experts. If she fell, she'd laugh and get up and disappear again, leaving poor Lewis struggling and falling. At the end of the day, Beth was ready to drink shooters; Lewis was ready to be shot.

His interest in skiing waned after that, although Lewis did admit to liking Deer Valley, the posh ski resort in Utah frequented by the rich and famous. "You know," he said, "they even carry your skis from your car to the lift. If only they'd ski for you, too."

I suspect Lewis really liked it there because he had found some snooty waiter he could harrass in one of the fancy restaurants.

When Lewis wasn't married, he had a terrible time managing the daily demands of life, things like having clean clothes in the closet and food in the refrigerator. So he came up with what he thought was a brilliant plan — he hired a "Girl Friday" to manage his domestic affairs.

Sue was a stunningly beautiful girl Lewis met while she was waitressing at Longhorn Steaks. The arrangement was OK for awhile, but that sort of thing works better on paper — or in a man's fantasy — than it does in reality.

Lewis had moved into a big new house on Atlanta's northside, and Sue moved in to manage the house. She ran errands for Lewis in his new black Mercedes convertible. I never asked her about her time living with Lewis, but having lived with the old boy himself, I know it was no bed of roses. Furthermore, Sue didn't exactly look like the kind who wanted to cook, clean, and pick up after others.

At any rate, Lewis was traveling a lot in those days, making speeches.

One night he returned to his house around midnight after cutting a trip short and couldn't find a place to park. Cars were everywhere.

Lewis walked into his living room and found it filled with partying strangers. He peered through the living room window and saw his hot tub filled with guys and girls. He made his way into the kitchen and was brushed by a young guy, obviously intoxicated, who said, "Who in the hell are you, buddy?"

Not surprisingly, Sue moved out shortly after that.

In the mid 1970s, Lewis and I had some great times on Peachtree, most notably at Harrison's on Peachtree, which in my considerably biased opinion was the greatest watering hole to ever grace the city of Atlanta.

But hear it from Lewis' typewriter:

Oh, those warm spring Friday nights at Harrison's on Peachtree, the singles bar that became an Atlanta legend.

The girl-children were flocking there. From places like Vidalia and Augusta and Montgomery and Birmingham and Ty-Ty and Albany (the Georgian pronunciation is "All-Benny") in the south, to Ringgold and Dalton (from whence came Marla Maples and Deborah Norville) to the north. They would wear those sun-dresses and you couldn't move in the place on Friday nights.

"This is living," Hudspeth would say, above the noise of the mating horde.

It was. There basically had been only one woman in my life since I was thirteen. But she was gone. And, once I had adjusted to bachelor life, this Harrison's on Peachtree was a veritable gold mine. I would have found it, of course, if Ron Hudspeth hadn't come to work at the Atlanta Journal, *but his divorce gave me a running mate.*

During the decade we both wrote columns for the *Journal-Constitution*, people who suspected competition between us always asked, "How can you guys be friends?"

It was easy. First, we knew enough on each other to hang one another. Second, writing a column is a lonely business and, in the end, no one really understands what it entails except another columnist. Instead of competitors, we were a support system.

Once in a while Lewis and I even used each other for column fodder. Hey, on a slow day, a columnist will sell his soul to the devil for a column subject. That guy you see searching under a garbage can lid is no street wino; he's a columnist looking for an idea.

Lewis did this one on me back in the early 1980s when my friend Norm Cates organized a roast for me at the Downtown Athletic Club:

Fellow columnist Ron Hudspeth is going to be roasted a week from Saturday at the new Downtown Athletic Club in the Omni Hotel for the benefit of the Scottish Rite Hospital for Crippled Children.

Ron asked me to be one of the roasters. I honestly would like to attend, but my dentist is giving a root-canal party the same evening, and that sounds like a lot more fun.

I have decided, however, to devote this valuable space today in an effort to explode some of the myths surrounding this giant of American journalism and to get even for the years he has gone around the city claiming to be my friend....

I thought the best way to handle this was with the question-and-answer technique. All you've ever wanted to know about Ron Hudspeth, but were totally uninterested to ask.

When did Ron first get interested in writing? *One day last week, but he had a couple of drinks and the feeling passed.*

How many times has he been married? *If you count common law, more times than I, and I'm ranked in the top 10 in both polls.*

How old is Ron Hudspeth? *No one is certain, but rumor has it he once voted for Roosevelt.*

Franklin? *Teddy.*

What is his educational background? *One night in a bar, he sat next to an encyclopedia salesman.*

How long does it take Ron to write one of his scintillating in-depth columns? *It depends on how sharp the point is on his crayon.*

Where was Ron born? *Harrison's.*

How does Ron keep his job at the newspaper? *I figure he has something on someone.*

A lot of people say Ron looks like Captain Kangaroo. Do you agree? *I think he looks more like E.T. with a scalp condition.*

What on earth do you call that ridiculous hairstyle of his? *Bald man's bluff.*

I confess I got Grizzard in trouble more than once. He was hardly skilled in after-dark life, something I definitely had honed to a fine talent many cold beers ago. In the later years, he'd phone occasionally with that lonely voice of his. Lewis could take misery to an art form.

"Meet me for a cold one," I'd always suggest and we'd wind up at some Peachtree watering hole trying to figure out what life was all about.

One particular evening we wound up at a Buckhead bar that bore a striking resemblance to the late Harrison's on Peachtree that we both had known and loved. By this time Lewis was a millionaire, his books were selling well, and from all outward appearances he had the world by the tail.

"But I ain't got nobody," he moaned, giving me that sad old hound dog look he could do so well, while sipping his second double screwdriver with a splash of orange juice.

I was headed out to a party for a group of reporters, so I said, "Come on and go with me."

"But I don't have a date," he said.

"We'll get you one," I said without thinking. Suddenly I realized I didn't have a clue how to fix up Lewis with a date at such a late hour. Then I remembered a piece of paper in my wallet.

In my research a few weeks earlier, I had stopped into The Cheetah to say hello to owner Bill Hagood, an old friend of mine. A dancer had walked up to me and said, "Hi, I'm Sally. I like your writing and Lewis'. I'd like to be a writer. Here's my number. Call me sometime." I dug in my wallet and there it was, Sally's number.

"Here, Lewis," I said, "this is the number of a nice girl I met at the Cheetah the other evening. She likes writers."

Lewis had had just enough double screwdrivers. In a matter of minutes he had bolted to a nearby phone booth, made a date with Sally, and sent a limo after her. She was to meet us at the party.

An hour later, all conversation at the party was cut short by

95

Sally's entrance. In she strolled, and I mean strolled, wearing a micro mini-skirt and black patent leather boots that climbed almost three quarters the length of her very long, shapely legs. All she needed was a whip. You could have heard a pin drop. There were maybe two dozen big mouthed journalists in the room, but Sally effectively shut them all up except for a few gasps.

That night Lewis and Sally became an item. Yes, she was a golddigger, but a nice one when she wanted to be. "I really like Lewis," she told me more than once.

Lewis had plenty of money and liked to spend it. That was OK with Sally, too. Actually, she fit Lewis' need for female company perfectly at that time. He wanted a woman around when he wanted her, didn't care how much it cost, and then he wanted his own space. That was fine with Sally, who continued to dance when she wasn't traveling with Lewis.

Lewis even lent Sally out as the entertainment at a friend's bachelor party. Problem was the bachelor party got a bit wild and some of the guys — all married — apparently wanted more than dancing. Lewis was asleep when he heard a knock at his door at 3 a.m. He staggered to the door, opened it, and found Sally crying, clad only in a man's sports coat. She had fled the bachelor party to be rescued by Lewis. I realize it's not exactly *Love Story*, but that was Sally and Lewis.

Once a group of us rented a villa in Jamaica, and Sally brought along a dancer friend as a gift for Lewis. After dinner one evening the two ladies rose from the table, grabbed Lewis' hand and led him into the bedroom. I couldn't wait to hear the story the next day.

"Well, it was kinda wild," Lewis said sheepishly. "There were these two beautiful naked women in bed with me and I reached out and...."

"Then what?" I asked with bated breath.

"I don't know," he said. "I fell asleep."

The old Grizzard would fall asleep anywhere, just like the young Grizzard. And I mean anywhere.

Lewis and Sally eventually parted company. "She could wear

out the lettering on your credit card," Lewis said more than once.

Last time I saw Sally she was driving Lewis' old Mercedes convertible. I think he gave it to her as a parting gift.

Little (and big) things I'll always remember about Lewis:

• When I met him, he weighed 225 pounds and could eat a dump truck load of hamburger steak and mashed potatoes in one sitting.

• He loved Cadillacs.

• Ditto for redheads.

• He, bless him, sometimes thought women attractive that other men unanimously agreed were absolutely homely.

• During one period he spent enormous sums of money at The Gold Club, an Atlanta club featuring nude dancing, but he quit frequenting the place when he got a conference call one rainy afternoon from the day shift asking him to come over to the club. "That was God's way of telling me I was spending too much time there," said Lewis.

• He loved his daddy more than the rest of the world put together.

• Making speeches was a love-hate addiction for him. He liked the money and the attention, but more than once he told me he despised doing it.

• In his next life, Lewis would like to be a country music singer. In the last few years, he began to sing during his one-man shows. That pleased him to no end.

• The time he sent me out to interview Billy Graham — who was preaching from a pulpit on the infield at Atlanta / Fulton County Stadium — and then entitled my story, "Salvation at Second Base."

• His favorite restaurant was the original Longhorn on Peachtree Street where he always ordered the T-Bone.

• He loved baseball box scores.

• He hated ties and socks.

• His one big claim to cooking was Grits Grizzard, a pot full of tasty, buttered grits mixed with crumbled bacon and cheddar cheese.

- He was unbelievably brave facing all those heart surgeries.

As Lewis himself might say, he was an "abso-byGod-lute" original!

Cold Climate, Warm Friends, Hot Business

BY TIM JARVIS

Tim Jarvis works in the mortgage industry as a broker account manager for LaSalle Bank in Northern California. He is down to a seven-handicap.

We met in Chicago in 1976. I was a native; Lewis was anything but. When I think back about Lewis in Chicago, I picture his leaky penny loafers in two feet of gray snow. He was the most out of place guy since Judas RSVP'd to St. Peter for the Last Supper.

I had gotten Lewis' name from the head pro at Midtown Tennis Center, which — with eighteen indoor courts — was the largest indoor tennis facility in the free world. I had just joined. Lewis had been playing there a few months but also didn't know many other members.

I had always thought that it was late 1975 when we first met, but a few years ago Lewis and I were talking about how long we had known each other, and he said it was actually March of 1976. He remembered because there was an NCAA tournament game on TV the first time I called him. Though we had this conversation fifteen years after we first met, he even remembered the teams that were playing, and that he was distracted because it was late in the game. Incredible as his memory was, not even he recalled the score, though.

We agreed to get together and play some tennis. I won the first three games; Lewis won the next eighteen, and I worried that he wouldn't want to play again. I was a little faster, a little stronger, and two years younger at twenty-seven. Lewis had been playing longer, served better, and was a great competitor. He served with a strange grip that he also used to hit a low, side-spin backhand that I couldn't handle. He could never seem to get out of that grip, so he was the only guy I knew who ran around his forehand to hit a backhand.

Of course, we did play again — maybe a thousand more times, starting with the four or five days a week we were good for during the next fifteen months before Lewis moved back to Atlanta. We played from 7:00 until 9:00 a.m. each morning on an early bird, half price special. His car had died in a snow drift somewhere, and he had abandoned it, so I picked him up almost every morning in my 1968 VW Beetle. That may be why he continued to play me even though he won our first 150 matches. The thing about tennis is that you can be fairly close to someone in skill level, but they'll just have your number. Lewis had mine.

We both had jobs where we didn't have to be to work until around 11:00 a.m. He'd kick my butt and we'd sit around drinking a Coke and shooting the bull for an hour, mostly about the hassles on his job as executive sports editor of the *Chicago Sun-Times*. Occasionally we would lose our minds and go get another court so we could simultaneously experience an intense hypoglycemic attack after about three games.

As autobiographical as Lewis' writing was, it's well known that he was very unhappy in Chicago. He was hired to redo the drab sports section of the *Sun-Times*, which he did. He completely transformed the layout of that paper, making it look much like sports sections you would see today. Dealing with the sports department personnel was another matter. Lewis was no Andrew Carnegie.

I remember a story he told me about the legendary and ancient Jerome Holtzman, the baseball writer who covered the Cubs for years. Jerome turned in his copy one summer day, and after reading it, editor Lewis suggested to him that maybe he was using too many clichés. What do you mean? replied Jerome defensively. For example, calling third base the "hot corner," Lewis pointed out. Jerome's response was that he was *the first* to call it that, and therefore he couldn't be guilty of using a cliché.

To make his stay in Chicago even more fun, Lewis' second wife had left him. Maybe if she hadn't, Lewis and I might not have become such close friends. There he was, as he described it many times, being held "prisoner of war" in Chicago. His dream job as executive sports editor of a big-time newspaper had become frustrating, he was living outside of Georgia for the first time, he had few friends in Chicago, and then his wife Faye left him. I think only tennis was keeping him afloat.

I did finally beat Lewis at tennis after nearly a year of trying. The match started out like his normal drubbing of me. He won the first set 6-1 and was leading 3-0 in the second. Mid game, a point ended with all the balls at the net, bringing us within close proximity. In an inspired, though not premeditated, act of gamesmanship, I uttered two words at the net that forever changed our tennis rivalry. I asked him, "How's Faye?"

The way Lewis told this story, as he did many times, he never won another game that day, and never beat me again. Saying that Lewis was prone to exaggeration was like saying Michael Jordan has an aptitude for basketball. But I did win handily that day, and he no longer had my number after that match. Eventually I was able to play more often, had fewer distractions, and started to win regularly. A few years later, when I had *his* number, Lewis quit playing me in singles so he could retire with a career winning record against me.

Our first really memorable doubles match was played in Chicago, and was one in which we were out of our league. We were playing the club champions, two 5'8" Italian guys by the names of Cuoso and DiOrio. It was obviously a soft spot in the schedule for them, but fortunately for us we played way over our heads out of sheer desperation. We lost, of course, but the match was close.

That day cemented our doubles partnership, as we caught a glimpse of the fun we were going to have with this sport in the next decade. It was also the first time I noticed a unique mental ability that Lewis possessed. Sometimes in tennis you have a great point, one that involves all four players hitting the ball, moving up, back, and sideways, probably for no more than fifteen or twenty seconds. But you feel like you just fought the Third Punic Wars, and you all end up staring blankly at the end of the point. Nobody has a clue what the score is in that game.

I remember this happening against Cuoso and DiOrio. One of the blank-faced Italian guys asked the score. In steps Lewis: "It's forty-love. On the first point, Tim hit a forehand return down the line, which Tom volleyed, I lobbed, and Bob put away an overhead. On the second point...." He recapped the entire game this way. In all the tennis I played with and against Lewis over the next ten years, I don't recall a single situation where he did not know the score. The man had almost total recall.

If Lewis ever listed the ten "low spots" of his life, I'm sure half of them involved heart surgery, and the other half probably occurred in Chicago during that next winter. The absolute lowest nonsurgical point probably was something I asked him to do.

The VW we used to get back and forth to the Midtown Tennis Center had frozen solid in the street. A tow truck never occurred to me. I either couldn't afford it, or didn't want to pay for it. There was two feet of old snow on the ground. My street wasn't plowed. There were just two ruts in the middle of it. I borrowed a garage, and I figured we'd just push the VW to the garage a block and a half away. There I would put a space heater near the car and would thaw out the crank case oil. I had a battery charger, which I could plug in inside the garage. That part of the plan was OK. Pushing it was the trouble.

Lewis never did buy anything more appropriate for two feet of snow than those penny loafers. It took about an hour and a half in sub-freezing weather to get that VW around two corners and into that garage, and we never would have made it if a couple of guys had not come by to help us. Lewis later told me that it was during that hour and a half that he resolved he was going to get his butt out of Chicago, some how, some way. Maybe if I had just called a tow truck, we'd still be where God's frozen people live. Naw.

In April of 1977, Lewis assigned himself to cover the Masters golf tournament in Augusta for the *Sun-Times*. I flew down to Atlanta during his trip to meet Lewis. He had also assigned himself to cover the Family Circle Cup tennis tournament at Sea Pines on Hilton Head Island, and we had rented a place at Palmetto Dunes.

After the long drive down I-75 South out of Atlanta, in a ten-year-old Pontiac Lewis had borrowed from his stepfather, the first thing we did was go out and play some tennis. Lewis ran into Curry Kirkpatrick from *Sports Illustrated*, and we played doubles against Curry and a friend of his. As a team, we got our first doubles win below the Mason-Dixon Line.

We weren't used to the hot sun and the clay courts, so it took us a couple hours to beat these guys. I was the original Pillsbury Doughboy, white as a sheet, at the start of the day anyway, and Lewis wasn't far behind. In Chicago, you sometimes don't see the sun for a month during the winter, and it was, of course, still winter there when we left in early April. I ended up about two shades of shocking pink past Lewis, with what could be called a farmer's burn on my neck and arms. There was even a cute, pale white circle around my right wrist where I had been wearing a sweat band.

On a close vote, we chose the Family Circle Cup over the burn unit and headed to the matches, trying not to touch anything on the way. Tracy Austin was thirteen, had just turned pro, and this was her first Family Circle Cup. I don't remember how she did, but she probably ran into the same buzz-saw as everyone else in the tournament. Chris Evert, on whom Lewis had a secret crush, was almost unbeatable on clay at the time. After she cruised through the final against Billy Jean King, 6-1, 6-0, Lewis wrote a story headlined "Break Up Chris Evert" (as if she were a franchise) for the next day's *Chicago Sun-Times*. I believe Lewis used the "Break Up Chris Evert" column, which was hilarious, and the others he wrote on that trip to help convince Jim Minter at the *Journal-Constitution* to offer him a job as a sports columnist. This job offer turned out to be Lewis' ticket out of Chicago a couple of months later, though I remember that he took a big cut in pay. Lewis wanted desperately to go home.

I missed Lewis terribly. He had become my best friend, and I was his. To try to soften the blow, Lewis gave me his press pass to Wrigley Field. I remember being able to drive that same Volkswagen that Lewis and I had pushed in the snow right up next to the building at Wrigley Field. With that pass, I could also sit in any empty seat in the ball park, of which there were many at Cubs games back then. I even sat next to Ernie Banks one day. I was in Cub fan heaven. The pass would have allowed me into the locker room, the press box, or even the Pink Poodle, whatever that was, but I never had the courage to venture into any of those places.

In the first year after Lewis moved back, I made eight trips to Atlanta and spent a total of two months there. I got to where it seemed like I had more friends in Atlanta than I did in Chicago. One of those friends both Lewis and I got close to during that time was Pepper Rodgers, the new coach at Georgia Tech. Neither Lewis nor Pepper had been back in town for very long. I don't think they had ever met, but of course they knew of each other. During one of my visits to Atlanta, Pepper called Lewis to see if he wanted to play some tennis on Pepper's private court. Since I was in town, we decided on a doubles match.

Pepper always seemed to have another quarterback for a partner. I guess old quarterbacks must hang around together. I remember Lewis and I playing on that court against Pepper and Steve Spurrier, against Pepper and Tech radio color man and local developer Kim King, and against Pepper and Eddie LeBaron. I think for that first match it was Pepper and Kim King. I don't remember who won. Lewis, of course, could tell you for sure, would probably remember the score, and could

Hot Competitors: Georgia Tech's Pepper Rodgers and Lewis after tennis.

give a good guess at the date as well.

We played a lot of doubles matches on that court over the next couple of years. Lewis always stuck with me as a partner, even though I was going through what he called my "Roy Rogers period" on my serve. I had developed a terrible hitch in my serve, which took various forms, but during this time it looked a lot like a cowboy getting ready to rope a steer.

Pepper ran in a lot of different partners trying to get a win against Lewis and me. I remember his being successful one time with a good player named Niles from the West Coast. And tennis was not his only talent. This man was possibly the greatest name dropper who ever lived. As Lewis recalled it, which he did many times, "Niles dropped the names of Ronald Reagan, the Queen of England, and three of the original four horseman on changeovers before we finished the first set."

At the end of July in 1978, I loaded everything I owned into a 1970 Volvo and headed to Atlanta. Lewis had a two-bedroom apartment at Mi Casa on Collier Road, and his buddy Ron Hudspeth lived in the next building. Ron and Lewis made Mi

Casa the headquarters of the late '70s singles scene in Atlanta.

I moved in with Lewis and split the rent. I didn't work for a while; Lewis called me the "pool fool." Neither of us was very domestic, so we never cooked; we'd pick up fried chicken, order a pizza, or walk across the street to Grandma's Biscuits. Friday nights we'd go to Harrison's on Peachtree, which was definitely the place to be at the end of the week in 1978.

About six months after I moved to Atlanta, Lewis bought a small house overlooking a little park. I moved there with him. The house had the steepest driveway I had ever seen. One day I left my Volvo, which had no emergency brake, at the top of that driveway, in what I thought was a stable position. When we came out minutes later, it had just started to roll backward. Since it was my car, I ran after it, managed to get the driver's side door open, but then made a split-second decision that I was too late to save it from going down that steep hill. I saved myself instead. It slammed into a tree at the bottom of the hill, and that was the end of my Volvo.

That house could have been the real estate poster child for functional obsolescence. It had one big living room and small everything else. It had three bedrooms but only one bath. Sharing a bathroom with Lewis is what eventually drove me out of that house to get my own place. These days, I'm messy; my wife will testify to that. Back then I was closer to a slob. Lewis, on the other hand, was way past that distinction into the oblivious range.

I didn't intend for this to be a "tell-all," but after all these years I feel compelled to tell the world that Lewis had a thing about toilet paper. He was a dedicated user. In the six to eight months I lived in that house with Lewis, he must have stopped up that only toilet a dozen times. I don't know what he did with all that toilet paper, but somehow half a roll would end up in the commode. He might as well have stuck in a giant redwood.

Maybe it was one of those taboo subjects between guys, but we never really talked about our plumbing problems, and I'm not really sure Lewis ever even noticed the situation. My choices were to drive to the gas station several times per day, or unstop that commode myself. Unstopping a toilet that someone else stopped up — that's friendship.

As far as Lewis' single life, he really hit his stride in that house. He once logged the "network triple," as we called it back then, when in one week he scored with a female employee of all three major TV stations, two of them on-the-air personalities. I doubt that this particular feat has been accomplished since.

In less successful (though no less active) weeks, Lewis would meet a "six" in Harrison's, drink her to an "eight," and then run her back to the house, which is where I would encounter them the next morning as they were trying to scurry away.

One evening a Lewis date volunteered to fix him dinner. It was one of those elaborate meals that included several sauces, each of which had to be cooked separately before bringing the whole concoction together. In the course of preparation, I believe she used every concave object in the house except the dirty ashtrays.

After dinner, no doubt with a full stomach and his judgment clouded by several beers, Lewis lost his head and told her not to bother with the dishes, he would take care of them the next day.

A month later, penicillin was discovered in those same pots, which hadn't moved from the sink. I admit, I really unstopped the toilet all those times more out of necessity than friendship, because I had no intention of doing the dishes for a meal I didn't cook or eat. As long as there was a clear path to the refrigerator, I was happy.

After about six weeks, when the microorganisms had flourished to the point of having their own smell, distinct from most of the other odors emanating from that house, I decided to put them in a box and take them outside. Had I known the Centers for Disease Control was in Atlanta, I would have borrowed one of their Level 4 biohazard suits. We almost always used the side door to enter the house, since it was right at the end of the driveway, so I put the box near the front door, which couldn't be seen from the road below due to the steep driveway. I swear to you, that box was still there when I moved out a couple of months later, and I imagine it had to be written into the purchase contract when Lewis eventually sold that house: "Buyer to pay for removal of box and various life forms contained therein from front steps."

Lewis' writing career was beginning to progress beyond his column. His first book was a smash, and his column was being syndicated nationally. Lewis once described his job to me as "remembering things that never happened."

Despite his career success, I often heard Lewis recall that he had only one major goal in life during the next couple of years: to finish his column early enough so that he could get to Bitsy Grant Tennis Center and we could get into a good doubles match before all the decent players were matched up and all the courts were taken. Soon we were back into our routine of playing tennis almost every day of our lives. Nearly all of my friends and many of Lewis' were from Bitsy. Some of the old guys from the Tennis Center, including Bitsy Grant himself, were ranked in the South or in the nation in their age groups. Lewis and I looked at them and believed we would play tennis until that age ourselves, as partners, of course.

Tennis at Bitsy Grant was not quite the same game as one might play with the Queen in attendance during the All England Tennis Championships at Wimbledon. It was a dusty, gritty, bad bounce affair that we cursed our way through, with our shirts off to get a good tan. On top of that, Lewis and I fell in with a bad crowd.

Together with our buddies, we formed an ALTA (Atlanta Lawn Tennis Association) team and played in the A-1 league, which at that time was the second highest of probably twenty different levels of play in the world's largest tennis league. We took our gritty show on the road, but it didn't play too well in the suburbs. In fact, we got into a bit of a brouhaha at one of the spiffier clubs during the first match.

By this time, I was out of my Chicago Pillsbury Doughboy mode, I was working on my "pool fool" tan, and I didn't understand why we couldn't play with our shirts off. The court we were on was right next to the club swimming pool, where people were practically "nekkid," as my partner would say. We argued about it for quite some time before I eventually relented.

Lewis and I ultimately got to match point on my serve, despite my hitching like I was in a rodeo. But I completely tensed up at match point, hitched a little extra, and actually hit the ball off the top of my racket, on a trajectory resembling that of a short, high lob. Lewis, wanting the match to end before his partner had a total body spasm, left at the sound of the ball hitting my racket. He was poaching. He got to the middle of the court, expecting our opponents' service return to already be heading his way for an easy volley, but nothing happened. In fact, my serve hadn't come down yet. Lewis decided he better go back and cover the spot he left open, which he did. He had plenty of time to get there, I might add.

Gravity eventually prevailed, my serve did come down, and, as luck would have it, landed in the appropriate service box, stunning onlookers and players alike. It was so slow, and bounced so high and fat, that one of our overanxious opponents miss-hit it right into the bottom of the net. We won the match and won our division. We disbanded the next season rather than move up to the AA-1 league and get killed.

The football season rolled around again. Bulldog fans will find it hard to believe, but Lewis didn't attend that many Georgia games in 1978 and 1979. We did go to a lot of Tech games, though. We were, in fact, on a double date to a Tech Game when Lewis met Kathy Logue, who later became the third Mrs. Grizzard. It was a half-blind double date. Kathy and Kim King's wife were good friends, and they set Lewis up with Kathy. Lewis was

On the Circuit: Another speech, another plate of peas

getting in deep with the Tech crowd. In fact, when Tech played Navy away, Lewis and Kathy, the Kings, ex-pro and Georgia Tech player Taz Anderson and his wife Gregory, and I all went to Washington. This was during the Carter administration, so we got the royal tour of the White House and briefly met the President. Tech won the football game the next day, as I recall.

By the time I moved to Atlanta, Lewis was already so popular that he was beginning to get requests to speak. He had done a few speeches but was yet to charge for them.

Pretenders: Grizzard and Jarvis at the Carter White House

We decided that since I wasn't gainfully employed at the time, I would be his agent. That way, he wouldn't have to ask for money himself, or turn down anyone who couldn't afford it. Lewis had trouble saying "no" all his life. When he first started charging, Lewis' speaking fee was $250. I got ten percent.

There are more than 150 counties in Georgia, and I bet Lewis spoke at the Chamber of Commerce annual meeting at half of them in his first three years. He spoke at practi-

The Real Thing: With first-brother Billy Carter in Plains, Georgia

cally every Quarterback Club in America, and they would want him back every year. He did Rotaries, Junior League meetings, conventions, and association meetings. Lewis would tell a raft of preacher jokes, knock Tech, Clemson, and Atlanta politicians, and end with Uncle Cleeve "risin' up out of that casket like he had good sense."

I had found a full-time job by March of 1979, but I was doing field service for the Maytag of medical equipment, so mostly I just stood by on the courts at Bitsy Grant Tennis Center. Lewis accused me of getting a beeper so people would think I had a job.

I remember that by April of 1979, Lewis was up to a whopping $350 per speech, and he was making about as much money speaking as he got from the *Constitution*. That month was already full — with ten speaking engagements booked — so when the daughter of a Saudi Prince who had a house in Atlanta called and wanted Lewis to do a luncheon speech, he said he didn't really want to. Rather than turn it down cold, he told me just to tell her his fee was $1,000.

I was a little reluctant to tell her that much, thinking that whoever had referred Lewis as a speaker probably told her what he charged as well. But I did what Lewis told me to do. She never blinked. We couldn't believe that someone would pay Lewis $1,000 to drive across town at lunch time and tell a few jokes and stories.

Soon after that, we decided that we'd better jump into this thing with both feet. We paid cartoonist Sam Rawls (Scrawls) $100 to do a caricature of Lewis, which I put on the front of our first brochure. We even got an audio guy that worked with Lewis' stepbrother, radio talk show host Ludlow Porch, to tape Lewis giving a speech. I spent several hours with him editing the tape, and we had the first recording of his speech material.

That recording was so good that, as Lewis' agent, I was able to sign him up with his first record contract. Here is how it worked: Lewis got twelve albums for ninety-nine cents, as long as he agreed to purchase eight more albums at regular club prices.

I guess I wasn't really that good an agent, but I didn't have to

The first official sales logo for Lewis Grizzard, newsman and entertainer.

be. Word spread fast. We kept going up on fees to $500, $750, $850, $1,000, $1,500, $2,500. If they weren't sure they wanted to pay that much, I would send them a copy of the tape. It worked every time.

Not being a complete dummy, I realized that there was potential for me to make money booking speakers other than Lewis. The ones that couldn't afford Lewis, I would usually steer toward Ludlow Porch, and I became his speaking agent as well. I'd call back the places where Lewis spoke the previous year. They'd want Lewis back but he didn't want to go, because at that time he had only one speech. So I'd book someone else in there.

Once Lewis got to about $5,000 a pop several years later, he decided that he needed a full-time agent and business manager. He offered me the job, but I didn't want to work for Lewis full-time. I thought that arrangement might interfere with our friendship. So Lewis hired Tony Privett to be his business manager.

I continued to act as Lewis' speaking agent for a couple more years, until Grizzard Enterprises started its own speakers' bureau. I remember once looking back and figuring that I had been Lewis' agent for some eight years, had booked his first six hundred speaking engagements, and had managed to parlay his popularity into booking another eight hundred speeches for other people. I still have that first tape, and it's still as funny now as it was then. I sold it via mail order at the time, to help defray the costs of the ones I gave away as promotional tapes. There's a collector's item for you.

During my first few years in Atlanta, Lewis and I played some memorable tennis on a court in Taz Anderson's back yard. A while back, my wife polished up a very tarnished old silver dish, which revealed from its inscription that we must have won the Taz Anderson Invitational one year.

I do know that event was the occasion for one of Lewis' funniest tennis lines ever. Lewis and I were playing Taz and one of his hard-hitting football buddies. It was a friendly but competitive match, with a considerable amount of banter about questionable line calls. Lewis was serving, and I was at the net. I leaned left and spit. Taz's wife Gregory, who was seated near the other side of the court, playfully said, "Tim, don't spit on my court."

I looked left and inspected the spot where I had spit, and I answered that it was just outside the court. Lewis, not wanting to miss a chance for another dig at our opponents, said, "Actually, he spit on the line and they called it out."

Although most of our tennis was still played at Bitsy Grant Tennis Center, we started making a few tennis trips. The first few were to Hilton Head, but later we settled on Sea Island, Georgia. Being used to the public clay courts at Bitsy Grant, where you could count on a bad bounce after a few shots, we were inspired by the perfect clay courts at the resort. We would play doubles from 10-12:00 in the morning, eat lunch, relax, and come back and play more doubles from 4-6:00 in the afternoon.

What we couldn't understand was why Lewis never seemed to be in as good condition as the rest of us, though year around we all played about the same amount of tennis. Even in the spring and fall, when it wasn't all that hot, Lewis would take off his leather tennis shoes at the end of a match and pour two to three ounces of sweat out of each one. He sweated more than anyone we had ever seen.

He'd do his best to keep up with us, but a long point would usually leave him winded and stalling for time when the rest of us were ready to play. Knowing what we know now, its amazing he didn't die on a tennis court in the early 1980s.

After the 1980 football season, when Georgia won the national championship, we started an annual pilgrimage to Sea Island, trying each year to be the first arrivals for the Georgia/Florida game. Most years, we both spent two full weeks in a "cottage," as the locals called those rentable five- and six-bedroom houses. It was a pretty good deal for me. Lewis got the house, and I got the chicken (brought the food). As game day drew closer, other friends would arrive to join us for tennis, golf, and partying.

Many of those trips eventually blurred together. Not even Lewis could keep the years straight. We used to refer to them as "the year we jumped buck nekkid in the pool," or "the year Booger Sealy ate the turtle," and so forth.

Lewis eventually went to see a doctor after his shortness of breath got worse. The doctors found that his heart was enlarged, and his blood pressure was 180 over zero. The way they explained it to him, his blood was leaking back into his heart through a faulty valve so severely that the forward movement of blood actually stopped during each beat.

He put off surgery for several months, during which time he was having problems with insomnia, maybe as a result of the substantial self-medicating he had been doing. That phrase in the song "Mr. Bojangles" — "he drinks a bit" — always reminded me of Lewis.

After the surgery, doctors predicted that he wouldn't wake up until the next day. What we all learned, however, was that Lewis had a tremendous capacity to remain alert. He surprised everyone by waking up in the early evening of the same day that he had the surgery.

He made a pretty complete recovery, and we had him playing tennis again after several months. That was still our main sport at the time. In fact, after that first surgery we got ourselves ranked in the Men's 35 and Over doubles in the state of Georgia. Not ranked real high, mind you, but we did beat some teams, and we even won a small tournament.

Only a couple of years later, during a visit to Russia, an infection on his replacement heart valve almost killed him. After surgery No. 2 at Emory University Hospital, Lewis again woke up about twelve hours before the doctors predicted he would.

Following that recovery, Lewis actually made another comeback to tennis. Our final conversion to golf, however, was hastened by playing legendary former Georgia Tech coach Bobby Dodd and "Brother" — Bobby Dodd, Jr. — a dozen or so times at Bitsy Grant Tennis Center. Coach Dodd was about a hundred years old, but it didn't seem to matter. He never would move more than a few feet one way or another. He had this huge snowshoe-type racket, and he had only one shot with it: no matter how hard you hit it, Coach Dodd would angle that racket out in front of him and push up another deep lob.

"Brother" was a great athlete who had played football at Florida. Other than a good serve, Bobby Jr. had pretty much one shot himself, and that was a buzz-ball forehand that I've only seen a couple of people hit. A ball hit off Bobby's forehand would have so much spin on it that the ball would actually change shape, becoming elongated. And when it bounced, it would jump at you. Unfortunately for us, neither Lewis nor I had a drop shot, because both Coach and "Brother" stayed mostly at the baseline.

We tried to stay away from "Brother's" forehand, so we always ended up hitting a series of progressively weaker and weaker overheads toward Coach Dodd, who would move about an inch, stick up that horseshoe racket like a backstop, and up would come another lob. Somehow we wound up winning most of those matches, but Lewis got to where he couldn't lift his right arm to brush his teeth in the morning, and my back got so bad that if I got out of a chair, it took about ten steps before I could straighten up. Rather than learn a drop shot, we took up golf.

From the start of our serious golf, Lewis and I were always about equal in handicap. The Sea Island trip eventually became all golf. One year, we played thirty-six holes a day for eight straight days before the start of the Gator Hater golf tournament. Another year, Mike Mathews, Lewis and I were playing the Island Club. On a short par three of about 120 yards over water, Lewis took a nine iron and knocked it on the green. The ball hopped twice and disappeared into the hole for an ace!

On the next tee, Lewis started to tee up his ball, hesitated a second as if he weren't sure that he had the honors, and turned to Mike and me and asked, "Anyone have a zero?"

Lewis wrote a great column about that hole-in-one for the next day's newspaper. I watched him write it in the house where we were staying on Sea Island. It took him thirty minutes. What I realized when I saw him do this is that he had actually written the complete "Hole-in-One" column in his head in the twenty-four hours since he had hit the shot. He had made absolutely no notes. Lewis Grizzard had refined the art of column writing to the point where the whole column was stored in memory in that word processing brain of his, and all that was left was just giving the signal to his fingers to type it.

We never bet on tennis, yet I don't think we ever played golf without betting. Lewis and I eventually worked our way up to $5 per hole and $2 for trash, as our normal bet on the first tee. Basic trash would be for birdies, greenies (closest to the pin on the tee shot on a par three), sandies (up and down out of the sand for par or better), and polies (making a putt or chip-in longer than the length of the flag stick for par or better).

Later we added Murphies and whammies. You got a Murphy by announcing that you would get up and down (one putt for par or better) from anywhere off the green. If you failed to get up and down, the other guy got the trash. None of us knew the guy named Murphy who apparently invented this game, but as far as I'm concerned, we might as well have called it a Grizzard.

Lewis always had a marvelous short game. He was relatively

short off the tee, and got shorter with each heart surgery, but he could get up and down from the parking lot. I never had the guts to call a Murphy, unless I was on the fringe about one blade of grass off the green, no more than fifteen feet from the hole. Lewis won a fortune on Murphies.

I sometimes got a little of my money back on whammies, which were awarded for being closest to the pin and on the green after three shots on a par five.

A Sure Bet: Lewis and Tim Jarvis on the course

One edge Lewis had over me and most of his opponents was that his comfort zone was higher than ours. He'd usually double the bet on the back nine, and then somebody else would double again, and before you knew it there was so much money at stake you could hardly draw a breath, much less hit a shot. Whenever there was big money at stake on the last hole, Lewis was a strong favorite to win.

Over the years we played golf on so many different courses in Georgia and Florida, I couldn't begin to name them all. Lewis, however, was different. I noticed that after we played a course for the first time, we'd be sitting around discussing the round, and Lewis would make references to hole numbers. I think I'm like most golfers — I've got to play a course several times before I can remember the exact sequence and layout of each hole. But not Lewis. Months later he could remember virtually all the holes on a course he had played just one time.

It's hard for me to express how important golf was to Lewis. Fortunately, he had the means to pursue this love. Golf has a fourteen-club rule, i.e., you can't carry more than fourteen clubs in your golf bag. Lewis thought that meant you weren't allowed to *join* more than fourteen different golf clubs, and he was working on it.

Although I was still living in Atlanta in April of 1989, my wife Rosel and I married in California, the state where most of my relatives and many of hers were living. Lewis flew there to be my best man. Afterwards, Rosel and I returned to Atlanta to live.

In July of 1990, Rosel and I and our daughter, Lewis' six-month-old goddaughter Gabriella, moved to California. Lewis and I talked about once a month on the phone, and I know neither of us ever sensed that the separation of two thousand miles affected our friendship. And, of course, we still had our annual two-week pilgrimage to Sea Island.

By the 1992 trip, Lewis' doctors were already telling him that he'd need a new heart valve. He put it off as long as he could, shoving it back into March of the next year. I flew out several days before the surgery. Lewis and I played in a member/guest tournament at Ansley Golf Club, which ended the day before the surgery. We finished second and had a chance to win.

I got to the hospital about 6:00 a.m. on the day of the surgery, and as it turned out, I left only one time, for about three hours, over the next four days. You'll read the details elsewhere in this book, but Lewis' heart wouldn't start beating on its own following the surgery. For four days he was on artificial pumps, and doctors didn't think he would live. Even after his heart miraculously started, he remained in a coma for nearly two weeks.

It's strange what you do in situations like that. The one time I left the hospital for about three hours, I went to Ansley Golf Club. If Lewis was going to die, I wanted the previous day's score card from the last time we had played golf together.

GA Bulldogs: The State's Majority Party

By Loran Smith

Loran Smith lives in Athens, Georgia, where he serves as executive secretary of the Georgia Bulldog Club. He is the author of numerous books and articles.

After Lewis returned from Chicago to Atlanta and began writing a daily column, one of the keen observers of his work was none other than Pepper Rodgers, Georgia Tech's head football coach. Pepper really liked Lewis and cultivated his friendship. They frequently played tennis together, and Lewis enjoyed Pepper's witty, caustic style. Both of them were great at one-liners.

Pepper knew what he was doing. He wanted this high-profile University of Georgia graduate in his corner. And when Lewis wrote columns about Pepper and his Tech team, what a coup that was. You don't denigrate or castigate your tennis partner, even if he makes a questionable third-down call. Even if he coaches the team that your friends from your alma mater detest.

At that point in his career, Lewis sincerely believed that as a professional newspaperman he had to maintain his objectivity. He felt he had to be above the intense Georgia-Georgia Tech rivalry.

Many of us in Athens thought, What's going on here? Lewis

didn't seem to be the kind of person who would forget his ties, his training, his alma mater. Especially his old friends. He was supposed to be a Bulldog and wear his feelings on his sleeve like the rest of us.

After the classic 1978 showdown — when Georgia came from behind 21-3 to beat Tech 29-28, in perhaps the most sensational game ever played between the two schools — Lewis wrote something to the effect that it was such a great game, it was a shame either team had to lose. Now, for a Georgia man to say it was a shame for Tech to lose really caused some head shaking. Dan Magill didn't like it. I didn't like it. Anybody I knew who knew Lewis didn't like it. That would be the last time Lewis ever made that mistake. His old friends let him know they didn't care for that kind of thinking. It was at that point, in my opinion, that Lewis began to understand Magill's slogan of many years: "The Georgia Bulldogs, the majority party of the empire state of the South."

Soon after, Georgia Tech fired Pepper Rodgers. One of Lewis' close friends said to him, "Now you can go back to hating Tech like the rest of us." Not long after that, Lewis was spending every weekend in Athens watching the Herschel Walker Show. Like a good Bulldog, he had lost his objectivity. He was screaming "How 'bout them Dawgs!" as loudly as anybody.

In his columns, he began taking blatant swipes at Georgia's biggest rivals, including Georgia Tech. He became the hero of the Georgia faithful. He said things the way they felt they would say themselves if they were writing a column. Bulldog fans were gleefully front and center. They had Herschel on the field and Lewis in the newspaper. For years Georgia fans had complained about the late Ed Danforth of the *Atlanta Journal* for what they perceived to be his biased support of Bobby Dodd and Georgia Tech. Now, with Lewis doing his thing, they were getting even. Bulldog fans were crass and without humility. They thought this dominance would go on forever.

Chafing and miserable were the Georgia opponents, particularly Florida, Auburn and Georgia Tech. Even if one of these schools got the best of the Bulldogs in football, Lewis found a way to insult their fans and delight his Bulldog brethren.

But he saved his best insults for Clemson, which seldom beat Georgia, despite its vast improvement in the early 1980s as scholarship rules leveled the field for recruiting. The game that hurt the Clemson fans the most, however, was the one they lost in Wrightsville, the rural, middle Georgia hometown of Herschel Walker. Clemson thought it had seduced Herschel before he signed with Georgia. Lewis liked to remind Tiger fans of how that recruiting battle turned out.

Along the way, Lewis had made an interesting discovery: Whatever he wrote and whatever he said brought a tremendous response from the people in the state who followed the University of Georgia. Like Dan Magill had said, the Bulldogs were the majority party. Lewis realized that writing to the Bulldog audience was good for him as a columnist. They hung on his every word. He was an old-shoe type and they loved him.

By the late 1970s his columns were so popular that several books of them had been published. They carried such funny titles as *Don't Sit Under the Grits Tree With Anyone Else But Me*, and *Shoot Low, Boys, They're Riding Shetland Ponies!* If a columnist can make it big with one or two of those type books in his career, he has done well. But Lewis was publishing a best-selling collection of his columns every year.

In the middle of the 1980 season, when it looked like Georgia was a team of destiny, Lewis came to Athens and had dinner at my house, which he did quite often. My mother and father, who lived on a farm near Wrightsville, kept my freezer stocked with vegetables, and whenever Lewis came over, my wife, Myrna, would set out those field peas, butter beans and corn from the freezer.

That night we sat up well into the evening, talking about how much we had enjoyed the Bulldogs' success to date, and wouldn't it be nice if Georgia could go all the way. We talked about Georgia's being a team of destiny.

There was something about Herschel and his magnetic influence on his teammates and the Georgia people. I sensed that he would take us to the top, and I had begun to make notes —

inside stuff from the locker room and private conversations with the coaches. My notebook was filling up nicely, but what was I going to do with it?

After dinner I began discussing my notes with Lewis. By the time I had revealed two or three of those inside vignettes to him, he was excited.

"I've got a good story, Lewis, but no publisher," I said.

"How about an editor?" he said. "You'll need an editor, too." We looked at each other, thinking the same thing, and embraced right there in my front yard as he and the latest Mrs. Grizzard were saying good night.

In a few days, he called to say that his publisher would be interested in producing a book on the Bulldogs, but both Lewis and I knew that it had to be a blockbuster year for such a project to succeed. The Liberty Bowl wouldn't be enough. Georgia had to go all the way.

After a thrilling comeback win over Florida the next week — on perhaps the greatest play in Bulldog history, Buck Belue to Lindsay Scott for a 93-yard touchdown in the last two minutes — Georgia finished the season by beating Auburn and Georgia Tech. The Bulldogs were ranked No. 1 at the end of the regular season, thanks largely to the fact that underdog Georgia Tech had tied then No. 1 Notre Dame midway through the season.

The publisher, Lewis and I all agreed that with Georgia being ranked No. 1 in the nation, we would do a book even if Notre Dame upset the Bulldogs in the Sugar Bowl. But Lewis and I knew that we were in trouble if that happened. Being No. 1 makes a big difference in a situation like that. Lose that national championship game and it takes the luster off a season and a story.

The month of December was agony, worrying about whether or not Georgia could pull it off. Lewis would call, hoping for some good news. "We gotta fight the ghost of Rockne," he said. "That's tough." Also there was the week or so when Vince Dooley was making a decision on whether or not to leave Georgia and return to his alma mater, Auburn. That would not have ruined the story at all, but whoever was the coach, Georgia had to beat the Irish.

We decided that since we were going to do the book anyway, we would be prepared to make it a story on Herschel Walker, who had become the most popular player you could imagine. His celebrity endeared him to the Georgia people because he seemed to be so modest and unassuming. He always said the right thing. He never called attention to himself. He always deferred to his teammates. Sports writers and television crews from all over the country were flocking to Athens.

What a story we had, but Lewis and I fretted over how to start, how to write about Herschel or the other players and games when we didn't know how the final game would turn out.

We decided that I would continue researching and trying to get as much detail as possible. Inside stuff that fans would cling to. The kind of things that you know about only when you are in the locker room — coaches whispering, players humming the national anthem, and somebody throwing up in the bathroom before kickoff.

Lewis loved it. "Hey," he said, "this is great. They'll go crazy when they read this. What a story, indeed!"

Glory! Glory! Lewis and Loran Smith with Bulldog head coach Vince Dooley

We published *Glory! Glory!* in the summer of 1981. As we toured the state selling books, Lewis and I signed until our hands ached. We couldn't just sign our names; we had to write a special Bulldog message in each one of them. At first Lewis, who knew what was in store, felt we shouldn't spend all that time doing personal messages. I said, "Lewis, we have to. These people feel so wonderful about the University of Georgia that we can't run the risk of offending them."

He grinned and said, "You're right. Suits me if we are here all night."

That tour over the state was a big success, but it was great fun, too. Tony Privett, our publisher's rep, drove the van, handled the money, set up the autograph parties, and made all the arrangements. Lewis rode shotgun, so he could manage the radio. He knew every country FM signal in the state, having gotten acquainted in the previous couple of years from making speeches in the hinterlands. I took the back seat so the smooth sounds of Lewis' favorite country artists would put me to sleep. But we didn't sleep very much. Mostly we swapped stories.

It was a laugh a mile. We talked about politics — not about who we agreed or disagreed with, but the colorful good-ol'-days style campaigning. We told sports stories. We laughed about how life was, growing up in the rural South.

Lewis was a gospel music fan. He grew up on the Atlanta Crackers and he read the comics first and the sports pages next. Except for the eternal emotional crisis of growing up without his father, life for young Lewis was simple and orderly. Down home living was in his bones, and he would never shake it. His stories about his small-town life and habits endeared him to people everywhere.

That's why he enjoyed storytelling so much. Everybody's family would sit around on the porch in the cool of the evening and spin tales. Children were not allowed to talk. They listened, but Lewis learned more than any of his family and friends realized. He would some day tell his stories and get paid as much as $20,000 a speech.

One of the colorful old Georgia pols that Lewis loved was

Marvin Griffin. I told him about going to see the former Georgia governor and spending an afternoon by a farm pond near Bainbridge, Georgia, listening to Marvin tell his favorite political stories. Lewis listened as if he were spellbound. Not by my delivery but by what I recalled Marvin's saying. We'd get in the car, headed to the next town and the next book signing, and Lewis would say, "Got any more Marvin Griffin stories?"

He had plenty of stories of his own that he had picked up through the years, but if you had a fresh one, he would laugh uncontrollably. Like the story about one long ago campaign for governor of Georgia, when Ellis Arnall ran against Gene Talmadge. This was in the stump and barbecue days. TV had not ruined campaigning.

Seems that Arnall was trying to convince a group of South Georgia voters that he was more honest than Talmadge. "If you go by old Gene's place, " Arnall said, "you'll find a paved road right up to his house. If you come to my house, you'll find a dirt road. Why would you vote for a fellow like Gene and not vote for me?" he asked.

A farmer in overalls raised his hand and replied, "I'll tell you why! We already paved *his* road."

A story like that always activated Lewis' laughter button. If you told it, he would never tire of your telling it again. More often than not it would wind up in one of his books or speeches, and the belly laughs would lift the roof.

That is the way it was on our book tour. We'd be riding down the road and Lewis would laugh out loud, recalling the punch line of a story one of us had told two or three days earlier.

On that tour he met a lot of people who became close friends. Lewis would see them at games in Athens and wherever the Bulldogs played on the road. He interacted with them, he partied and celebrated with them. They liked his good ol' boy style and they cheered his speeches and bought his books. He bought them drinks and dinners. He could never have become the sensational hero of Bulldog fans, as he did, by being neutral. Or objective. His fans believed that he hurt when Georgia lost. And in truth, he did.

In Athens, we were always having parties during football season. Many people — some I had never met — showed up at our house, and I am sure that Lewis' being a frequent guest was often the motivation for that heightened attendance. Two particularly memorable parties were when Lewis turned forty and when his journalism degree became official.

Years after he attended his last class at Georgia, Lewis commented one day that he really wished he had found a way to complete his degree requirements. He had taken a job in the *Journal* sports department only three courses shy of graduation. So I called the dean of the journalism school, Tom Russell, and asked him if something could be worked out. In an odd sort of way, I felt I was following through on the promise I had made to Charlie Harris years earlier, when he had asked me to help young Lewis Grizzard.

Two of the journalism courses Lewis never took at Georgia were News Writing and Reporting, and Advanced Editing and Make-up. The other was a physical education course. The dean said that he would ask for a waiver on the P.E. course and that Lewis could go through the challenge process for the other two courses. Most universities have a procedure for challenging that your professional experience would exceed anything taught in the classroom. By that time, Lewis could have taught the courses in News Writing and Reporting and Advanced Editing and Make-up better than the professors themselves. So it was no problem for him to satisfy his journalism requirements using the challenge procedure. There was a problem, however, with the P.E. course.

Physical Education Department officials were adamant that Lewis would have to do something physical. It looked for a while that he might have to enroll in P.E. at Atlanta's Georgia State, but Dean Tom Russell personally lobbied the P.E. staff with information about Lewis' bad heart, and the requirement was finally waived.

When I called Lewis to give him the good news, he was happier than he was when Herschel scored two touchdowns over Notre Dame in the Sugar Bowl for the National Championship.

But there was not a lot of shouting and screaming, as you might think.

"You don't know what this means to me," he said humbly and appreciatively. "I never thought that it would happen without me coming back to Athens and physically enrolling for those courses. Tell Dean Russell I'll remember him in my will."

Lewis could never remain somber for any extended period of time, but of all the things that were ever done for him, getting that degree was one of the most important.

"This calls for a party," I said, and we planned a big one with many of Lewis' friends following a home game. I considered a cap and gown ceremony or maybe inviting one of Lewis' big critics, like the Clemson coach, to do a commencement address. But we finally settled on having Dean Russell officially present Lewis with his diploma — live on the air of our pre-game radio show.

After the game, we celebrated some more at my house with Lewis entertaining everybody. I almost got the best of him, however, when I insisted that any Georgia graduate has to be able to sing the alma mater. Lewis didn't know the words. He couldn't do it. But he laughed long and hard at this incident.

The party that topped them all, however, was the celebration of Lewis' fortieth birthday.

We hid all the guests in the basement of my house, and Athens friends Billy and Nancy Anderson brought Lewis by, trumping up some story about plans for the evening. At the appropriate time, everybody came up from the basement to the back yard, singing happy birthday.

We had organized a little show to go with the celebration. Lewis always enjoyed poking fun at waiters, especially the great number of gay waiters he seemed to encounter at the many restaurants he frequented. "Hi, I'm Brad, and I'll be your waiter tonight." Lewis would say of those experiences in his speeches. Then he would counter with, "Hi, I'm Lewis, and I'll be your customer, but that's as far as it goes!" We put together a script for a college student to imitate a gay waiter; it was a successful put down of Lewis, and he roared with laughter.

With a local minister, we reenacted his three marriage ceremonies. His third wife, Kathy, who was coincidentally in town for the game, actually participated by playing herself in his third marriage ceremony.

But the hit of the party was Don Beasley, who was one of our football managers. Don is a dwarf, and in planning the party, I asked Don if he would consider playing the part of Lewis' fictitious little brother, Joey. Those who heard Lewis speak will recall that he always brought up little Joey's name, suggesting that Joey was in need of a serious operation and that it would mean a lot to Lewis if all those in attendance would go out and buy one of Lewis' books or tapes so he could raise enough money for Joey's operation. Then he would say something like, "I get two dollars and little Joey gets a nickel."

We had a clever script for Don to follow, and he followed it to perfection, chastising Lewis for his phony act, his greed, and his failure to give Joey any money. He let Lewis have it for wearing Gucci shoes, vacationing at Sea Island, Georgia, riding in limousines, and getting rich off the emotional appeal to help Little Joey — but in truth, never really doing anything for Joey.

We even had country music hall of famer Bill Anderson, a long-time friend of Lewis', sing a nonsensical song that Lewis' manager, Tony Privett, had written to gig Lewis. Bill laughed at the weak lyrics, but the song left Lewis laughing too.

Lewis could not have been more pleased by our antics at his expense. He literally laughed until he cried, wiping his eyes with his handkerchief as he laughed uncontrollably. When you got a good one on Lewis Grizzard, he enjoyed it as much as anybody.

At The Reins Of A Runaway Rocket...

BY TONY PRIVETT

Tony Privett is corporate communications manager for the City of Lubbock, Texas. He resides in Slaton, Texas, with his wife Judy.

Waldenbooks, the national bookstore chain, brought me to Atlanta from Texas in 1977, and brought Lewis Grizzard and me together two years later. I was District Manager over a dozen Southeastern bookstores when Lewis began writing his *Atlanta Journal-Constitution* column.

I first noticed Lewis' sharp wit in the column where he explained how his name was properly pronounced. The "GrizZARD, not GRIZzerd" story was a witty, self-deprecating bit that he learned from his father and continued to use in his stand-up routine for the rest of his life.

Like thousands of Atlantans in 1979, I was drawn to the six-times-per-week column's fresh humor. But Grizzard could also turn on a dime and pull your heart up into your throat. And then he'd hit you over the head with seething, self-righteous anger over a crooked politician or a senseless murder.

When Helen Elliott, the charming founder of a recently-formed Atlanta book publishing company, signed Grizzard to a contract to bring out a collection of his best-loved columns in the fall of 1979, she launched Lewis on a book publishing career that would eventually rival the top living authors.

With a $500 advance against royalties, Peachtree Publishers bought the rights to *Kathy Sue Loudermilk, I Love You*. Lewis delivered the manuscript to the publisher in a brown paper grocery sack, a tradition he carried on for many years. And with this clever title, Lewis began a signature style of titling his books that in later years would cause him to joke, "The damn titles take more time to come up with than the rest of the book."

Kathy Sue Loudermilk was a popular character Lewis created for his columns. Unlike many of his childhood friends who found themselves in his writings, Kathy Sue was more of an idealized male fantasy. He may have even used the name "Kathy" because he was dating Kathy Logue, the woman who would soon become "the third Mrs. Grizzard."

Even though Helen Elliott was confident of the success of this book project, she had to swallow hard when she ordered the first printing of 10,000 copies. In later years, initial print runs for Grizzard books would grow to 150,000 copies.

Fortunately for everyone, *Kathy Sue Loudermilk* took off. I had placed a modest initial order in September for my Georgia Waldenbooks stores. They were gone in about a week. As Thanksgiving approached and we could see that the book was turning into a blockbuster, I called Peachtree to place a third order.

But I was dismayed to learn that the Rich's buyer, Faith Brunson, had already spoken for the remaining first printing inventory. The second printing would not arrive until after Christmas!

I knew that Helen had been seeking the counsel of Miss Brunson, the long-time Rich's book buyer, and Faith had taken Helen under her wing and supported Peachtree's early books with Rich's prestigious author signings.

In my disappointment, I complained to Helen that, "No matter how big Rich's is in Atlanta, ultimately Waldenbooks' national presence is more valuable to your company."

Helen was a savvy businessperson and found a way to get

Waldenbooks a thousand copies to carry us through most of the Christmas season. I always wondered how Helen explained "the missing thousand" to Faith.

Flush with my new inventory, I asked Peachtree to do an autograph party with Grizzard. Helen informed me that Rich's had already sewn up *all* of his Atlanta appearances. This was the second of many examples I would see of Faith Brunson's shrewd business dealings.

I took my lumps and scheduled Lewis for a signing in Albany, a city in south Georgia where we could piggyback with a speaking engagement Lewis had on his calendar. The autographing was one of the few in Lewis' career that was poorly attended. His column had just been picked up by a national newspaper syndicate, but in Georgia it was available only in the *Constitution*. The Atlanta newspapers did have a statewide readership, but Lewis' column was not yet stirring up the same attention outside metro Atlanta.

On this particular day in the fall of 1979, we probably drew fifteen or twenty folks. I found Lewis to be rather demanding and surly to me, though charming to his fans and friends. When a local television news crew showed up to get an interview of Lewis while he signed books, Lewis' mood brightened. Though twice-divorced, Lewis had just written a column telling his fans that he was getting married for the third time. It was big news. I was amazed at how interested people were in Lewis Grizzard's personal life.

As the TV crew began filming, one of Lewis' fans expressed apprehension at being filmed. Since she was a customer of mine, I asked the cameraman to wait until she got her book signed before he began filming. He ignored my request and kept filming.

I was not aware at the time how arrogant the media could be, so thinking that he just hadn't heard me, I stepped in front of the camera to get his attention. Again I asked, "Would you mind not filming until this woman leaves, as she does not want to be on camera?" The reporter acted as though I had insulted him, and it also made Lewis furious. Grizzard later told me, "The only good thing to happen at this autographing was some television publicity, and you even screwed that up."

Needless to say, Lewis and I didn't get off to a great start.

But Helen Elliott and I did. Like most people I knew who came in contact with Helen, I adored her. She had a magical charm and grace and, as her husband Leonard often said, "a need to mother the world." Since Lewis was always in need of mothering, their relationship grew on several levels.

In 1980, mostly through the success of Lewis' book, Peachtree Publishers had grown to the point where it needed sales and marketing help. During a conversation with Helen, I casually mentioned that I would be interested in moving into the publishing side of the business. A few months later, I became Peachtree's first Marketing Director.

Peachtree would be publishing a second Grizzard column collection in 1980 and had national sales expectations for it. Though Lewis was still somewhat leery of me, he signed off on Helen's decision to hire me.

My first task with Peachtree was to smooth over my working relationship with Grizzard, so that we could work out a marketing and promotion plan for his second book, *Won't You Come Home, Billy Bob Bailey?* In my first few days on the job, Lewis was making a speech to an Atlanta business group. The popularity of his column had triggered a growing demand for him as a speaker. I was to meet him at the speech and we would talk afterward.

I could not believe how funny he was in person! He kept us all in stitches, and I found out later that he was paid $1,000 for the speech. At that time, I didn't know *anyone* made $1,000 to tell jokes as an after-dinner speaker.

Afterward, Lewis informed me that he needed me to take him to pick up a rental car, as he had to drive to another speech in Jacksonville, Florida, the next day. We managed to spend a few minutes talking about plans for his next book during the fifteen minutes it took to get to his rental car, and as he got out he asked, "Could you loan me some money?"

Here was a man with a $1,000 check in his pocket, on his way out of town to make another $1,000, and he had no money.

I had $40, which I gave him.

I would learn that this was the normal way Lewis operated. He seldom planned ahead, was constantly on the run, and was almost totally incapable of managing his time or money.

I would also learn that Grizzard was a man of many contradictions. He was spoiled and selfish, yet generous to a fault with his money. He was one of the most unhappy people I ever knew, yet could find humor in even the darkest moments.

When I returned to the office that afternoon, I laughingly related the story of our jet-setting author who didn't have a dollar on him. Helen's husband, Leonard, repaid my $40 and told me not to bother mentioning it to Lewis.

Though Leonard ran his own separate electronics business in the office suite with Peachtree, he was an invaluable financial and marketing adviser to Helen. On many occasions, his advice and business acumen saved Helen from costly mistakes.

I began work on selling Lewis' second book to a national audience by recruiting a group of sales representatives around the country and by calling on the national bookstore chains. I fully expected my former employer, Waldenbooks, to make a significant purchase, but found that it was my old competitor who was first to spot the rising Southern star.

With the help of Annie Henry Sillman, a North Carolina woman who bought regional books for B. Dalton Booksellers, *Billy Bob Bailey* made some national sales lists in the fall of 1980. Annie relived her southern roots through Lewis' column, and his growing audience made it possible for her to justify ordering his books for a wider geographic area. Publishers in New York began to take notice of this hot new author.

But something else was happening in the fall of 1980 that was more important to Lewis Grizzard. The University of Georgia was in the middle of a remarkable football season, led by a freshman running back sensation from Wrightsville named Herschel Walker.

At lunch in late October, Lewis told Helen, "If Georgia were to go undefeated and win a national championship, this state will go berserk." As a relative newcomer to Georgia from Texas, home of the then-mighty Southwest Conference, I was skeptical. I would later learn how sharp Lewis' instincts were.

About two weeks later in Jacksonville, it appeared Georgia's hopes and Lewis' dream were about to die when Georgia was behind late in the Florida game. Grizzard, who lived and died with his Bulldogs, had given up in disgust and left the stadium when it appeared hopeless.

But a miracle Buck Belue-to-Lindsay Scott pass late in the game preserved the undefeated season another week. After writing a great column admitting that he had deserted the Dawgs before the end and didn't see the miracle play, he promised it would never happen again. And it didn't.

Lewis and Helen began planning *Glory! Glory!* in earnest, co-written with longtime UGA insider and friend Loran Smith.

With the storybook ending win over hated Notre Dame in the Sugar Bowl barely over, Loran, Lewis and Peachtree went into overdrive. Lewis was right: Georgia fans were hungry to buy any and everything related to this team. Since the book needed to be published as soon as possible, the brutally short deadline pressure for *Glory! Glory!* — along with his column deadlines and speeches — forced Lewis to experience sleeplessness for the first time in his life.

Lewis was no stranger to hard work or odd hours. His night and early-morning shifts at newspapers over the years and his taste for non-stop partying had seen to that. But a new marriage with stepchildren, a large mortgage payment, five column deadlines a week, and a growing speech schedule that required him to be on the road three or four nights a week was taking its toll.

He and Loran persevered through their labor of love, and the book was published in the spring of 1981. Lewis, Loran, and I promoted the book with a barnstorming tour of the major Georgia Bulldog clubs around the state. It was a promotional tour unlike any I ever experienced, and one I will never forget.

Loran Smith was instrumental in getting Lewis his first job in Athens after high school. Lewis was forever grateful for the help, and the two struck up a friendship that grew beyond their University of Georgia connection. Lewis often said of Loran, "He is one of the few people who always makes me feel better when he walks in the room." Loran shared a keen appreciation of great stories and could match Lewis' own incredible collection.

One morning while we were on the *Glory! Glory!* tour, Lewis got a call in his motel room from his wife, informing him that one of their cars had been stolen from the driveway of their home. The car turned up a day or two later, but Lewis worried that since he was now a celebrity, the story would make the news and "cause my mom more reason to worry about my living in the big city."

A couple of weeks later, I was shocked to read a column Lewis wrote about the theft and return of his car. When I asked him why he wrote about it, in light of his mother's anxiety about his living in Atlanta, Lewis replied, "Sorry, Mom, I needed a column idea."

Lewis initially wrote six columns each week. In time, the column was reduced to four but the distress over "the next column idea" was unrelenting throughout his life. When Lewis had the column worked out in his mind, he could pound one out in thirty minutes. But as friends would prod him about the apparent easy life he lived, he'd say, "It ain't how long I spend at the typewriter that counts, it's the lying awake at night coming up with the idea."

Any episode from his life, his friends' lives, or any comment he overheard was fair game to wind up in his column. He even wrote about a touching moment when his childhood sweetheart (and first wife) came to see him at a Rich's autograph party for his book. It was obvious from reading the column that he still had deep feelings for her. The third Mrs. Grizzard was not pleased to see it in print.

Shortly after the *Glory! Glory!* tour was over, Lewis was finishing up a column at his newspaper office. His secretary had stepped away from her desk, and when the phone rang he picked it up and gruffly answered. It was an elderly man from a small Georgia town, and although Lewis was in a hurry, he had a soft spot for old men. "I've just finished readin' your book about the 'Dawgs, Lewis," the caller began. It was only late morning, but Lewis suspected the caller had been drinking. He went on for a few minutes telling Grizzard how much Georgia's national championship and the book had meant to him. Overcome with emotion, the old man finally closed by weeping, "We whupped they ass, didn't we?"

Lewis would recount this story many times, and this caller represented one of the reasons for the enormous staying power of his column in the South. Lewis never forgot that a huge part of his audience was living in, or like himself had grown up in, a small Southern town. And unlike the changing management of the big city newspapers, Lewis and his core audience continued to look at the world from the small-town perspective.

This outlook would cause much conflict between Lewis and his bosses at the newspaper in years ahead. But at that moment, the Dawgs were national champions, his popularity and bank account were rapidly growing, and Lewis was on a roll.

After spending time on the road together promoting his second and third books, Lewis and I forged a friendship from our shared small-town backgrounds and the love of a good quip.

His career continued to move upward. In the fall of 1981, Peachtree published his third book, *Don't Sit Under the Grits Tree with Anyone Else But Me*, yet another column collection. Booksellers, as well as the publisher, wanted Lewis to write an original book, but the demands on his time were prohibitive.

The books' sales continued to grow, along with the number of newspapers who picked up his column around the country. But ninety percent of the sales still came from the South, and the syndicate found problems getting his column placed in larger markets. The money he was making as a regional success was impressive, approaching $200,000 a year. Lewis Grizzard's future seemed incredibly bright.

Then one night in January 1982, Kathy Grizzard told her husband, "Quit shaking the bed." After a few moments they realized that Lewis' heart was pounding so strongly that it was causing the bed to shake.

Grizzard was known to his friends as a major-league worrier and borderline hypochondriac. A hangnail could appear to him to be the early stages of leprosy. But now, Lewis' doctors would give him no reason to exaggerate. A birth defect in his heart would force him to have replacement valve surgery right away.

Lewis told me about his forthcoming surgery during lunch at one of his favorite country food restaurants. Not surprisingly, he was not very talkative that day, but as I drove him back home he smiled and said, "If I survive this thing, you'd better batten down the hatches, because I'm gonna raise some hell."

His surgery created an unbelievable media event. There were regular news bulletins during surgery and an incredible outpouring of concern and support from his readers. It was an eye opener for all of us in the business of promoting Lewis Grizzard, especially the management of the *Journal-Constitution.*

Cards and flowers poured in by the truck load. Fans who shared his wacky sense of humor sent a variety of caps, beer, barbecue, and T-shirts. Someone even sent a hockey puck. Though he didn't know what it meant, Lewis loved it, thanking the unknown sender in a column after he got out of the hospital.

Six days after his surgery, Grizzard went home with coverage on the evening news. Eight days after surgery, he wrote his first column. With great pain, using only one finger to type, he felt the need to respond to his readers by letting them know he got their messages of good will.

He would take more time off before resuming his regular column, but he was proud of the effort he had made to get that first column done. He asked his secretary what his editor thought about the column and was crushed when she reported that he said, "It's not his best effort."

Lewis' editor at the *Journal-Constitution* was Jim Minter, a man of few words and high standards. Lewis had a complicated relationship with Minter, but he viewed him with the fear and respect that a soldier would have for a field general who demanded his men give their all to the cause.

Minter was Lewis' champion at the paper. He had first hired

Lewis as a sportswriter when Jim was the *Journal*'s executive sports editor, and as Lewis rose through the ranks of the paper, Jim would promote and rehire Lewis several times. But like most people who worked for Jim Minter, Lewis lived in fear of him and knew that Jim would fire him, in spite of their long-standing friendship, if he felt it was in the best interest of his employer. Lewis respected that.

The increasing demands of publicizing books and travelling to speeches in the early 1980s had caused the quality of Lewis' columns to suffer. Plus, he quit going into the office at the news-paper to write his column, which became a constant source of irritation between Lewis and the newspaper's management.

Grizzard was as concerned about the quality of the column as his bosses, but he couldn't understand what difference it made *where* he was when he wrote his columns. He also found that the ever-growing distractions at the office made it a more diffi-cult place to write. He made his deadlines, and his incredible popularity said to him that he was doing something right.

But his growing absence at the paper did not allow him to write a column that responded to a breaking news story, as he had done when he went into the office every day in years past. It also caused grumbling among jealous newsroom staffers. And on top of that, some of Minter's bosses wanted to be able to schmooze with their new star and introduce him to visiting friends and associates.

Management felt that since they sent Lewis a check every two weeks, they had the right to require him to show up at the office. As editor of the *Journal-Constitution*, Jim Minter was caught in the middle of this conflict.

But what happened on the ninth day after Lewis' heart surgery would test not only his relationship with Minter, but would shake the walls of his marriage. It was time to "batten down the hatches."

After Grizzard had been home from the hospital for a couple of days, Helen Elliott walked into my office at Peachtree Publishers and asked, "Do you know where Lewis is?" I did not.

Helen informed me that Lewis' wife, Kathy had just called her, wondering where he was.

Helen suggested that Kathy call Lewis' secretary at the paper. But Kathy had already done so, and "Miss Wanda Fribish," as she was known to Lewis' readers, was not in.

I didn't think anything about it until the next day when Helen once again asked me if I had heard from Lewis. I still hadn't. Helen learned that Lewis and his secretary were both missing, and that Lewis' bosses at the *Journal-Constitution* were also in the dark.

Later that day, Lewis finally called in. He told his boss Jim Minter that he had called the office and asked his secretary to come to his house right away. When she arrived, he told her that he wanted her to take him to see a young woman who lived in a small Alabama town — a three-hour drive from Atlanta.

Miss Fribish, of course, couldn't believe that he was serious. The man could barely walk across the room. But he was most serious, and they were soon on their way out of town to see a young woman fresh out of Auburn University whom Lewis had begun seeing before his surgery.

Lewis' young friend was home visiting her parents, telling them about her new job in Atlanta and privately wondering about her relationship with a local celebrity. Then the doorbell rang. Imagine her surprise to see a frail Grizzard in Alabama, only nine days after heart surgery. He stood on the front porch with a smile and a ten-inch chest scar. In the getaway car was his secretary and a bag full of medicine. They had not even packed.

Though they stayed only one night in Alabama, all hell broke loose when they returned. Kathy Grizzard was incredulous and humiliated, and Jim Minter wanted both their heads. Lewis was able to keep his secretary from being fired by explaining to Minter that he had ordered her to drive him to Alabama and not call anyone at work.

After he'd been back a few days, I went to Lewis' house to deliver a manuscript. Kathy was clearly upset but told me I could find Lewis in his basement office. When I went in, Grizzard was alone and deep in thought.

Lewis told me that his marriage was over, and he was getting almost universal anger from his friends. Not having had much contact with Kathy, I held no strong feelings about what was right for him to do. As I got up to leave Lewis surprised me by saying, "I feel like you understand me better than any of my other friends. They all hate my guts for leaving Kathy, but you just want me to be happy.

"I'd be the same way with you," he continued. "If you told me today that you had left your wife and run off with two twelve-year-old girls, and had robbed a bank on the way out of town, I'd still be your friend. As long as the twelve-year-olds were good looking, of course," he closed with his typical dead-pan humor.

I was taken aback by his expression of friendship, which was more heartfelt than the words might convey. In later years, I realized that Lewis was in dire need of approval, and my lack of disapproval was enough to qualify me as a "new close friend."

Lewis' self-centered nature, lack of faithfulness, and alcohol abuse doomed all of his female relationships. As soon as the "new" wore off, his eyes would begin to wander. Since he liked to frequent bars where young single women came to be seen, his eyes had plenty of reasons to wander.

Although I thoroughly enjoyed my work at Peachtree Publishers, I knew that the future was most uncertain. I didn't believe that we would be able to hold onto Lewis forever, and his books were the only real successes we had.

Of more concern was the owner's health. Helen Elliott had seemingly won a serious bout with cancer several years before, but she let me know that she was uncertain about how long she had to live.

In the fall of 1982, a tantalizing job opportunity presented itself to me with *Texas Monthly Press*. This was with the book division of a very successful regional magazine in my home state. Personal factors also entered into my decision to seek the job, which I was able to get.

Just before I left, I had dinner alone with Lewis and his girlfriend in their apartment in northwest Atlanta. Lewis was happier than I had seen him since Georgia won the national championship. He did something that evening I never saw him do again in the fifteen years I knew him. He cooked dinner.

Actually, he burned some steaks on an outside grill, but we had a pleasant, melancholy evening. I told the young lovers I was envious of their happiness. As I left, we shared a toast to Lewis' new heart and my new job in Texas.

About six months after I left, Helen Elliott passed away. Lewis and I shared a deep affection for Helen and reminisced about her remarkable life many times.

The Grizzard newspaper column generated plenty of opinion and occasional controversy. In the early '80s, he wrote a column off a news story that would never stop following him.

During a trip to Alabama, Lewis saw a news story about a man who had become infatuated with a woman in a laundromat. At some point during their discussion, the man touched her on the butt. Her boyfriend punched the offender in the mouth and the woman brought charges against the man.

In court, the man tried to defend himself by telling the judge that the woman's jeans were so tight he couldn't resist a quick touch. The judge was not impressed, and on top of his sentence even endorsed her boyfriend's on-the-spot justice.

Lewis wrote a column that appeared under the headline: "A stitch in time, ladies, will save us from crime." In his column about the incident Lewis didn't condone the man's actions but said, "I often have a difficult time feeling sorry for women when they scream about being sexually harassed in, say, their offices after they show up at work wearing something that would have embarrassed Mae West."

In his attempt to create some humor about women's choices of dressing and the reactions they cause in men, Lewis appeared somewhat sympathetic to "the tush toucher," saying that, "If the woman in Birmingham had heeded the rule about an ounce of prevention...the laundromat Lothario would be a free man today."

Naturally, there was a firestorm of condemnation. Women's

groups had something concrete to hold up to prove what they already knew, that Lewis was a sexist. Their consensus held that this was a perfect example of how a woman can get blamed for anything that happens to her if a man finds her dress provocative.

Amazingly, there were a large number of letters to Lewis from his older female audience that *agreed* with his column. But rather than denounce it for a weak attempt at humor that failed, Lewis tried to defend the column.

How the column ever made it past the editors at the *Journal-Constitution* was beyond belief. I wondered if it was allowed to slide through by a newsroom enemy with hope that it would damage Lewis' career. A petition circulated at the Atlanta newspaper, calling for his resignation. His secretary even signed it, and she was severely criticized for doing so. "You don't sign a petition against your own boss," she was told. "If you don't agree with what he writes, then quit."

"Miss Fribish" didn't quit, and although Lewis held it against her for a long time, he wisely didn't fire her. She was the first secretary he'd found that he was happy with, and he still owed her after she had risked her job to take him to Alabama.

One of the problems with being a celebrity in today's media environment is writers' ability to find quickly almost everything that has ever been written on any person or subject. Something that has been reported before becomes a "fact" and is almost never checked for accuracy. I could find an item reported in error in an early feature story on Lewis repeated again and again "as fact" in dozens of subsequent stories.

Though the facts in this case were not erroneous, many reporters elevated the "tight jeans column" to a defining statement of Lewis' sexism. He would have to explain and defend writing this column dozens of times. But he never backed down or admitted that he shouldn't have written it.

Journal-Constitution editor Jim Minter told me that he felt this column was an example of how Lewis' career was hurting his column writing, that he was dashing off columns without giving them enough thought due to his heavy travel schedule.

Lewis and I continued to keep in touch during my time in Austin. I would send him funny articles I found, and he would call from time to time to ask my opinion about a publishing problem. Lewis' newspaper syndication agent was pushing hard to get Lewis to move his books to a New York publisher. Given his devotion to Helen Elliott, it might not have happened when she was alive. But his incompatibility with her son, who had become president of the company, had escalated to the point where Lewis was ready to bolt.

His ambition made him want to try it. "I've always wondered if I could make it in New York," he mused. I advised him to give it a try, if he was so unhappy. "You can always return to Peachtree if you're not happy with a New York publisher," I reasoned. I also told him that I missed Atlanta.

In February of 1984 Lewis called again with something else on his mind. "Privett, my life is out of control," he said. "Do you know anybody who could be my manager?"

He described a position that would entail someone balancing the demands on his life. Though he had quit doing television commentaries, his speeches, books, publicity tours, and column deadlines were pulling him in too many directions. I jumped at the opportunity and returned to Atlanta to begin work for Lewis on April 14, 1984.

When I returned to Atlanta in the spring of 1984 to manage Lewis' career, he was earning more than $300,000 per year and living in a $400,000 house with a black Labrador pup named Catfish.

The columns Lewis wrote about Catfish were some of the most popular ever with his fans. To this day, when Lewis' name comes up in a discussion, invariably the first question I'm asked is about Catfish.

While Catfish chewed up a significant portion of Lewis' contemporary furnishings, Lewis was chewing up the Georgia highways. His aversion to flying and the lack of time to keep up with day-to-day necessities had led Lewis to buy a conversion van and to hire a full-time driver. He also owned an old Cadillac

Seville and a new black Mercedes 380SL convertible.

Before Lewis hired a young man to assist him with his driving, he had put well over 100,000 miles on his Seville going from town to town for speeches. Many times Lewis would finish an evening speech in one city and drive several hours across the state to the location of his next day's speech. He spent those nighttime driving hours listening to Braves baseball on Atlanta's clear-channel WSB-AM radio station.

One late evening in south Georgia, Lewis was on his way to Savannah. He had just purchased a twelve-pack of beer and knew that the Braves were playing the Dodgers in Los Angeles, so he would be able to listen to them while he drove. It was a cool spring night and Lewis was driving alone with the windows down, an activity he greatly enjoyed.

On a dark stretch of highway, he reached into the floorboard of the passenger seat to retrieve another beer. As he raised back up and looked down the road, he saw a man standing in the road directly in front of his speeding Cadillac. Lewis slammed on the brakes and swerved violently. After he came to a stop, he could not believe that he had missed the man. He turned the car around and in the headlights could see the man still sauntering down the road.

Severely shaken, Lewis drove slowly back to find a drunk man apparently unconcerned that he'd almost been a bug on Lewis' windshield. Lewis dumped all the beer out of the car and decided that he didn't need to be drinking and driving any longer. By hiring someone else to do his driving, he would gain in several ways: it would allow him the chance to work or relax during his trips, would prevent him from getting a black eye in the press with a drunk driving arrest, and would enable him to drink more freely.

For my first road trip with Grizzard, I joined him and his driver in the brown van to head for Callaway Gardens, where Lewis was to speak for a country music awards banquet. The evening's event at Callaway involved quite a few big-name Nashville stars. Lewis was a huge country music fan and promoter of traditional country music — just the style that was

being pushed aside by the Nashville music machine in the mid
'80s. Powerful friends in the media like Lewis were few, and his
support was appreciated by the old guard entertainers.

As we were leaving the building, I heard someone shouting
Lewis' name. We turned to find Tom T. Hall running down the
hallway to say hello. Tom T. Hall was one of Lewis' all-time
favorites, and in a few years Lewis would even perform his classic "Old Dogs, Children and Watermelon Wine" on stage. Lewis
had often praised Tom's music and the entertainer wanted to
thank him.

After a few minutes of
conversation, they said
goodbye. As we got in the
van I remarked to Lewis,
"You're a bigger star than I
thought when Tom T. Hall
runs after you to say hello."

Shortly after I came to
work for Lewis, he signed a
multi-book contract with
Villard Books, a division of
one of the most prestigious
publishers in the world,
Random House. In a spirit-
ed "auction" where a num-
ber of publishers made

*Privett trying to manage 'a bigger star
than I thought'*

offers for his books, Villard offered Lewis over a million dollars
for three books, the largest offer made.

At that time, Lewis was still pretty much an unknown entity
to the New York publishing community, but he had made a personal connection with a Villard editor and was ready to "make
it in New York." Grizzard's career would introduce him to
dozens of New York publishing types in the coming years, but
he seldom enjoyed the relationships.

Lewis' first Villard book would not come out for two years,
since he still had two books under contract with Peachtree.

They had planned a book to arrive in October of 1984 entitled *Elvis Is Dead and I Don't Feel So Good Myself.*

This was Lewis' sixth book in six years. The first three were column collections and this would be the third original work. The concept of *Elvis Is Dead...* was based on the premise that Elvis was the pied piper of Lewis' generation. Elvis' death was the wake-up call that his fans were moving into middle age, and as they looked around they saw that the world was changing in ways that left them confused and uncomfortable. In Lewis' case, the discomfort was reaching the extreme.

Enthusiasm for the book was high, and shortly after its release, an interview took place that would prove to be one of the most influential media "breaks" of Grizzard's career.

Art Harris, an Atlanta-based correspondent for the *Washington Post*, had pitched doing a feature on the Lewis Grizzard phenomenon. Art was an Atlanta native and probably had to introduce Grizzard to his Washington D.C. editors, since the Georgian's impact inside the Beltway was minimal in 1984. But the assignment was made, and Art did several interviews.

I don't think even Art realized the response Lewis created in Atlanta until he followed the author to one of his first autographing sessions for his just-released *Elvis Is Dead...*. When they walked into Rich's and saw a line of several hundred people snaking through the store and out into the mall, Art found a ready supply of Grizzard fans eager to tell him why they loved the rascal columnist.

The resulting story in the *Post*'s "Style" section captured the devotion to Lewis' humor and celebration of the South that his fans so admired. It also created a huge impact on Grizzard's career and helped vault *Elvis Is Dead...* onto the *New York Times* best-seller list, his first of many such appearances. Writers, editors, producers, and agents from New York and Hollywood began calling me at Grizzard Enterprises with inquiries about Lewis. I knew how influential the *Washington Post*'s political reporting was, but I was unprepared for the ripples that continued to reverberate off this feature story for months. Lewis had truly broken outside his Southern boundaries.

Of course, that meant that folks who weren't nearly as predisposed to understand and agree with his Southern white male perspective would be taking a look at his message.

One such reviewer in the *New York Daily News* wrote in a scathing review of *Elvis Is Dead...* that, "He's not simply a gay-baiter and woman-hater. Grizzard rejects most of post-war, or rather post-Elvis, society. Or at least he purports to. What makes the skin crawl in reading his attempts at reactionary humor is that one suspects it's a pose."

Because of the huge volume of mail and reviews, I generally showed Lewis only the most complimentary or venomous, and always those published in the nation's most influential media. Lewis' reaction to a review like this one was usually, "Screw 'em if they can't take a joke." But I came to understand that Lewis took his criticism hard.

I did write this reviewer a response to her review, stating that I had no problem with the fact that she did not care for Lewis' message, but that, "Most absurd are your assertions that Lewis' stances are 'a pose.' Lewis may make you laugh, cry, or fume...but he writes from the heart."

As Lewis would often tell people who asked whether he really believed the things he wrote, "What you see is what you get...I am your mother's worst nightmare."

Another defining event in Grizzard's professional life occurred in the fall of 1984. Atlanta Mayor Andrew Young made a disparaging comment about the Walter Mondale campaign staff, and Lewis knew instantly that he had a "no-brainer column."

Under the headline that stated "Andy put me in my place" Lewis wrote:

I would like to take this opportunity to thank Mayor Andy Young for finally finding a place for me in this multistructured melting pot of a society in which we live.

As most everyone should know by now, Mayor Andy last week became disturbed because the Mondale campaign staff wasn't consulting him in regard to finding a way to get Wrongway Wally elected president in November. After much thought, I am certain, he decided to blame it all on the fact that the Mondale campaign is being run, in his own cleverly chosen words, by "smart-ass white boys."

As soon as I read that quote I said to myself, "That's you, Self. You are a smart-ass white boy, an S.A.W.B. if I ever saw one.

Lewis' column created an attitude that took on a life of its own across the South, far beyond people who read his column. "SAWB" t-shirts, caps, and bumper stickers appeared from dozens of sources, and Lewis had ten good minutes of comedy material to entertain Southern audiences for several years.

Andy Young was a regular source of fodder for Grizzard's columns over the years, but Lewis also admired the Mayor's courage and willingness to speak his mind. If Grizzard was the "racist" some critics accused him of being throughout his career, he would not have praised Andy Young in his columns. I observed a cordial relationship between these two men as their paths continued to cross, and I noted that Mr. Young responded to an Atlanta television station's invitation to come on the air and reminisce about Lewis' life after he passed away. I don't believe Andy Young would've done that if he felt that Lewis' columns espoused racism.

Lewis was feeling his oats as 1984 came to a close. We had doubled his speech fees and cut the number by one-third. The syndicated column was gaining momentum, and we had a plan in place to release his first comedy album the following spring. He was working less and earning more. Lots more.

In addition to two full-time staffers, Lewis was occupying a significant amount of an accountant's time and was doing a fair amount of business with a stock broker. In true Elvis style, Lewis started referring to his business associates by mafia-esque names (like the King's "Memphis Mafia"). I was "Tony Bananas," his accountant was "Al, the shark," and his broker was "Lucky Churnola."

When *Elvis Is Dead...* made the bestseller list, we threw a party at Harrison's, his favorite Atlanta watering hole. It was a small gathering to thank the staff of Peachtree Publishers.

Those of us in his mafioso showed up wearing spats.

The evening was somewhat uncomfortable, given that Lewis had recently announced he was leaving Peachtree Publishers for Villard, but we raised a toast to everyone's success over a cake which was decorated with a *New York Times*-style headline that read, "Ain't White Trash No More."

Let's Make a Deal: 'Tony Bananas' on the limo phone

I was the keeper of Lewis' appointments calendar, and as I looked ahead into 1985, I always made sure that the sacred dates were put on the calendar in ink. When I came to work, Lewis told me there were three things that could get me fired: early meetings, booking him in a parade, and doing anything that messed up his going to a University of Georgia football game. He was dead serious about number three. We never booked anything on a fall Saturday until we had the final Georgia football schedule.

We also put the Masters golf tournament, Braves home schedule, and, in later years, all of the Ansley Golf Club tournament dates, on the calendar first. Any speeches, promotional appearances, or other business would have to be worked around these dates. As Lewis started earning money in the million-dollar-a-year level, he would think nothing about turning down a $20,000 speech to be in Athens to watch his beloved Dawgs play football.

Looking ahead, I saw much good on Lewis Grizzard's horizon. We were changing him from an "after dinner speaker" to a "concert performer." The first three January dates in Chattanooga, Huntsville, and Atlanta had sold out. Calling them "An Evening with Lewis Grizzard," we were recording these three performances for Lewis' first live comedy album to be released in the spring. We formed a partnership with long-time Nashville songwriter Bill Anderson and legendary Atlanta record publisher Bill Lowery to edit and distribute the finished product. We named the business venture "Six Silly Beans," after the Daffy Duck cartoon version of "Jack and the Beanstalk." This venture would produce a half-dozen albums and bring a serious new revenue stream into Grizzard Enterprises.

There were other deals cooking, too. But underneath the seemingly unlimited opportunity I felt a nagging concern: Lewis was a very unhappy man and was not taking care of himself.

Although he had divorced Kathy, his third wife, in 1982, she was still a big part of Lewis' life when I came to work for him in 1984. They had dinner together fairly regularly and I felt there was a chance they might get back together. They shared a keen sense of humor, and their closeness caused problems for more than one of his girlfriends.

He also took Kathy and her children on a few trips after their divorce. In the early months of 1985, they all boarded a Delta jet for a skiing vacation in Utah. During the middle of the night after their evening departure for Salt Lake City, I was awakened by the telephone.

It was Lewis on the line. He was almost incoherently drunk and weeping uncontrollably. After several minutes of conversation, I was able to discern that he was alone with no money at the Salt Lake City airport, and that Kathy had left him behind without any tickets or reservations information. He had no idea what to do. The last flight of the night had departed and the airport was closing. He said there were no ticket agents at the counter to help him.

With no other option, I suggested that Lewis find a security guard and ask for help. I knew full well that he might be arrested for public intoxication, but I felt that was better than his being found passed out. I also called the Salt Lake City Police and Delta Air Lines and asked if they could possibly use their connections to get someone in the airport to find him.

Lewis was one of Delta's biggest (and, I'm sure, most troublesome) customers. He loved Delta's friendly service and frequently praised the company in print, but he never conquered his extreme fear of flying and would always precede his boarding a jet with a number of stiff drinks. I only flew with Lewis when I had to, because his drinking made him difficult to control. He would lose all good sense, manners, and patience. Any minor irritation could set off a flurry of slurred obscenities and off-color remarks which were heard throughout the first-class cabin. Delta's stewardesses were quite adept at handling his drunken behavior, but I know they dreaded the sight of him wobbling onto the jetway.

It was a long flight to Salt Lake City, and Lewis would've had time for a few extra drinks. Plus, he

Turbulence: Lewis and Tony preparing for another flight

had mumbled something about an altercation on the plane. Now, all I could do was sit by the phone and wait. I didn't hear from Lewis again. I worried that he might have left the airport on foot and passed out in the freezing Utah night. I dozed off by the phone.

The next morning I went to the office and called the travel agent to get the number where Kathy and Lewis had planned to stay. When I called, Kathy answered. Lewis had found his way to them by getting a cab and going from resort to resort until he recognized the hotel name. Kathy let him in and paid the cabbie. He was incredibly lucky.

The altercation on the plane had been about smoking. One of the passengers in first class was forced to sit near Lewis in the smoking section, although she didn't smoke. She asked Lewis not to smoke. He declined. She went to the stewardess and complained. After some deliberations, the stewardess informed Lewis that under FAA rules, if someone forced to sit in the smoking section did not want to be near smoke, the airline had to enforce a no-smoking rule for the whole smoking section. Lewis didn't think that was right, given the fact that the woman had been upgraded to first class and had not paid to be in that section. He also reminded the stewardess that he was something of a celebrity and one of Delta's biggest customers.

Nonetheless, he was told he would have to refrain from smoking. Lewis went ballistic. He shouted and made threats. Kathy could not restrain him. She was sure that he would be arrested as soon as the plane landed. She was so angry and disgusted over the incident that when they landed she took the kids and jumped into a cab and left without him.

But she did let him in when he arrived at the condo, and after sleeping it off everyone wound up staying for their skiing vacation. It was the last trip they ever took together.

The drunken episodes in airports and restaurants were becoming more frequent. When he returned, I expressed my concern about his dangerous drinking habits and pointed to the damage that it was doing to his life, relationships, and career. Mine was not the first appeal of this kind Lewis had heard. By this time, almost all of his close friends and business associates had spoken to Lewis about his alcohol abuse. All were dismissed, just as I was. He didn't want to discuss his drinking or smoking, and if he was pressured too hard, he would distance himself from the person causing the irritation. I backed off, for the moment.

Working for Lewis was exciting, challenging, and maddening. On any given day, I could be negotiating with Hollywood agents, magazine editors, corporate presidents, and unhappy women who were waiting in vain for Lewis to show up for a date made the evening before. And there was always Catfish to deal with.

When University of Georgia football coach Vince Dooley gave him a black Labrador pup, Lewis didn't have a back yard because his house was built on the side of a steep hill. He wanted Catfish to have a yard to run, so he charged me with finding a new house with a some acreage that would allow the energetic pup to roam at will.

The house he bought had no fenced back yard but was on a large lot full of trees, which would give Catfish his space. Selling a $400,000 house and moving to another one in the same price range so that his dog could have a place to run was a classic example of the unreal world to which Lewis had grown accustomed. He was a little boy in a big candy store with a pocketful of money...which he often gave away as freely as he spent.

Lewis appreciated the absurdity of how he lived. And as Hollywood came calling, it moved to a new level. One of Norman Lear's companies, Embassy Television, expressed an interest in developing a situation comedy on Lewis' life after reading the *Washington Post* feature on him. We had a number of discussions about possible scenarios and had begun to settle on the idea of a storyline that took place when Lewis was the sports editor in Chicago. That was a time of great unhappiness in Lewis' life and he wrote about it many times in columns and books. The small-town-boy-out-of-his-element-at-a-big-city-newspaper setting did offer plenty of opportunity for dramatic tension and comedy, and in January of 1985 we were closing in on a deal with Embassy to make a pilot. A pilot is what Hollywood calls the first episode of what they hope will be an ongoing sitcom. If the pilot gets good ratings and advertiser support, they will then make additional shows. There are dozens of pilots made each year. Many are never even shown.

We had retained an entertainment attorney to advise us in the slippery maneuvering of Hollywood deals, and we knew that the chances of this making it as a series were slim. But it was an entertaining exercise, nonetheless. Lewis got plenty of mileage out of talking about it with his friends and dates.

It was during this time that the second major entertainment "break" of his career occurred. As Lewis' book stayed on the *New York Times* best-seller list for a number of weeks, it caught the attention of a producer on the "Tonight Show with Johnny

Carson." Carson was one of Lewis' idols, and after several days of chatting about some possible funny stories Lewis could tell on the show, the Carson show booked Lewis to appear on February 26.

Lewis was beside himself with excitement. The only problem was that he wanted to do some of his well-worn material on the show, but Carson did not want any of his guests doing old material. As his was the top entertainment venue, he demanded — and got — what he wanted. In Lewis' case, that meant fresh stories.

The producer isolated several "topics" that Lewis could expect Johnny to pick from to discuss, but Johnny was also known to ignore all of them and talk about anything that popped into his mind. Lewis had a quick mind and in an informal setting could banter with anyone. But he was seldom spontaneous in a professional setting and was not very good at it.

As we had been planning a trip to Hollywood to talk to Embassy Television, we arranged to meet with them when we flew out to do the "Tonight Show."

Lewis had recently begun seeing a professional model, who was the most self-obsessed person I had ever known. She was also off the scale for being late. I hoped that Lewis would not bring her along on the trip to Los Angeles, because experience had shown that travelling with this princess was an exercise in frustration. He did want to take her along, but fortunately she had a modeling job that she couldn't cancel.

Lewis got to sleep on the flight and was fairly alert when we arrived in Los Angeles. We were met at the gate by a limousine sent by the "Tonight Show." The driver was an African-American man in his late fifties from Birmingham, Alabama. This was a good omen. Lewis did not deal well with people from outside the South. We had a great conversation with the driver, and he assured Lewis that Hollywood was every bit as undesirable as he suspected.

We checked into the Beverly Hills Hotel, amid the aromatic fragrance of night-blooming jasmine, and Lewis got his second wind. He went to the bar while I went to bed. We were in a suite but had only one phone line. About the time I was drifting off to sleep, the Princess called. Her photo shoot had been cut short, and she wanted to fly out to be with Lewis in the morning. But she needed to get his credit card number to charge the ticket. I told her that Lewis was out, and that I would have him call her. I heard Lewis when he came in but I decided not to tell him about the call.

It didn't matter. The phone rang again and Lewis answered. The Princess was on her way. I asked Lewis what was going on and he said, "Go back to sleep. You're in a Fellini movie."

The next morning we had a ten o'clock meeting at Embassy television. Lewis had one of his rare hangovers, the worst I ever saw him suffer through. Like many alcohol abusers, Grizzard seldom suffered any debilitating morning-after effects. On this, the biggest day of his young career, he was not starting at the top of his form.

The scene at the sit-com producer's office was not one that inspired much confidence. We met in a room full of toys and overstuffed couches with four television executives. I would guess the oldest member of the group was no more than thirty years old. None had spent much time outside southern California. This didn't look good.

While Lewis drank a Coke and stared at the floor through his sunglasses, I tried to convince these arbiters of the nation's evening television programming that sitting across from them was, indeed, the hottest property in the southern United States.

Incredibly, before we left, an agreement was reached to make a pilot. As we got in our limo, I asked Lewis, "Could it be that the people who brought us 'All in the Family' will soon bring the life of Lewis Grizzard to all of America?"

Lewis had no interest in acting, but we hoped to get a small piece of a show that would require no ongoing work. A program that stays on the air for several years and gets into syndicated reruns could earn Lewis a nice amount of money for a long time. None of this happened, of course. We saw how the television industry does business when, after Embassy pitched our idea to numerous studios, one of them took the same basic storyline and started a series without us. Happily, it failed miserably.

Lewis and I had planned to play tennis when we got back to the Beverly Hills hotel, alongside the Hollywood big shots, but his headache didn't permit it. He went back to bed, after making arrangements for a limo to pick up the Princess. She was scheduled to arrive about 2 p.m., more than two hours before we would be picked up to go to the NBC studios to tape that evening's show. I knew as sure as Ed McMahon would laugh at Carson's every joke that Her Majesty would make us late. I was right.

There are people who are always five to ten minutes late. There are others who are perpetually a half-hour late. This woman redefined late. She once made a date with Lewis to come to his house, and showed up at the appointed time — three days later.

After Lewis' nap, he came down to the pool to find me sitting in a cabana and talking on the phone. For years, we laughed about the absurdity of the scene. "How quickly a couple of small-town boys can assimilate upward," Lewis joked in his best new-money voice. We sent the pool boy off for two more Cokes and watched people watching each other.

As the time arrived for us to leave for the "Tonight Show," I headed out for the limo while Lewis left a note for his date, who had not yet made her Beverly Hills Hotel entrance. We were already ten minutes late leaving the hotel. I did not think our scheduled arrival time at the "Tonight Show" was something to miss. As Grizzard was walking toward the car, the Princess-bearing limo pulled up.

It seems that she had a couple of stops to make on the way to the hotel. Now she would need time to get ready. We gave her limo driver directions to the studios and left. "There is a God," I breathed. I felt confident for the first time that we might actually make the show.

Traffic was bad, so we wound up arriving only about twenty-five minutes before the "Tonight Show" was to begin. Lewis had never really gotten over his hangover and was not mentally sharp that evening. Plus, he was anxious for his girlfriend to arrive. Every time the door in his dressing room opened, he expected it to be her.

To top it off, the producer we worked with popped in one last time as the show began and excitedly reported that, "Johnny just told me as he walked down the hall that he was reading some of your book today and would not be using the suggested talking points!"

By this time, we were both nervous wrecks. Lewis declined the opportunity to sit in the Green Room, where the guests can gather to wait and talk with their respective entourages while the show is taped. Instead, we watched the show from his small, sparsely decorated dressing room. His producer stuck her head in every few minutes, going over the details of when she would come get Lewis to take him backstage. We watched the monologue. The producer came in to say, "It ran a little long, but don't worry because Johnny will cut some of the first guest's time."

After the first guest's time was over, she came in to tell us that, "He is still running behind schedule, and if he gets any further behind, it's possible that Lewis might be pulled from this evening's show and invited back another time." But we shouldn't worry, she said, "because the next guest is off the wall, and I doubt that she and Johnny will have that much to talk about." She took Lewis backstage to get ready, and I waited alone in the room.

The producer was right. Johnny had trouble finding that much to talk about with the second guest. But she was dressed in a most revealing manner, and Johnny was in no hurry to move her along. There was a large clock on the wall just above the television monitor. I watched the minutes go by while Johnny leered and flirted. She giggled and flirted back. I could see the headline in the next day's Atlanta paper: "A Star is Born, Grizzard Waits Backstage."

Finally, Johnny cut to a commercial and I looked at the clock. Grizzard was supposed to be on by now. Will they bring him on? After what seemed like ten minutes of commercials, Johnny came back on and began introducing Lewis. The band played, the curtain opened, the spotlight came on, and Lewis appeared. He turned to the left and took a step, then found Johnny on his right and made his way to television's most famous chair.

Watching him on television, I saw how labored his movements were. Lewis walked slower than anyone his age I'd ever known. When he watched a tape of his Carson appearance later, he observed, "I walk like an old man."

Lewis knew that his time with Carson had been cut short, and in his desire to make up for the lost time, he was stiff and spoke too fast. And he resorted to his oldest, most familiar material. It was over in a moment.

After the show, the producer told me that she was disappointed in Lewis' performance, but she said that it was understandable given the lack of time they gave him. She promised to try to get him back on.

Lewis showed up in the dressing room a few minutes later, and he was concerned that he hadn't done well. He told me that when he came out the spotlight had blinded him, and it took him a second to spot Johnny's desk. He knew that it hadn't gone as well as he had wanted, but the important thing was that he had made it on the "Tonight Show." Like the University of Georgia's national championship, he could put the newspaper story about it in his wallet and nobody could ever take it away from him. His appearance was featured in the *Atlanta Constitution* the next morning.

We caught our breath for a few minutes, and then Lewis asked if his date had ever shown up. She hadn't. As we laughed about it and headed out for the limo, in the door she waltzed. Lewis had spent over a thousand dollars to fly her out to see him do the "Tonight Show," and she arrived fifteen minutes after it was over! Lewis was right. We were all in a Fellini movie.

The year had started with extreme highs and lows, and I could see that they paralleled Lewis' own life. Seldom was Grizzard lukewarm about anything. Whether he was commenting on a plate of fried chicken or a movie, Lewis saw every event as either "the greatest..." or "the worst experience of my life."

When he bought a cabin at Big Canoe, a mountain golf resort ninety minutes north of Atlanta, in the spring of 1985, Lewis instantly called it "the best investment I've ever made." He spent only about seven nights in the cabin over the next two years, and he also became disenchanted with the slow pace of play at the golf club. In a couple of years, I would sell this "best investment I've ever made" for a loss.

At this same time, Lewis began having anxiety attacks. These were sudden spells of gut-wrenching terror, accompanied by extreme sweating, racing heartbeat, and gasping for breath. Once in the throes of an attack, the victim is convinced he is dying. Doctors were not able to give Lewis any diagnosis, but they guessed that his fast-paced lifestyle was exhausting him, making him vulnerable to unresolved conflicts.

Grizzard's attacks seemed to come when he was on his way to a destination that he was dreading. The first few attacks sent him to the emergency room. These hospital visits were noted with small news stories.

I worried that the panic attacks might be related to the combination of his drinking with medication. After Grizzard's first heart surgery, he began seeing a psychiatrist on a weekly basis. Lewis was told that this is advised to help patients readjust after traumatic surgery. Lewis had continued seeing his psychiatrist, who was also prescribing sleeping pills for him. When I questioned his combining these pills with alcohol, Lewis assured me that his doctor had told him, "There is no problem with drinking and taking these pills."

Doubting this and knowing Lewis' ability to hear what he wanted, I contacted his psychiatrist to make sure he was aware of the amount of liquor that Lewis sometimes consumed while taking this medication. Lewis was not the best at managing his medicine, and I knew that it was possible he could take too many sleeping pills when impaired. I hoped that the psychiatrist would become an ally in my growing efforts to pry Lewis away from the bottle, but that did not happen. One of Grizzard's girlfriends even told me that the psychiatrist had given Lewis "a liver test" and the results "proved that Lewis is not an alcoholic."

The panic attacks eventually went away and, sadly, so did his third ex-wife Kathy. Soon after Lewis gave her money for cosmetic surgery, she surprised him by marrying and moving to Montana. Lewis was sorry to see her go and so was I. Though they were never going to remarry, Kathy was a positive influence on Lewis, and he needed all of those he could get.

Later that year Lewis was offered the chance to go to Russia. A new group called The Friendship Force was orchestrating trips for groups of American citizens to travel to other countries and, at the same time, inviting their citizens to spend time in America. The organization was based in Georgia and was looking for well-known participants to help encourage participation. Lewis enjoyed travelling and was fascinated with the thought of getting to see The Evil Empire first-hand. The trip was set for two weeks in August, and Lewis planned to spend some time in London on his way home.

About this time, Lewis' drinking had taken a turn for the worse. I became aware of a technique called "intervention" used by friends and family of alcoholics to coerce them into seeking treatment. The idea of an intervention is that *all* of the abuser's closest friends and family surprise him by walking into his room unannounced. Guided by a facilitator, each participant tells the subject how much he is loved, why the friend is concerned about his drinking, and then gives a specific incident that illustrates the problem. After each person delivers the message, the subject is strongly encouraged to go directly from the room to a treatment center. A reservation for the person has already been made, and his room is ready.

This is a very dramatic effort, involving tremendous pressure on both the family and the abuser. Intervention statistics claimed a high rate of success, though it was possible that the subject would reject all pleas and isolate himself from everyone who had a part in it. I knew that I could lose my job by trying this, but I believed that Lewis' life was at stake.

I was convinced this was the only way that we could get Lewis' attention. Most alcoholics have to "hit bottom" to realize they need treatment. Since Lewis had no wife to lose, could manage his career around his drinking, and could afford a driver to avoid the inevitable drinker's smash-up, he would not likely receive any of the "wake-up calls" that most drinkers do.

With encouragement from several of his close friends, I began calling others in the inner circle to organize a meeting to discuss an intervention for Lewis. There were about twenty names on the list. I was shocked and disheartened by the responses. Several of Lewis' friends said, "I just can't imagine Lewis without a drink in his hand." A few felt that the surprise approach was somehow dishonest. Most of the others didn't want to risk losing the status or monetary benefits of being Lewis' friend by trying to help him beat his addiction.

Out of the twenty names, only a half dozen agreed to participate. In a meeting with the facilitator a few weeks before Lewis was scheduled to leave for Russia, only four of the six showed up. The facilitator told us that an intervention for Lewis had little chance of success without at least twelve of his close friends. We talked about what was ahead for Lewis, how we could best help him, and when we might consider the coercion option again in years to come.

As I left the meeting, I was torn between relief and disappointment. Attempting an intervention was a very risky proposition for me, but I was afraid that it was going to be impossible ever to close the circle of Lewis' friends around him.

When Lewis left for Russia, I was in discussions with "CBS Morning News" executives. They had just gone through yet another general turnover in on-camera personnel and were mired in third place in the morning show ratings. Lewis' name had come up as a possible daily or weekly humor contributor, but we didn't get very far in the discussions. Every one of Lewis' attempts at television commentary had been utter disasters, and CBS wanted his on-camera appearances to be live from New York. We were on the lookout for a national television format for Lewis, but this wasn't it.

Plenty of good things were happening in Lewis' life. The comedy album was hot, Peachtree's final Grizzard book, *Shoot Low, Boys — They're Ridin' Shetland Ponies*, was due out when

Lewis returned from Russia, and we had a full calendar of speeches and promotional appearances lined up. And Lewis was anticipating an exciting Georgia football season, which opened with a Labor Day game against Alabama in Athens.

I didn't hear from Lewis while he was in Russia. He called from London, saying he hadn't enjoyed much of the trip and wasn't feeling well. I didn't think much about it, because Lewis chronically complained about not feeling well. The next day, Lewis' travelling companion called to say Lewis had gotten worse and was on his way to the emergency room.

Lewis was told that the doctors were very concerned and wanted to begin a series of tests. Knowing that the Georgia-Alabama game was less than a week away, Lewis checked himself out of the hospital against the doctor's wishes and caught the next flight home. His condition worsened, and when he got through customs at the Atlanta airport, he was taken directly to Northside Hospital.

He did not improve right away, and he was despondent to learn that he would miss the Georgia-Alabama game. He'd been looking forward to it since last football season ended. At least it would be televised. Lewis lethargically watched the game with numerous tubes and probes connected to his body. As time was running out, Georgia was behind. Suddenly an Alabama turnover led to a Georgia touchdown to put the Dawgs ahead. Rising from what had seemed all evening to be his deathbed, Grizzard leapt out of bed and danced around the room in jubilation. His actions set off electronic alarms that brought nurses rushing into the room.

"A miracle has happened!" Grizzard sang to the nurses. Unfortunately, Alabama had a miracle left and came back to win the game. Lewis returned to his funk.

The next day, Grizzard's cardiologist found that Lewis' refusal to deal with a nagging tooth problem before he left for Russia had led to a serious infection in his mouth, which subsequently had spread to the replacement valve in his heart. He was to be moved to Emory Hospital for heart valve replacement surgery right away.

Lewis' bright future suddenly turned dark. When I entered his hospital room after Lewis got the news, I found him resigned yet not completely despondent. He asked his other visitor to give us a few minutes alone to discuss some business. After the usual comments and hopes offered at a time like this, we discussed what I needed to do regarding the cancellation of his commitments. High dollar speeches to the top rung of American corporations now seemed so meaningless. Lewis was understandably quiet. Then he dropped one more bombshell on me.

"I know about your efforts to get me into an alcohol rehabilitation center," he began, "and I know that you did it because you care about me." My mind was reeling. "But I want you to promise me that you'll never do it again."

After a few moments of sorting out my thoughts, I asked Lewis how he found out about the intervention discussions, and he told me. I asked him if he wanted my resignation. He assured me that he didn't. I went over a few of the reasons why I felt it was necessary for this attempt, and then I promised him I would never do it again.

Lewis' ideals of loyalty to one's football team, country, or friends (not to be confused with one's wife), were among the most strongly felt sentiments he held. That he could overcome the sense of betrayal he must have felt as a result of my actions was most surprising. Grizzard usually saw things in black and white: You were either for him or against him. Readers usually loved or hated him. It took Lewis and me some time to get beyond the problems that this caused, but we did. It took me much longer to get over my anger with the person who had told Lewis about the intervention discussions.

Lewis stayed in the hospital nineteen days after his second heart surgery. The scar tissue on his heart prevented the surgeon from getting as tight a seal between the new valve and Lewis' heart as he'd wanted. Plus, Lewis had resumed smoking and was not exercising as much as after his first surgery in 1982.

As Grizzard began to get his spirits back, his next crisis concerned the juggling of girlfriends in the hospital. He had recently begun seeing a woman that he was very interested in, but he still wanted to see a couple of others. Some days it felt as though we'd moved from Fellini to "I Love Lucy" with Lewis' sending one girlfriend on an errand so she wouldn't be in the room when another one came in. The Hollywood Princess even made some late-night appearances, made possible by special arrangements with the night nurses. As we checked out, Lewis told me that the doctors knew he was ready to leave the hospital because his heart had gotten some heavy workouts during the Princess' midnight visits. "They are almost enough to make me sad to leave this place," he joked.

Lewis got out of the hospital three days before South Carolina was scheduled to play the Dawgs in Athens. He had missed two Georgia football games and was not going to miss another one. It had been a month since Lewis' last drink. I held out some hope that this forced sobriety, along with the time to mull over his friends' concern, would encourage him to make an effort to stop drinking. In spite of the heavy dosages of antibiotics he was still taking, and being well aware of the effects that alcohol has on antibiotics, Lewis took his first drink the day he got out of the hospital. I knew at that moment that the cause was lost.

After a few weeks off, Lewis jumped right back into his schedule. He made his first appearance on CNN's "Larry King Live" and closed out a disappointing Georgia football season with one of his most memorable columns ever. After the Dawgs lost their final game to a mediocre Georgia Tech team, Lewis wrote a column that consisted of one sentence: "Frankly, I don't want to talk about it." The remaining space where the additional seven hundred words of his column would have normally run was left blank.

It was a brilliant idea on Lewis' part, but it took some talking to convince the editors at the *Constitution* to go along with this unconventional idea. Once again, Lewis' instincts were on target.

Tech fans who had to endure merciless insults and ribbing from Lewis' columns and speeches year-round loved the fact that at last, they'd shut him up. Georgia fans loved it, too, because it expressed just how they felt. The "shortest column

Grizzard ever wrote" received widespread attention.

Though Lewis' love of college football was well known, it did not extend to the professional variety. This was partly the result of his sports editor days at the *Atlanta Journal*, where he covered the perennial losing teams fielded by the Atlanta Falcons. After he gained notoriety as a columnist, Lewis was invited every year by friends to accompany them to the Super Bowl, but he always turned them down.

In January of 1986, Grizzard found himself in New Orleans as a guest of the Pepsi-Cola company during Super Bowl Week. He was in town to speak to a gathering of Pepsi executives and their customers. Lewis was now commanding over $10,000 per speech, along with first-class airfare and hotel accommodations for two. This speech also included two prime game tickets, but he flew out of New Orleans right after his speech the day before the game. Friends thought he was crazy to pass up great seats to the Super Bowl, but Lewis considered pro football to be the rough equivalent of professional wrestling, and the New Orleans scene to be a zoo.

He returned to Atlanta in the midst of another "zoo." Grizzard had endless problems finding someone to decorate his house in the manner he wanted. The latest round of decorators had his house torn up, and he was going bananas. When I walked into his house in late January, I was ready to hear another horror story. Instead, I found him glued to his television set. The Challenger space shuttle had just exploded.

Moments later Grizzard's boss, Jim Minter, called and told him to get on the next plane to Florida and cover the story. Lewis asked me to go with him, and thirty minutes later we were on our way to the airport.

It was a bright, sunny day as our Delta jet began its descent toward the Melbourne, Florida, runway. Our flight was full of journalists from all over the country on their way to cover the national tragedy. We looked out the window to our left as we passed the launch pad. On final approach, Lewis said, "I'm not as worried about flying today. The odds are slim that there could be two major air disasters within miles of each other on the same day."

As soon as the words left his mouth, our jet took a violent, hard right turn. Lewis looked out the window and shouted, "Oh my God!" Then the plane took a hard left turn. Lewis turned to me and said, "We just missed hitting a single engine plane!" Before we exited the aircraft, Lewis talked to the pilot and learned that a student pilot had strayed in front of our jet and then froze. The Delta pilot, who had heard the tower's repeated instructions for the other pilot to turn to his right, waited as long as he could. When he saw the small plane make the correct turn at the last possible moment, he veered around it. Our pilot guessed that we came within one hundred feet of a mid-air collision.

Lewis had his first story done within thirty minutes of our landing. Imagine the Atlanta newspaper's famous columnist, who is afraid of flying, being involved in a near mid-air collision on the way to cover the Challenger explosion. While Lewis called in the story to the Atlanta papers so they could get it into the afternoon *Journal*, I fought the crowd of media types for a rental car.

It was late afternoon as we headed straight to NASA. We stopped at the guard house and found yet another hectic scene. Lewis' press credentials would get him inside the gate, but they would not let his "research assistant" come in with him. As we left to find a place for me to wait, I drove through an open gate that led onto the grounds of NASA. When we arrived at the central office, Lewis headed off to find his story while I went inside to explain how I had inadvertently bypassed the guard station and to ask for permission to wait in their office for Lewis to return. NASA staffers' nerves were completely shot by this time, and I soon found myself under house arrest for trespassing on a federal compound. After about an hour, as I was explaining my story for the third official who had been brought in to interrogate me, Lewis came back.

"Do you know a good attorney?" I asked. He then told the authorities the same story of what had happened, and in summing up the incident he said, "This has just been a big mistake."

The NASA security officer replied, "We don't make mistakes."

Lewis opened his mouth but immediately thought better of the obvious comeback he had in mind. I knew exactly what he was thinking. After another half-hour of negotiations, they finally agreed to release both of us if we would leave the grounds immediately. Lewis had his second story, so we were only too happy to comply.

Once safely outside the compound, Lewis told me that he had seen a dazed young man walking around, so he struck up a conversation with him. The man was the teacher who was slated to go on the Challenger mission if Christa McAuliffe had not been able to fly for any reason. Lewis wrote a poignant column that included a description of the man's shoes.

"The part about the shoes is a nice touch," I commented back in the hotel room after Lewis finished writing the column.

"Minter always told us to write about their shoes," was Lewis' reply. He was referring, of course, to his editor at the newspaper, Jim Minter. In coaching young writers, Jim had impressed upon them the story that a person's shoes could tell. Lewis never forgot it.

Before we turned in for the night, Lewis insisted that I find an alternative route home. We wound up driving to Daytona Beach for our return flight, thereby avoiding the Melbourne airspace. We learned that there was a large pilot school based in the Melbourne area, and that the airspace was regularly dotted with student pilots earning their wings. Lewis had no intention of flying in or out of this airport again. I was in full agreement.

The next day, Lewis was shocked to find out that his paper didn't run the story of his near mid-air collision. To add insult to injury, they *did* run an Associated Press version of the story the following day written by someone else on the plane. Lewis was incredulous, and it reopened his growing anger with the way he felt the Atlanta newspapers treated him.

First, he had grown to be the most popular feature in the paper, yet he felt management hadn't raised his salary accordingly. And then there were the perennial problems Lewis had with editing and headline writers, as well as a growing number of anti-Grizzard letters to the editor being published. Lewis felt that the letters editor was intentionally using the page to snipe at him, rather than publishing a representative number of positive and negative letters.

After he returned from Florida, Lewis was hard at work on his first Villard book, the story of his relationship with his father. His routine was to get up about eight, read the paper, and write a column if one was due that day. Then he would eat lunch, play golf, and return to the typewriter for four to six hours of work on his book.

The title of this book was quite a challenge to settle on. Since this was the most serious book Lewis had written to date, he didn't want the same kind of lighthearted title he'd always used. We'd pretty much settled on *The Marvelous Major: The Good Times and Hard Life of Captain Lewis M. Grizzard, Sr.* But when the publisher made its initial calls on the national bookseller chains, they expressed disappointment with the title. They wanted the "typical Grizzard title."

We finally reached a compromise on *My Daddy Was a Pistol and I'm a Son of a Gun,* a line from "Dang Me," an old Roger Miller song. This book was Lewis' literary search for the meaning of the relationship between him and his rogue of a father. Lewis poured his heart and soul into the book, and I have always considered it his best work.

Because he pushed the deadline for turning it in, he gave me his original manuscript with his handwritten editing comments to retype before we sent it to New York. Villard was hounding us to get it in, so I divided up the manuscript among the three Grizzard Enterprises staffers, and each of us went to our separate offices to pound out a clean draft. We typed furiously all day, and I was stunned by what I was reading.

As is well documented in Lewis' writings, his dad had a drinking problem. In *My Daddy Was a Pistol...,* Lewis told numerous stories of having to bail out, sober up, and cover up for his drunken father for about fifteen years. For the first time, I realized that Lewis had lived the life that I and others around him were now living. Just three months after our discussions about his drinking problem, Lewis was reliving these same gutwrenching and frustrating memories of times with his father. I felt renewed hope that Lewis would make some connections with his father's hard life and early death and begin to make some changes in his own life.

Tears came to my eyes as I typed the last pages of the touching memoir. As my two coworkers brought their finished portion of the book into my office, I could see that they had been crying, too. Lewis always had the ability to grab your heart.

I believed that this book would take Lewis to a new level of critical acclaim, but it turned out that the subject matter was too heavy for his usual audience. Sales were somewhat below his previous book, in spite of a brutal national tour in the fall.

Lewis' golf game continued to improve, and he developed a daily habit for the game. That he was able to stick with golf through the early months of playing it so miserably was a testament to his strong will. I had played golf in high school and college and enjoyed picking the game back up. We began booking golf games for Lewis when he travelled to make speeches. He would always get an invitation to play with his hosts at the finest local golf clubs. Through these business contacts, we were able to play many of the top golf courses in the world, and Lewis even made his first trip around the hallowed pines of Augusta National in the spring of 1986.

Through the graces of our Augusta National host, Lewis and I were able to spend the night in rooms located in the clubhouse after our magical day on the course. But when we got ready to leave the next morning, the battery on my car was dead. Lewis always kidded me by saying that having a dead battery at the Augusta National Golf Club was a sure sign I'd never be asked to join. Something akin to a "litmus test for white trash," he said. But I found a way to get even with him.

On a desktop publishing system, I designed a lookalike Augusta National logo and addressed a letter to Lewis "from the membership committee." I left the letter sitting in a stack of mail which he went through one night when he got home.

I was spending the night at his house this particular evening and had already gone to bed. When he read the letter, he immediately told his girlfriend "this is a joke." She was in on my scheme, however, and played it straight. He kept picking up the letter, rereading it. After about an hour, his ego finally took over. Lewis looked at her and said, "It's about damn time they invited me!"

He grabbed up the letter, walked into the bedroom where I was sleeping, turned on the lights and said, "Get up, Tony. Life as we know it is over!"

I started laughing, and in a second Lewis knew he'd been had. He was almost embarrassed that for a moment he had let himself believe that he'd been invited to join such a staid, conservative club. But he never tired of telling the story on himself.

Lewis had trouble finding a regular group that could play every day when he was in town, and also could afford to jet out of town for three- or four-day golf weekends at resorts like Hilton Head or Sawgrass. Until he was able to get a regular foursome, I would spend time many mornings helping him round up players. I didn't enjoy playing every day, but if I wasn't able to find enough players, he'd pressure me to fill out the foursome. Nobody believed that I had to argue with my boss *not* to play golf. And those who did believe me didn't give me any sympathy.

On Mondays, when most country clubs are closed, Lewis found himself on the "Charity Celebrity Tour," which was what we called the Monday charity golf tournaments. Atlanta's sports and entertainment celebrities were recruited to play in each foursome at these tournaments, so that organizers could attract paying customers who wanted to rub elbows with celebrities. The same crowd of notables saw each other almost every Monday during the spring and summer, since it was the only way they could feed their daily golf habit when most courses were closed.

Lewis also tried to plan a golf resort trip almost every month, although most of his friends didn't have the time or money to handle that type of lifestyle. So Lewis often paid for his play-mates. In time, he would find a small group of friends who could pay their own way, but many of Lewis' friends found themselves "on scholarship" during these trips. When you figured first-class airfare, daily resort green fees, dinner, and drinks for four, he easily could spend $5,000-$10,000 on every trip.

In addition to golf weekends, Lewis' largesse could include trips to Georgia football games, vacations, and, in 1986, a wedding present honeymoon trip to Hawaii for two close friends. (Lewis and his girlfriend went along with them.)

Another rising expense line in Lewis' credit card bills was caused by the women he began running around with — women who cared more about his spending power than who he was. The Hollywood Princess was particularly aggressive in raiding Lewis' pocketbook at this time. All of Lewis' credit card bills came to my office to be paid. When I opened one during the summer of 1986, I was astonished to see a $4,100 bill at a trendy Galleria (Atlanta) clothes boutique. I immediately thought that Lewis had lost yet another card and that someone

Exotic Golf: (L-R) Lewis, Pete Moore, Tony Privett, and George McKerrow Sr. in Scotland

had run up a big bill. I was only half wrong.

Someone had indeed run up a bill, but Lewis had not lost the charge card. I asked him if this was for a designer dress. In fact, the young lady had bought a closet full of clothes. It took seven pages of sales slips to detail each item she purchased. When I asked Lewis if he was aware of this bill, he said he had no idea of the total when he signed the sales slip, but he didn't care. They had just spent the night together at a plush hotel, had enjoyed a champagne brunch, and Lewis was interested in getting her back to the room. Both parties knew what costs were involved on the date. It was nothing more than a genteel version of the world's oldest profession, and Lewis was leaning more toward this kind of relationship that did not require any emotional commitment.

But whatever gains Lewis felt with the absence of commitment seemed more than offset by their growing demands for money. Most of these young ladies were shockingly aggressive with their abilities to get Lewis to give them large sums of cash. Lewis was never one to handle business very well, and he was an easy mark in the hands of these street-wise women. One even wound up with his black Mercedes convertible.

In the fall of 1986, Kathy Logue Grizzard Schmook, or "the third Mrs. Grizzard," published a book about her marriage to Lewis. *How To Tame a Wild Bore* was published by his former Atlanta publisher at the same time his new Villard book was hitting the shelves. It was a shrewd idea by Peachtree Publishers, and it sold very well. Kathy gave readers a hilarious account of her years with Lewis, and though it wasn't overly malicious, several parts of the book stung him.

But Grizzard was able to laugh along with it for public consumption; he swallowed the hurt he felt and helped promote it by writing a column about the book and regularly mentioning it during interviews. He even mentioned it on his second visit to the "Tonight Show."

Lewis turned forty in October, and he was surprised by seeing his likeness on the cover of the University of Georgia football program for the Vanderbilt game. The Sanford Stadium crowd even sang "Happy Birthday" to him before the game. Lewis was an unapologetic and rabid supporter of the Georgia football program. He fought the Dawgs' fights, defended their honor, and ridiculed their enemies in his column. He had been through the highs of the national championship and the great teams that followed it. But now, Georgia was mired in a series of mediocre teams and had just come out of the difficult and humiliating Jan Kemp period.

Jan Kemp was an instructor at the University of Georgia. When she complained that athletes were being passed out of remedial courses without earning their grades, she was reprimanded and later fired. Ms. Kemp filed suit to get her job back, reportedly even offering to settle. No settlement was made, so the Georgia football program was dragged through the mud in the media for months. It made Lewis' life miserable, and the damage to the program's reputation was evident for years. Grizzard's passion for the University never wavered, though; he remained a large financial contributor to the program.

The Georgia schedule included an annual game in Jacksonville against the University of Florida. As Georgia fans called themselves "Gator Haters" during this week, Lewis started an annual Gator-Hater invitational golf tournament at Sea Island Golf Club. Grizzard had begun taking two weeks vacation prior to the Georgia-Florida game at the lovely Georgia coastal resort. On the weekend of the game, the normally sleepy island was overrun with rabid Bulldog fans. Lewis would invite about forty of his friends to play a two-day golf tournament. He always called this time "the best two weeks of my life," and it wasn't his usual exaggeration. He had all the elements of the idyllic life around him at Sea Island: The weather was almost always perfect, he had golf buddies scheduled in and out throughout the two weeks, and he rented a huge house where everyone could stay, which reminded him of his college fraternity house. He normally took a vacation from his column writing this week, so that deadline was gone, and he got to anticipate the classic football game that always brought the vacation to a climax.

The crowd at Lewis' tournament was rowdy, even by his standards. At his last Gator-Hater tournament in 1993, Lewis' ill health kept him from his normal revelry. Afterward, he told a friend that, "This is the first Gator-Hater where I've been sober for the whole time. Now I realize I don't even like most of these people."

For the second fall in a row, catastrophe struck Lewis Grizzard when he learned that his boss and friend, Jim Minter, had been moved out as editor of the *Atlanta Journal-Constitution*. The changeover occurred on Veterans Day, ironically, as Lewis considered Jim the consummate patriot. Lewis was extremely upset about it. Although his conflicts with newspaper management had escalated over the years, he never considered Jim to be any part of the problem.

Over the next week, Lewis called the paper twice late at night, quite drunk, telling whoever he talked to, "I quit." I heard about the calls the following mornings and counseled him to come to his senses. The publisher of the paper was giving Lewis some line to run out his anger, but Lewis responded by stepping up his verbal bashing. Shortly after the announcement of Minter's move, Lewis walked into Creekside Cafe, a favorite hangout owned by close friends.

"Dom Perignon for the house!" he said as he hit the bar. "I want everyone to raise a toast to the greatest editor of all time!" Lewis' friend behind the bar surveyed his condition and made sure that he indeed wanted a glass of $100-per-bottle champagne for everyone in the bar. Lewis confirmed the order.

After all the glasses were delivered, Lewis made a rousing toast honoring Jim Minter while slamming the newspaper. Grizzard then told everyone in the room that he was putting the $1,500 tab on his *Journal-Constitution* credit card. The total included a $500 tip for the waitress, who later told Lewis that she didn't know how she was going to be able to afford her college textbooks until his generous tip provided the answer.

As Creekside Cafe was also a media hangout, the Dom Perignon toast on the *Journal-Constitution*'s tab was the buzz of the morning talk shows. Lewis' bosses were not amused, and he was notified that the bill would be coming out of his check. Of course, he didn't care. He had plenty of money and just wanted to exact revenge.

Unfortunately, the bitterness would only increase as time wore on. The *Atlanta Journal-Constitution* would have two more editors during Lewis' remaining years, and he had little interest in making an effort to work with either one. By this time, Grizzard knew that his popularity had made him almost indispensable to the Atlanta newspapers, and as much as he hated to admit it, he needed them to keep his hometown pulpit (not to mention his health insurance.) It was like two nine-hundred pound gorillas locked in a small room with their hands tied behind their backs. Since neither one could kill the other, aggravation was their only option.

As I reflect on the final years of Lewis Grizzard's life, it's difficult for me to get beyond the feeling of overwhelming sadness.

Lewis had so much talent, but much too short a life to use it. He was handsomely rewarded for his hard work, but he couldn't buy his way out of the fear and loneliness that haunted him every day. An acquaintance once complained to Ludlow Porch, Lewis' stepbrother, that Lewis was not handling his success very well. "Don't forget," Ludlow countered, "that Lewis never handled failure very well, either."

Lewis traced the restless emptiness in his life to the moment his father left home, but I suspect it was passed on from his father at birth. He deeply loved (and never stopped loving) several women during his life, but he was not happy living with any of them for very long. He yearned for the idealized image of "the old days and small-town ways," but he chose life in the fast lane. His happiness could only come in fleeting moments.

In several heart-to-heart talks with Lewis during his last years, I came to an understanding of the opposing forces that pulled at his life and mind. Grizzard was desperately insecure, and no amount of success or praise was ever enough to ease the fear of failure or rejection.

Coupled with his insecurity was a need for constant gratification and self-absorption that prevented him from sustaining any long-term relationship. From his female companionship, he required ongoing sexual attraction. But he also expected to be waited on hand-and-foot like he was as a child. Before long, his young "knockouts" would wind up acquiring a "mother" image in his mind, and he would be back out on the street looking for the titillation he craved. The cycle played itself out over and over again.

For all of Lewis' nostalgic reminiscence about his old small-town Methodist Church, he was never able to buy into religion's premise. He wanted to believe in the power of prayer and miracles, and he was humbled by the outpouring of spiritual support during his times of crisis, but wasn't able to make the personal leap of faith until his final days.

Grizzard took a fatalist's view of his life. He knew that the drinking and smoking would kill him, but he also believed that his heart problems would beat them to the punch. It was a vicious circular argument that did not allow him to consider the "quality of the journey" over the "time of arrival at the end of the line."

But I also have many happy memories of my years with Lewis. I remember the times I would sit in his kitchen, waiting for him to finish a column. I can hear the sound of his pounding the words out on his old Royal typewriter. A cigarette is hanging out of his mouth and Catfish is curled up at his feet. The back door is wide open, the air conditioner is set at meat locker temperature, and every light is on in the house. When he finishes, we head out to a favorite country cooking cafe and eat fried chicken and fresh vegetables. No one ever enjoyed a good meal more fully than Lewis Grizzard.

We shared so many great career successes, all originating from his sharp wit. I miss Lewis the most when I hear a rich story or joke that I know he would have appreciated.

And then there are hundreds of great golf memories. From the camaraderie of the regulars at Atlanta's Ansley Golf Club to the gloriously unforgettable days on the ancient Scottish links; from the times we spent walking in the legends' footsteps at Augusta National to the day we played with Arnold Palmer.

Lewis loved to be surrounded by his friends, and he would regularly invite more people to "ride to the game in the limo" than the stretch could possibly hold. But even though he took on some of the ego trappings that accompany the life of a celebrity, Lewis never lost sight of who he really was. This was clearly illustrated when, in 1991, he backed out of a long-planned trip to play at the prestigious and ultra-exclusive Pine Valley Golf Club in New Jersey. Lewis decided he'd rather accept an invitation to partner with a good friend in an Albany, Georgia, Member-Guest Tournament. Said Grizzard, "I'd rather be with my friends at a small-town country club than spend a day with a bunch of Yankees on a world-class course." No one was ever more passionate about good friends and golf than Lewis, and I would take him as a partner against anyone with all the bets doubled on the last hole.

And that's exactly how my friend LG played out his life...double or nothing.

Vicarious Philandering With Lewis

BY ROBERT L. STEED

Robert L. Steed, an occasional columnist for the Atlanta Journal-Constitution and a practicing attorney, lives in Atlanta with his wife, artist Lu Steed. He is the author of five books, including A Ship Without an Udder.

Although the epitome of a Southern "good ol' boy," Lewis Grizzard, the late, great Muse of Moreland, was a man of many parts. (This doubtless explains why he provoked so much laughter when he appeared *au naturel* in the Ansley Golf Club steam room.)

I had known Lewis casually and pleasantly for many years (we both began writing a humor column for the Atlanta newspapers in 1978, his a professional effort, mine a *dilettante* spasm), but our friendship really began in 1982, the year of his first heart valve implant. I was so dazzled by the universality of the humor in his columns dealing with his ordeal that I wrote him an unabashed fan letter suggesting that he pull the columns together between hard covers and, as an example, sent him a copy of a little known 1915 humor classic by Irving S. Cobb, *Speaking of Operations.*

Soon after that, I got a call from Lewis thanking me for the idea and sending me a copy of a manuscript for that soon-to-be brightly blazing star in the American literary firmament, *They*

Tore Out My Heart and Stomped That Sucker Flat, with a request that I review it for the Atlanta papers.

In an otherwise glowing review, I did offer one criticism of the book, which was that after giving us the clinical details of the pig valve procedure, Lewis left his readers hanging as to one of the most important questions raised by his story — what became of the pig whose heart valve the doctors put in Lewis?

I went on to answer my own question by reporting that I had learned from insiders at the prestigious Emory University Heart Institute and Ear Piercing Clinic that when they put the pig valve in Lewis, they put Lewis' old valve in the pig, which, as might be imagined, underwent a severe personality change. I revealed that the pig had grown a mustache, was wearing Gucci loafers, industrial strength cologne, gold neck chains and open-front polyester shirts, hung out at singles bars, and was writing a newspaper column under the name of Ron Hudspeth.

Our mutual friend Hudspeth was not amused, but Lewis was so appreciative that one would have thought I had removed a beer can opener from his paw. We became fast friends thereafter, though he was always faster than I.

The friendship was characterized by an ongoing exchange of insults. In one review of mine, I wrote that Lewis was amazing in that he was one of the few University of Georgia graduates I know who could write sentence after sentence (many of them containing both a noun and a verb). As difficult as it is for Georgia Tech graduates to accept, "Go Dawgs!" is a complete sentence.

Lewis retaliated in kind with a blurb for a column collection of mine entitled *Money, Power and Sex (A Self-Help Guide for All Ages),* which read, "Bob Steed knows as much about money, power and sex as Boy George knows about testosterone."

A subsequent Grizzard blurb for another of my meager endeavors said simply, "With this book, Bob Steed has done for literature what Jimmy Swaggart has done for cheap motels."

I once wrote that Grizzard had been married so many times, he was the only person I knew who had rice marks on his face.

The friendship survived, indeed, thrived, on the obloquies each of us directed at the other, and, grounded on our common

West Georgia upbringing (with the emphasis on "common"), our view of life through mutually jaundiced eyes and our passion for golf, offered us opportunities for many grand adventures.

I think I was drawn to Lewis' dangerous lifestyle flame because my own, as a buttoned-down, three-piece suit, staid lawyer lifestyle, was so different. However, my participation in his more raunchy adventures was all vicarious, primarily because I could never get late permission from my wizened wife of long standing, who feared I might be tempted to put pale lascivious thought to vivid action. Beyond that, Lewis' nocturnal drinking patterns were often so rowdy, raucous and ribald that, while I enjoyed hearing about them, I was too prissy to enjoy them in person. Our greatest common ground was on the golf course.

I was chaperon to Lewis on his first round at Augusta National (he said it was like "playing golf in a cathedral"), and was with him when he first played Peachtree Golf Course and a host of other links in Scotland and Ireland, including St. Andrews, Carnoustie, Muirfield, Royal Dornoch, Nairn, Prestwick, Lahinch, Ballybunion, and our mutual Scottish favorite, Western Gailes. He was serious about his golf and was a great competitor, always formidable on the closing holes where the bets begin to throb with fierce fiscal implications.

In 1987 and 1989, Lewis and I organized a small band of sturdy and avid golfers to attack the golf courses of Scotland and Ireland. It's a wonder that our visits didn't cause a suspension of diplomatic relations between the U.S. and Great Britain.

At times Lewis seemed to be the ultimate embodiment of the Ugly American Abroad, particularly when he was so deep in Screwdrivers that he was courting a citrus virus.

On our first trip over, Lewis confirmed his legendary pre-flight jitters by ordering our band of merry men to the first-class lounge where he managed to get on the outside of an extraordinary number of powerful potables in a very short time. Although carried aboard the plane, he played high stakes gin in an alcohol haze all the way across the Atlantic. When we arrived at London's Gatwick Airport, Lewis took on another round of booster shots to fortify him for the trip to Edinburgh and, once there, commandeered the bus and ordered it to make frequent stops for schnapps shots along the way to our hotel.

He was in such wretched shape when we arrived that he was put to bed. The next morning, as we were all having breakfast and getting up for our first round of golf in Scotland, we noticed that we were flying missing-man formation — Lewis was nowhere to be found. The manager of the inn overheard our concern and gravely volunteered, "Yes, Mr. Grizzard had a rather rough evening. He was up at least three times trying to check in the hotel."

We finally roused him and he managed nine holes at Gleneagles before he had to go back to the hotel and "speak on the Big White Phone."

Except for that outing, I never knew him to fail to show for a scheduled round of golf.

As a rule, Lewis was conscientious about avoiding strong drink during golfing hours, turning toward the bar only after his rounds had been completed and he had collected his bets from all involved.

The long bus trips between golf courses were memorable and we passed the time by coming up with column suggestions for Lewis, who would polish them up and call them in to his secretary in Atlanta.

He also organized a lascivious limerick contest and, while I can't remember his entry, it was so concupiscent that it even embarrassed some of the grizzled veterans in our group.

Thanks to my vaunted pornographic memory, I can still remember my contribution to the effort:

"There once was a lass named Hannah,
Who, in search of sexual Nirvana,
Booked a trip to Kilwinning
For two days of sinning,
And was multi-orgasmic, Hosanna!"

Once when our group was flying from Shannon, Ireland, to Dublin and Edinburgh, Lewis again allowed himself to be "over served" and, after the first leg of our trip, was yawing about the lounge in the Dublin airport looking like a man walking on a trampoline. He was so drunk he could not have hit the ground with his hat. As our group was boarding a bus to be taken to the plane, Lewis noticed a gasoline truck nearby and decided he would take it for a drive. Friends interceded and coaxed him out of the cab of the truck before the police arrived. In the U.S. this misadventure would have resulted in conversations with the FBI and perhaps a change of zip code by federal authorities.

Lewis fully prepared for his flight to Scotland

However, the Irish are more forgiving in matters involving strong drink.

Leaving the bus for the airplane, Lewis decided to circle the plane and kick the tires. When he was finally poured into his seat by anxious companions, he began to rail about why our group wasn't flying first class. The plane was a small single-class plane, but he grew more agitated and profane and his travel companions became increasingly anxious. Finally, he spotted a young Irish nun in the row of seats ahead of him and, while all the group held its collective breath, he leaned over and accosted the nun. He said, "Sister, can you bless us?"

She replied, "Only a priest can give a blessing."

"Can you pray for us then?" he asked.

And she said, "Yes, of course."

He then bellowed, "Well, it's a good thing because this f—-ing plane is going down!" With that he collapsed in his seat, put his head on his tray table and, much to the relief of his traveling companions, disappeared for the rest of the flight. The stewardess wisely refrained from asking him to put his tray table up.

At the end of the trip our group of golfing revelers found itself

Tony Privett, seated next to the enlightened Irish nun, ponders absolution.

in Nairn in the northern reaches of Scotland.

Lewis, in particularly good postprandial form, announced at the end of our closing banquet that he would be leaving our merry group to travel as an unaccompanied adult by train, to London, where he had arranged to meet a "ballerina" from Atlanta's Gold Club. They would, he announced, be enjoying a liaison at the Savoy Hotel.

All of us were a little thunderstruck at the prospect that Lewis would be traveling alone by train to London. Complicated travel arrangements in strange cities and copious quantities of alcohol had always proved to be an unfortunate mix for him, and many of us thought when he was poured into a cab for the train station that we had seen him for the last time.

Months later, he and I were playing together in a local golf tournament and, while waiting for our tee time to be announced, I asked him how he enjoyed the Savoy Hotel (hoping for yet another cheap vicarious thrill). Lewis allowed that it was a terrific encounter. He went on to say that the ballerina had flown in the evening following his arrival and, as they were having dinner in the opulent dining room of the Savoy, she gingerly approached the subject of birth control, informing him delicately that she had no "protection." Lewis said he immediately left the table to take care of the problem and had his first encounter with one of the legendary English Hall Porters, who, sympathetic and helpful, sent him to a chemist in a nearby arcade to procure some condoms.

Lewis was surprised to learn that the commodities he sought could only be obtained in packages of twelve but, undaunted, he bought a dozen, and when the Hall Porter inquired if he had been successful, showed him the box. (The fact that he had left his date at his dinner table and the fact that he showed the condoms to the Hall Porter convinced me that he was in that state of bliss he customarily achieved after a bout of freestyle imbibing.) Later, Lewis said, he and his companion were in their room when, in the heat of passion, he discovered that he had lost the condoms. (I had a mental image of a very surprised busboy clearing the Grizzard table after dinner.) Lewis went back to the chemist in the arcade but found it closed, whereupon he went back to the same Hall Porter and told him he would need some more condoms.

"Lawyer Steed," Lewis said, "you should have seen the look of awe and admiration in the eyes of that bloomin' Hall Porter."

As the story suggests, Lewis was probably a victim of testosterone poisoning. He seemed to be at his best at rowdy all-male gatherings and endeavors and at his worst (or, at least, at his most ill-at-ease) in the presence of intelligent and independent women. His passions, in addition to his golfing addiction, included macho movies, adult beverages, nude dancers, steak and french fries, Sprayberry's Barbecue, big black dogs, parental-guidance-advised jokes, ranch-against-the-riverboat gin rummy, cigarettes, and University of Georgia football. He had an antipathy toward anything even vaguely cultural or pretentious, as well as toward hunting, fishing, men with earrings, political correctness, sanctimonious editors, militant feminists, New Jersey Americans (his term for anyone living north of Richmond), neckties, and, of course, socks.

He was, perhaps because of his porcine plumbing and his

father's early death, as fatalistic as a rock star. He abused his body to an extraordinary degree with tobacco, strong drink and hard living. His fatalism, however, did not extend to flying in airplanes, and getting him on one was like putting toothpaste back in the tube.

Though his humor was underappreciated by most literary critics, it was widely and wildly enjoyed from sea to shining sea by readers of the more than 450 newspapers which carried his column. His after-dinner speeches and stand-up comedy routines fetched breathtaking fees. His point of view was, at the same time, unique and universal. One respected source of criticism, the *Encyclopedia of Southern Culture*, did applaud his work, saying he was the Faulkner of the common man.

W. J. Cash, in his epic, *The Mind of the South*, spoke of the Man at the Center. And, in a sense, Lewis Grizzard was that Man at the Center, the unreconstructed and vigilant guardian of the Southern *status quo*, always resisting any homogenizing influence on the South wrought by television, liberal thought, New Jersey Americans, or change of any sort. And, for those New Jersey Americans who, in the name of progress and enlightenment, suggested that the South might be improved if it moved away from the *status quo*, Lewis had a ready answer: "Partner, if you ain't happy down here, Delta is ready when you are."

His marvelous insights, his wry eye and his humorous harrumphing will be severely missed, and it appears that there is no one around to take his place.

Highs And Lows: Life On The Road

BY STEVE ENOCH

Steve Enoch is president of Atlanta-based Enoch Entertainment, which provides management and financial planning for artists and entertainers.

I met Lewis Grizzard for the first time on January 2, 1988. Appropriately enough, we met on the practice range of a golf course.

My then-wife and I had gone to the Melrose Club on Daufuskie Island, South Carolina, for New Year's Eve. By January 2, the only people left at the club were Lewis and his date and me and my wife. When he started looking for a golf game, I was the only choice. For the rest of that week, we played daily.

Lewis was a fairly good golfer. He had an excellent short game but couldn't hit the ball very far; he was small to begin with, and heart surgery — which required cutting through muscles — had left him with very little upper body strength. I had grown up playing a good deal of tournament golf, so I gave him tips on how to improve his swing, and he seemed to be truly grateful.

After our rounds, we would go to the bar and drink, smoke cigarettes, and talk — all of which Lewis loved. He also said he appreciated the fact that I didn't look down my nose at him if he overindulged; I didn't because I was prone to do the same things myself.

We met later that year in Williamsburg, Virginia, for dinner and more golf, and we talked on the phone occasionally, but my next lengthy encounter with Lewis came when he asked me to be his partner for the 1990 Melrose member/member golf tournament. On the first day of the tournament, Lewis shot 84 and I shot 81, leaving us disappointed and in the middle of the third flight. The next day, however, I shot 69 (one of the best scores I have ever had), and we vaulted over everyone to win the entire tournament. Lewis had never won a golf tournament before, and he was ecstatic. When asked if he contributed to our win, Lewis replied with his usual wit, "Hell yes, I helped him. I said, 'Good shot, partner!' all afternoon."

Our friendship was really cemented later that spring during another get-together at Melrose. As was our habit, we went to the bar after a round of golf and spent the entire evening telling stories and getting plastered. Somewhere deep into the night, I remember lying down on the sofa in the bar. The next thing I remember was waking up about 8:30 the following morning — still on the sofa and still wearing the same clothes from the night before.

With drums pounding in my head and what felt like fuzzy sweaters on my teeth, I walked outside the clubhouse. Through the haze I saw Lewis hitting balls on the practice tee a couple of hundred yards in front of me. I slowly walked over and asked him, "Did you get the number of the truck that ran over me last night?"

A grin spread across Lewis' face. "Are you just getting up from the bar?" he asked.

"Yes, I'm afraid so."

"All right!" he said too loudly. "That makes you OK in my book."

It was at that moment we officially became pals.

About the same time, Lewis began asking me questions about my business background. After years in the insurance business, I had joined with my father to form a consulting business for small-sized companies, and Lewis seemed particularly interested.

"Any time I ask my manager or accountant a Yes or No question," he said, "I never get a Yes or No answer. Would you be willing to take a look at my operation?"

Within a couple of months, Lewis had hired me as his business manager.

Lewis' situation was pretty simple: All of his income was coming from writing columns and books, performing on stage, and doing after-dinner speeches. "It's wearing me out, Buddy," he said. "Isn't there some way I can make money that isn't so labor intensive?"

Lewis didn't live an exorbitant lifestyle. He didn't care about fancy cars, clothes or jewelry. He had a nice house that was nicely decorated, but it wasn't extravagant, and he had a second lakefront home in a golf course development. He did belong to several golf clubs and he enjoyed a good time, but mostly what he wanted to do was play golf, eat country cooking, and listen to country music. He was making about $1.2 million a year when I went to work for him, and a year or two later that had increased to about $1.6 million annually. That should have been more than enough to take care of his needs and wants.

At that income level, it is necessary to make business investments. Lewis' previous financial manager had tried that during the '80s with a number of limited partnerships, but those investments — driven largely by tax benefits that had disappeared — seldom returned any cash. In fact, as partners defaulted on their commitments, Lewis (who was usually the largest investor) ended up holding the empty bag. For example, in the mid-'80s Lewis and four other people formed a limited partnership to buy eighteen acres of raw land inside the perimeter highway of Atlanta for $2.3 million. When the property didn't escalate in value, some of the partners dropped out. Lewis was personally left with a $90,000 per year obligation to keep from losing that entire investment. Unfortunately, that wasn't the only such deal on his ledger.

Complicated business dealings often frustrated Lewis. Instead of hearing explanations about his "worth," he preferred a simpler approach: "If I wanted to leave town tonight, how much money could I put in a brown paper sack to take with me?" He asked that question over and over; to Lewis, that was the only "worth" that counted.

So most of my first year as Lewis' business manager was spent getting him *out* of deals rather than getting him into deals. And he had to keep making money the old-fashioned way while we tried to right the ship.

During the first year I worked for Lewis, I commuted from my home in Florence, South Carolina. Whenever I came to Atlanta, I stayed at his house. That was a perfect arrangement for both of us, because Lewis despised being alone. One Saturday in August of 1991 I arrived about 5 p.m.

"Partner," he said as I walked in, "tonight I've got a special surprise for you. I have the lovely Juanita coming over from the Spring Street Ballet, and she's bringing her roommate to escort you." The "Spring Street Ballet," as Lewis called it, was also known as the Cheetah III, a nude dancing club. "The four of us are going to Chops restaurant for dinner. And you'd better hurry, because the ladies and the limo will be here in about forty-five minutes."

When I came back downstairs from changing my clothes, the two "ballerinas" were already there, both smacking gum. We had a couple of drinks and departed for the restaurant. Almost as soon as we arrived, our dates headed for the restroom — "to reload their gum," Lewis said.

As we sat at our table awaiting their return, we noticed a very attractive, dark-haired woman standing at the bar talking to another woman. We rushed over to the bar where Lewis introduced himself, and the woman, Dedra, did the same. "Well, Dedra," said Lewis, "I would love to get together with you and go out sometime. The problem is, however, that I currently have a date, and she's probably flushing at this very moment. If you would kindly give me your telephone number, I would like to call you sometime." Dedra wrote her number on a napkin, Lewis stuffed it in his pocket, and we returned to await the ballerinas.

And so began the relationship between Dedra and Lewis that would last beyond his death. Before Dedra came along, Lewis had been dating a number of women, including "ballerinas." I had taken it upon myself to try to get him away from such types because I felt they were bad for him and his reputation. These women tended to take advantage of him when he had too much to drink. They would ask him to buy them expensive things, and ol' big-hearted Lewis would open his wallet. He needed someone stable in his life, someone to look after him, not just to use him and move on.

Dedra was not only attractive, she was also amicable and gracious, and her young daughter Jordan proved to be a great influence on Lewis.

One of the most gruelling parts of Lewis' life was his annual book tour, following the publication of a new book. Between mid-October and mid-December, we would travel to about fifteen different cities for book signings and media promotions. A typical day included radio and/or television interviews, a newspaper or local magazine interview, and one or two autographings — each lasting approximately two hours. And, of course, Lewis still had to write his three columns a week for the newspaper. At the end of those days, we would have a big dinner in the nicest restaurant we could find, have several cocktails, and then crash and burn until the next morning, when we'd get up and do it all over again.

Lewis' deal with his publisher provided him two first-class airline tickets and all expenses (thus the nice restaurants) for these tours. The second ticket was because Lewis hated flying alone even more than he hated being alone. But even flying first-class was a problem for Lewis; he hated flying no matter what class he was in.

One fall Villard Books (Lewis' publisher and an imprint of Random House) had him going to Kansas City and then St. Louis for signings. "Look," I said, trying to save my own sanity as well as Lewis', "are you trying to sell books or just to get some press in bigger cities? If you're trying to sell books, you're going to the wrong places. Lewis will sell more books in Dothan, Alabama, than he'll sell in Kansas City and St. Louis combined." Although Lewis' column was published nationally and he was certainly well known in all areas of the country, the South was still his most devoted region.

Since the publisher had already committed to cover the costs of the tour, I asked them if they'd be willing to pay us the cash instead of reimbursing expenses. My plan was to buy a limousine and hire a driver to take Lewis from city to city. I assured Villard that he would arrive in much better spirits, and it wouldn't cost them a dime extra. They agreed.

The book tour was supposed to start in three days in Charleston, South Carolina, so I had to move quickly. First I located a limo for sale in Greensboro, North Carolina, and flew there to look it over. It was the longest car I had ever seen — a 113-inch stretch that was so long it had five doors and two televisions. I bought it and drove it back to Atlanta the next day.

James Shannon and Catfish prepare to load up for another road trip in the stretch limo.

191

Then, through a friend, I located a man in Greensboro, Georgia, who had driven limousines and was looking for a job. I hired James Shannon, and we were set to begin the tour.

As we pulled out of Lewis' driveway the next day, headed for Charleston, Lewis said, "P.T., this may be the best idea you've ever had."

"P.T.?" I asked.

"Yeah, for P.T. Barnum," said Lewis. "You're a lot like him, because I never know what you're going to come up with next."

James Shannon became one of Lewis' best friends and actually lived in Lewis' house for awhile. He loved Catfish, the black lab, almost as much as Lewis did, and the three of them spent many hours together.

One night about 2 A.M. we were returning from doing a live show in Birmingham, Alabama. James was driving and Lewis and I were relaxing in the back of the limo. Lewis asked James to pull over to the side of the road so he could go to the bathroom. (Lewis liked going outside more than anyone I've ever known, and he went on the sides of more roads than you could count.) But there was an exit just ahead, so James said he'd pull off there. In the confusing maze of roads and medians at the end of the ramp, James accidentally turned the wrong way, and we were headed in the wrong direction down a one-way stretch. We didn't have to worry about crashing into another car, however, because we were surrounded by police cars before we had gone a hundred yards; Alabama law enforcement officers were everywhere!

We could tell James was nervous and jumpy as one of the officers asked for his driver's license, insurance card, and the registration of the car. When he couldn't find any of them and the officer told him to get out of the car, James turned around and yelled, "Mr. Lewis! Mr. Lewis! Come up here and help me! These men are gonna do the Rodney King thing on me!"

Lewis was always very popular with police officers throughout the South. He respected them and the jobs they did, and he often said so in his columns. When Lewis identified himself and flashed his honorary deputy's badge from Greene County, Georgia, one officer got on his radio and told the others who they had stopped. Within minutes, with the limo still on the wrong side of the road, Lewis did an autographing for probably a dozen officers. We stayed there thirty minutes before continuing on to Atlanta. James, needless to say, was relieved.

One of the strangest autographing events I ever witnessed happened in Charlotte, North Carolina. A fairly young man, about forty years old, patiently waited in line to meet Lewis. When his turn came, he greeted Lewis and said, "My daddy was your biggest fan." We had heard that line before, but never what followed: "As a matter of fact, my daddy said that when he died, he wanted to be cremated with your book *My Daddy Was a Pistol and I'm a Son of a Gun*. So when Daddy died last year, we cremated him with your book. And do you know...we could tell which parts were Daddy and which were your book." That could only happen to Lewis.

While Lewis underwent heart surgery at Atlanta's Emory Hospital in 1993, and subsequently was unconscious for nearly two weeks, James Shannon had angioplasty at nearby St. Joseph's Hospital. Fortunately his clogged arteries did not require surgery. Lewis and James both recuperated at Lewis' house.

A year later, when Lewis died, James became unemployed. We had sold the limousine a month and a half earlier when it became apparent that Lewis would not be going back on the road anytime soon. James had remained as Lewis' righthand man. Today he still lives in Greensboro, Georgia.

Catfish, the black Labrador retriever, was the one constant thing in Lewis' life. If Lewis had to be without human companionship, he could always count on Catfish to keep him company. Lewis often said that Catfish's love was unconditional: Unlike women, no matter what time Lewis came home, no matter what his condition, Catfish never asked any questions and was always glad to see him.

Through Lewis' writings, Catfish became a celebrity in his

own right. Almost every year he was invited to be the grand marshal at the annual Catfish Parade and Festival in Scottsboro, Alabama. Catfish rode in a police car with the siren on, wearing his grand marshal's ribbon, sitting up like he was king of the world.

He certainly was king of Lewis' house. Lewis had a large green sofa in his living room, and he and Catfish always sat on one end and watched television together. Anytime Lewis wasn't playing golf or writing, he and Catfish were watching old movies on that sofa.

The day Catfish died was one of the worst I ever spent with Lewis. On Thanksgiving Day, 1993, Dedra called and asked me to join them for a family dinner about 5:30 p.m. I arrived just before 5 p.m. but Lewis wasn't there yet. Six o'clock came; still no Lewis. He was playing cards in the men's grill at Ansley Golf Club and was more worried about his hand than the time. About 6:30 he showed up with three of his buddies, and they'd all been drinking. They marched right through the house and

Boys Club: Lewis enjoyed cards and camaraderie in the Men's Grill at Ansley Golf Club.

onto the back deck, where they continued talking. Dedra was hot; the food was cold.

I was in the living room with James Shannon when Dedra came in and suggested that we start a fire in the fireplace to liven up the atmosphere. In all the years I'd been going to Lewis' house, I had never seen a fire in the living room fireplace, but it sounded like a nice idea. So we put two artificial logs in the fireplace and lit them. About four minutes later, the entire room started to fill with smoke. The fireplace was either bricked up or the flue was closed. Suddenly the fire alarm went off — an ear-splitting shriek that sounded throughout the house. Of course, nobody knew the security code to disarm it, but everyone was running around the house trying to do *something*.

I couldn't take it anymore: Lewis' attitude, Dedra's aggravation at Lewis, the fire alarm blaring, and everyone walking around yelling. I picked up a cold drumstick and headed for home.

Lewis called me early the next morning to tell me that Catfish, who had not been well and had been staying at the veterinarian's, had died Thanksgiving night. The vet said he had waited until the following morning to call with the bad news so that he wouldn't spoil Thanksgiving for the family.

The minute I hung up, I went to Lewis' house. As I stepped on the front porch, I listened hopelessly for the sound of Catfish barking at the door. Lewis was sitting at the kitchen table, where he had just finished his column about the dog's death. The last line read, "My heart, or what is left of it, is breaking." It was a miserable Thanksgiving.

Outside of golf and Georgia football, there was nothing Lewis enjoyed more than watching old movies. He was a student of old war movies in particular and knew the names of nearly every actor who played in them. Lewis, who often talked about his father's military service, felt the ultimate "gut check" was hand-to-hand combat, and he was awed by the courage required to do battle.

He appreciated the values reflected in the old movies. He always said they were "very pure." Women were comfortable in their roles as wives and mothers, men were loyal and honest, no one used profanity, and — for the most part — all the movies had happy endings, for that was the American way. Lewis often said that if everyone watched old movies, we would all be awakened to the ideology that people's lives are important and good.

Another aspect of "pure" values, according to Lewis, was gospel music. Once Lewis came back from a Christening service in a Methodist church where the choir sang three songs. Lewis was incensed that he didn't recognize any of them. He immediately wrote a column saying, "No wonder church attendance is down: They've gotten rid of all the old-fashioned hymns we used to sing."

Lewis had basically memorized the Methodist Cokesbury hymnal. He would often quote page numbers of his favorite hymns: "Amazing Grace," page so and so; "Precious Memories," page so and so. He received an overwhelming response to that column from readers who agreed with him that old-fashioned values were reflected in those old-fashioned songs. He also received more than fifty copies of the Cokesbury hymnal from fans.

Nothing electronic ever worked right around Lewis. Hair dryers, radios, electric razors, remote controls — you name it, it wouldn't work for him. Once we were in Richmond, Virginia, for a live performance. We checked into the luxurious Jefferson Hotel about midafternoon and went to Lewis' room to relax by watching an old movie.

He got comfortable on the bed, with his Tab and cigarettes nearby, and punched in movie No. 103. Unfortunately, he meant to punch in movie No. 106. When No. 103 started playing, Lewis said, "That's not the movie I wanted! Call down and get 'em to switch it to No. 106."

I called the front desk and reported the problem, but the clerk said, "I'm sorry, but if you punched in No. 103, you'll just have to watch No. 103. It's going to play until it's completed, two hours and eleven minutes from now, and there's nothing we can do about it."

Lewis and I took turns changing the channel and turning the TV on and off, but the only picture we could get was movie No. 103. "I can't have this," Lewis said. "Steve, you've *got* to take charge and get this fixed."

I suggested moving to another room, but Lewis wouldn't hear of leaving the suite for a regular room. So I called the cable company, which was in Washington, D.C., figuring Lewis would be impressed even if I couldn't get the movie changed.

"We're in room 1215 of the Jefferson Hotel in Richmond," I explained. "My friend accidentally punched in movie No. 103, when he really wanted to see No. 106. We admit that the mistake is ours, and we're certainly willing to pay for the movie. But we're going to be here for only a short period of time, and we don't want to spend that time watching movie No. 103. Isn't there something you can do to help?"

About an hour later, a worker in Washington, D.C., threw a switch that turned off movie No. 103 in our room in Richmond and turned on movie No. 106. Lewis was elated; he had prevailed over the system. "Thank you, partner," he said. "Sorry I hit the wrong button."

Another time on the road he woke me up at 5 a.m. with the ribbon from his old manual typewriter half off the spool. He wanted me to help him rewind it. I think that was the same typewriter he used to write one of his earlier best-selling books. Just as he was beginning that book, the letter *e* broke off his typewriter. He wrote the entire book without an *e*. When he turned in the manuscript to his editor, he said, "Every time you see a blank space, put an *e* in there." Only Lewis could have gotten away with that.

Lewis was very superstitious about the number 11. According to him, the obsession started one night as he was driving to a speech and began pondering if there were ever a point in time when the exact time, day, and date were all the same number. The only digit that worked was 1: it could be 11:11 in the morning or evening, on November 11 (11/11), in the year 1111. Lewis became so superstitious that he wouldn't fly on

November 11 of any year. And anytime he spotted a digital clock reading 11:11, he got spooked.

The last time I was aware of 11:11 was Christmas of 1993, Lewis' last Christmas. On my way to Florence, South Carolina, to visit my daughter and son, I went by Lewis' house to exchange gifts. He had just gotten out of the hospital a few days before; in fact, he had spent most of the year in the hospital, and he was still very weak. Christmas depressed Lewis anyway, because his parents were both dead and he felt alone, and his medical problems had left him feeling even lower.

I considered staying with Lewis that day — he was such a pitiful sight — but he encouraged me to go ahead and visit my kids. I'm sure he was thinking of all the Christmases he never saw his father. So I said good-bye, went to the car, and started the engine. The digital clock on the dash flashed 11:11. Two days later Lewis entered the hospital again, and from that time until his death, he spent more time in the hospital than out.

Lewis loved the Waffle House. He *adored* the Waffle House. He often said that it and Catfish were the only things in his life he could count on: "It's always open, the bathrooms are always clean, and the food always tastes the same no matter which one you stop at."

Whenever he did live shows with "The Lewis Grizzard Trio" — Dick Feller on guitar and Timmy Tappan on piano, with Lewis singing lead — we would rent a tour bus to travel in. The shows usually ended around 10:30 p.m., and generally by 11 we'd be on the bus headed out of town. Almost immediately Lewis would holler to the bus driver, "Stop at the first Waffle House you see once we're out of town."

If he went inside, he always ordered the steak. But if he didn't want to be recognized and delayed, he'd send us in for his usual — sausage and egg sandwich, white bread, with extra pickles.

In early December of 1993, Lewis was finishing his book tour for *I Took a Lickin' But Kept on Tickin'*. We were driving from Atlanta to Birmingham in the limousine when Lewis said, "James, stop at the Waffle House so I can get me a sandwich." Sausage and egg with extra pickles.

As soon as we arrived at the mall for the autographing, Lewis began feeling bad. He said his stomach hurt, and he began to perspire. Lewis refused to cancel the autographing with fans standing in line, but the bookstore personnel were so concerned that they sent a nurse over to check on him. One of the things she suspected was food poisoning. As soon as the signing was over, we loaded Lewis into the limo and drove straight to Emory Hospital.

Doctors ran tests and took x-rays before Lewis' cardiologist, Dr. Randy Martin, came in and explained the situation: "Lewis, you've had an aneurysm in your spleen. Basically the blood supply has been cut off to the majority of your spleen. The pain you felt was the blood filling up in the sac around your spleen."

When the doctor finished his explanation, Lewis looked at me and said, "Ah ha! The Waffle House has been exonerated!"

Once we were doing a live show in Montgomery, Alabama. One of the backstage security folks — an off-duty policeman — struck up a conversation with Lewis, telling him how much he liked his writing. Lewis asked, "Do you have any kids?"

"Oh, yes sir, Mr. Grizzard, I've got two children. My daughter's name is Liberty, and my son's name is Justice."

Lewis looked over the top of his glasses and said, "Liberty and Justice?"

"Yeah," said the policeman, "I wanted to have a third child and name it For All, but my wife had her tubes tied first."

Lewis laughed so hard he almost made a spectacle of himself. But the real spectacle occurred after the show as we prepared to leave.

The head of security — another off-duty policeman — said, "We want to escort you, your bus, and your folks out of town to make sure you get out of Montgomery safely." We said that wasn't necessary, that we shouldn't have any problem, but the man insisted. "Just follow me," he said.

We boarded the bus, the police escort turned on his blue lights, and then over the patrol car's loudspeaker we heard "Hail to the Chief." At each light through downtown there were police roadblocks, and "Hail to the Chief" played over and over.

I had never seen anything like this. Lewis, who was still laughing, turned to me and said, "I'm *big* in Montgomery!"

After my divorce, I lived in Lewis' house for a little more than a year. One morning I went downstairs and poured myself a glass of orange juice. Lewis was at his usual morning post — the kitchen table — hammering out a column on his manual typewriter, with coffee and cigarettes close at hand. "You want a glass of orange juice?" I asked.

"I don't drink orange juice," he said. "Don't like the taste of it."

"But I've seen you drink orange juice with vodka a thousand times," I said.

"Yeah," he answered, "but I do that only because if I drink straight vodka, people will say I have a drinking problem. If I order vodka with a glass of orange juice, then I don't have a problem."

Lewis was aware that he often drank too much, but nonetheless he tried to justify it. Since he had been drinking continually throughout his impressive career, he was afraid that if he *wasn't* drinking he might not be funny. Quitting drinking, in his mind, could have destroyed his career.

Of course, that didn't happen. In the last year of his life, Lewis didn't take a drink. During that time, he wrote some of the funniest and most poignant material of his career. He never acknowledged that fact, but I'm sure he finally knew the truth — he didn't have to drink to be funny.

When he got philosophical, Lewis often would say, "Everyone tries to make life a lot more complicated than it really is. Life is like a public bathroom: Some people go in and leave it better, or at least no worse, than it was when they went in; others do whatever they can just to mess it up for the next person who comes in." Givers and takers. Lewis was a giver.

Any time he saw a bum by the side of the road holding a sign that said, "Please help me," or, "I need money," Lewis would always give the man or woman at least twenty dollars. In explaining his actions, he said, "Every time I see a person like that, I think about my daddy and how hard his life was and how he begged and borrowed money from people. I always try to do what I can to help them out."

He frequently came to the aid of needy people in his column. Two such instances were Peggy and Daniel.

Peggy was a thirty-five-year-old nurse in a small south Georgia town. She had two children and acute kidney failure. Without a transplant, she almost certainly would die. The administrator of her hospital called to ask if Lewis could help them raise money to deal with Peggy's huge medical expenses. Lewis did his show *gratis*, and $33,000 was raised that night. He also wrote a column about Peggy the next day, and another $66,000 in donations resulted. With one show and one column, he raised almost $100,000 for Peggy.

Daniel's story started out small but became a major event in Lewis' life. One night before a show in Shreveport, Louisiana, a woman came up to me and said, "My son is Lewis Grizzard's No. 1 fan." I had heard it a thousand times. "He is twelve years old. He's been blind since birth."

I decided that Lewis might enjoy meeting Daniel, so after the show I took him backstage. As they talked, it became clear that Daniel was something of a savant on Lewis' material; he knew it inside and out. Rocking back and forth, he would ask Lewis a question and Lewis would answer, but sometimes Daniel would say, "No, I know that can't be right, because in your fourth book you wrote...." The kid was truly amazing. His mother had read all of Lewis' books to him, and he had all of Lewis' books on tape and comedy albums. Lewis was completely taken by his new young friend, and when he found out that Daniel was being raised solely by his mother, he was even more committed.

The Shreveport performance was taped and later became the comedy album, "Don't Believe I'da Told That." Lewis dedicated the tape to Daniel, and he later wrote a column about the boy. Doctors at the Emory Eye Clinic read Lewis' column and offered to check Daniel for free to see if they could restore his sight. Daniel and his mother flew to Atlanta and stayed in

Lewis' house. Unfortunately, nothing could be done for Daniel's sight, and we all felt a little disheartened.

Some time later we saw a commercial for a machine manufactured by Xerox that is capable of reading several languages and has several different speaking voices. Singer Stevie Wonder did the commercial and endorsed the product. We arranged to buy one for Daniel; approximately $1,500 of the $10,000 purchase price was donated by citizens of Shreveport, and Lewis and I made up the difference. After another live show in Shreveport, we led Daniel up on stage and presented the reading machine to him. The grin on his face was so bright it could have powered all of Shreveport.

Lewis Grizzard was a giving man.

One night over dinner at the Ritz-Carlton in Kansas City, Missouri, Lewis broke a lengthy silence with this assessment of his life: "I've spent most of my life doing work I loved; I've played with Arnold Palmer, had a hole-in-one, shot par, and won a tournament on the golf course; sang 'Georgia' with Willie Nelson at the White House; the Georgia Bulldogs have won a national championship during my lifetime; and I've written best-seller books and received standing ovations at my concerts. Yeah, I've had a good life."

A Tale Of Too Many Broken Hearts

By Dedra Grizzard with Judson Knight

Dedra Grizzard is the widow of Lewis Grizzard. She lives in Atlanta and is partner with Steve Enoch in Bad Boot Productions, which controls the intellectual properties of Lewis Grizzard.

Lewis had to have a new heart, but there was no guarantee he'd get one. A heart being such a precious thing, much sought after and meant to be cared for, they don't just give them away to anyone who asks. Someone had to speak up and say *why* he deserved a new heart.

And though he had the gift of spinning out words just as smooth as his mama's biscuits, this time he couldn't do the convincing himself. Not when he was fighting for his life and struggling to take every breath.

Someone else had to make his case for him, to say that Lewis McDonald Grizzard, Jr., should be awarded the gift of time itself: another few hundred million heartbeats. Just a few more years, a few more laughs, a few more fights, a few more times to look back upon and reminisce.

That was all I asked.

It was March 1993, and Lewis had just had his third operation at Emory Hospital. When they opened him up, they found his heart valves covered with scar tissue from the second operation eight years before; one of the doctors said it was as though a hand grenade had gone off inside his aorta.

He very nearly died on the operating table. Afterward the doctors had to put him on a ventricular assist device, which acted in place of his heart and gave his own a chance to rest. But it was possible to stay on that machine for only a short time before other major complications would arise.

Several times they turned the tempo down on the assist device so they could evaluate the functioning of Lewis' heart, hoping it would start beating on its own. But it didn't respond. And so we began to consider the possibility that Lewis might need a transplant to survive.

Seconds counted now: This was more than the two-minute warning, more than the bottom of the ninth with the score tied and bases loaded. This was Lewis' life.

I was approached by the transplant team, who had plenty of questions for me. It was then I realized that you have to *qualify* to receive a new heart, and the standards are high. The reason for this is obvious: Many critically ill people are awaiting hearts all over the country. Therefore, a person about to receive a hard-to-find organ has to make certain promises and must agree to live by certain rules.

I was told that a smoker — that is, someone who wouldn't put away the cigarettes — would never qualify. Likewise, a person who drank alcohol, and kept it up afterward, would definitely not be a viable candidate for a heart. Did I believe that Lewis could or would change his lifestyle?

Now, that was *not* the question I wanted to answer.

They didn't ask me, for instance, if he *needed* the transplant. We all knew he might — that was obvious. They could see him in the intensive care unit every day, gasping to hold onto life. It wasn't a question of need.

And it wasn't a question of whether I could *make* him change his old habits. It wasn't up to me. I'd learned a long time before that what Lewis did was by his choice, and the surest way to get him *not* to do something was to insist that he do it.

So, the question remained — would he or wouldn't he change

his ways? The clock was ticking.

I didn't know what to say. Anyone, I thought, can change if his life depends on it. But he was not just "anyone." This was Lewis Grizzard they were talking about.

I thought about how he would feel when, partially as a result of my decision, he woke up with a new heart. At first, all I could imagine was how happy he would be that he was alive: now we could get married, and he could father that child he'd never had, and he'd have someone he could teach how to play HORSE.

But then I pictured his recovery. After I told him he had a brand-new heart and another decade or so added to his life, I'd have to tell him the catch. "Lewis, darling," I'd say, "I've got a few little things to tell you. First of all, I've flushed your Marlboros down the toilet, and secondly, you're never going to come close to alcohol again unless it's on a gauze pad. Third, I know you've been thinking about a big plate of fried chicken floating in enough grease to lubricate a Ford Explorer, and you can have it — at Jimmy Carter's re-election party. In the meantime, I've fixed you a nice tofu-soybean steak with steamed radishes, and grapefruit slices for dessert. Now, last but not least, you don't have to worry about making any more plans, because we've got the rest of your life planned for you: five-mile walks every day, a pill diet that would make Elvis squeamish, and lots of quality time with a couple hundred of your favorite doctors and nurses at Emory."

After he heard all that and had a heart attack with his second heart, what would we do?

With all the pills they'd have to give him to keep his body from rejecting the new heart, he would experience severe mood swings, something he already had a problem with. Like a lot of writers and other dynamic-type people, Lewis had a hard time shutting off his mind at night. He'd always be thinking about the next column, the next speech, the next book.

So his doctor had prescribed Imipramine, of which he took six every night to help him sleep. He was fine if he took them, but if he somehow missed his pills and lost sleep, he'd have heavy bouts of depression. Now they wanted to load him up with God knew how many other chemicals, and I wondered if he could stand it.

Lewis loved his freedom, a fact I'd learned over and over and in many ways — both good and bad — in the three years I'd known him. And now he'd have a doctor monitoring his medications and his eating, wanting to know about his exercise habits. And in Lewis' case, that would mean he would have to *develop* some — other than swinging a golf club or doing vodka curls.

And so in the back of my mind, in my soul, I tried to sort out the facts of the present and the prospects for the future. Under any circumstances it would have been hard to make that kind of decision for someone else, but it was especially hard knowing Lewis as I did.

In the end, however, it was like the old saying about a second marriage — the triumph of hope over experience. Yes, I said to the transplant team, yes, he'll change his ways. Give him a new heart and I'll give you a new man!

I begged for that heart, and made all kinds of promises I knew I could never keep if Lewis had a different mind about things than I did. Maybe if he realized how close to death he'd come, it would frighten him into clean living. But then again, maybe not.

Fortunately, we never had to find out.

After four days Lewis' own heart began to beat again, and with a sigh of relief we all watched the EKG begin to register the regular rhythms of Lewis Grizzard — himself, unaided.

I was relieved beyond words. Changing his lifestyle would have been a monumental task, and though I knew that I was willing to give it all I had (and probably Lewis would have done the same), there was no guarantee of success.

Lewis got lots of interesting calls, including some from people wanting to donate their hearts to him — yes, actually wanting to give their living hearts to the man who'd made them laugh so many times. In other cases, people had relatives who were clinically dead and would never recover but had perfectly good body parts. One phone call came from a nun who said she would let Lewis Grizzard have her heart. Can you imagine Lewis waking up and being told that (1) he had a female heart, and (2) it had come from a nun? That's something he *never* would have forgiven me for!

At the same time that I'd been pleading his case before the Emory transplant team, I had also gone to a much higher authority. Sitting in the hospital through those long, long days and nights when we never knew what the next hour would bring, in my heart I'd gone down on my knees. God, I prayed, please give me one more year with him. Just one more year.

And God heard my prayer. He was faithful to my request — very faithful, as it turned out. That extra year made all the difference in Lewis' life, and in mine.

But on the day we took him home from the hospital in May 1993, we had no idea what lay ahead. All we knew was that we were relieved.

During Lewis' hospital stay, I'd had to leave my four-year-old daughter with her baby-sitter (or my family) much of the time. Now I was ready to go back to being the family we'd been before: Lewis, Jordan, and me. And Lewis, of course, couldn't wait to get home. Yet I can't say we were any more excited than the staff at Emory. In fact, *ecstatic* might be the word for them.

Now, that excitement came partly from the empathy of medical professionals who've made a psychological connection with the patient, who've rooted for him and are thrilled to see that, partly through their efforts, he has made it. But it also had something to do with the fact that they were glad to get rid of the most crotchety, cantankerous, and just plain ornery patient they'd ever seen.

During his stay in their fine facility, Lewis had harassed the nutritionist, attempted to strangle the physical therapist, badgered every nurse within yelling distance, and roundly cursed the "bloodsuckers" who came to take samples from his veins.

I remember one poor nurse who especially got the brunt of his abuse because she had the misfortune of looking just like Hillary Clinton. She could have been the nicest person in the world, but there was that resemblance, and Lewis wasn't very nice about it. I felt sorry for her, but then again, imagine Hillary Clinton in a nurse's uniform!

There were only two nurses in the ICU who could get him to behave and obey hospital rules: one was Gabriella (or "Gabby"), and the other was Mary German, the head nurse. Gabriella was beautiful, and I think Lewis wanted to be nice to her for that reason if nothing more, and Mary was very strong and to-the-point. This was her second open-heart surgery with Lewis, and she'd become something of a confidante to him. But they were just two people, and unfortunately they had outside lives and other patients — not to mention the fact that they had to sleep. When they weren't around, everyone else was in danger.

While he was struggling to stay alive, Lewis couldn't be much trouble to anyone, but as he began to recover, it was like watching a bear wake up out of hibernation. Nobody wanted to get in his way.

And rightfully so — he had seventeen scars with stitches from his neck to his groin area, and every move he made sent intense pain throughout his body. Even a more mild-mannered person might have gotten a little irritable in the circumstances, and with Lewis, any traits a normal person had were multiplied many times over.

Now the nurses were releasing him, and giving him to lucky old me.

We left in the middle of a swarm of newspaper and TV people. Usually Lewis had been on the other side of the news, not reporting it so much as commenting on it in his own way; now he *was* the news. He wanted to thank his fans for their many prayers, a thing he'd learned to value during his close brush with death, but he didn't have the strength to address the reporters. All he could do was wave and cry, and I waved and cried with him. We were on our way home at last.

To my home, that is. Because of the media and occasional drop-ins, Lewis had decided not to spend his recovery period at his place, a house whose location many people knew. At that time I still lived in a high-rise in Buckhead, which had a security guard who had a way of making unwelcome visitors feel even more unwelcome, so Lewis hid out there.

We rented a hospital bed and set him up in the living room. His cardiologist, Randy Martin, had said we would need round-the-clock care so he could receive his antibiotics and in case he should spike a temperature, etc., so I called up Home Health Care and they sent us over a nurse.

She seemed sweet, and after I had introduced her to Lewis, showed her around the house, and gotten her situated, I felt completely confident to leave her alone with him while I ran some errands. But when I got back, I found Lewis by himself.

"Where's the nurse?" I asked him.

He told me he'd fired her because "she looked at me funny."

I said OK, and I called HHC for a replacement.

They sent a new nurse the following day. Nurse No. 2 seemed like a quiet, bookish type — exactly what Lewis needed at a time like this. I went out to pick up Jordan from school, and when I came back, once again I found him alone.

Not only had this one stared at him, she breathed too loudly. The third nurse was sent and dismissed just as quickly, because she got twisted in the IV too often.

They got to know my voice quite well at HHC, and I became more and more specific each time I requested a nurse to replace the one Lewis had just sent packing: someone who doesn't stare, can't talk, and is definitely competent enough to keep the IV from twisting around her body.

If I were to give a blow-by-blow of the entire nurse saga, it would be about as boring as a round of "Ninety-Nine Bottles of Beer on the Wall." Suffice it to say that Lewis fired every nurse employed by Home Health Care. I don't think Florence Nightingale would have lasted in that environment, and it did-n't seem to matter how competent they were: if I so much as left to go to the bathroom, I'd come back and find that the nurse of the day had been dismissed.

It took me awhile, but eventually I realized that Lewis want-ed me there, and only me, to hold his hand, to rub his forehead, to calm his fears. He could hear his heart pounding with his new

St. Jude's mechanical valve, and he was petrified it would stop. He had never liked being alone, but during this time his phobia intensified greatly.

We finally settled into a pattern where the HHC nurse would come in only to administer his antibiotics every four to six hours, but the rest of the time, I'd take care of him. This made everybody happy — even me.

My only regret was that I couldn't make time pass any more quickly for him during those difficult days of recovery. But I didn't mind being his nurse. We spent many tender hours talking together on the couch, getting to know one another more closely, and he never went a day without telling me how much he loved me and how much he appreciated my sticking by him through the rough times.

During those weeks, he suffered a great deal of pain, not only physically but perhaps even more so emotionally. Lewis had always been such a go-getter, a loose cannon, living hard and fast, and now he'd been stopped in his tracks by his illness. His competitive spirit thrived within him, but his body just wouldn't go.

He loved golf, and he didn't just *want* to get out on the course — he *had to* play. It was like a drug, and knowing he couldn't play for a few months made him very unhappy.

But not nearly as unhappy as watching daytime TV made him. By noontime, Lewis would already be irate with the happenings of the world. Oprah and Montel and Sallye Jesse — with all the nutcases they would bring out of the woodwork on a daily basis and hold up as examples of ordinary American life — drove him crazy. It isn't pleasant to watch a man with a heart condition shout at a television set.

The more simple life he had known — the postwar small-town Georgia that he'd idealized in his columns and books — was disappearing. "Our world is full of smut," he said to me many times, his irritation always showing through on that last syllable as though he had just stepped in dog poop.

To me that meant there were a lot of things happening that Lewis didn't understand or agree with — nor did he want to try.

His basic view of the world wasn't likely to alter significantly if he lived to be a hundred.

And yet in the three short years I'd spent with him, I had seen him change a great deal on the inside. As simple as his tastes could be in many things, there were a number of layers to the man, and I was still coming to understand him.

In our last year, the layers were peeled away. If he'd died right after that third operation, I wouldn't feel like I had really and truly known Lewis. And so I will always be thankful to God for that last year — for those thirty-one million more heartbeats — with Lewis Grizzard.

I suppose it's fitting that the man who claimed credit for inventing the Tomahawk Chop ("The restroom's over there") would have entered my life at Chop's restaurant in Buckhead, the heart of Atlanta. Come to think of it, the restroom had something to do with it, too.

It was July 28, 1990, the day I turned thirty. Up until a few months before, I'd been living in Ft. Lauderdale with my husband, the father of my eighteen-month-old baby girl. But the town held too many temptations, and the effect it had on Dean was enough to make me decide that there were worse things for a child than having divorced parents.

So, taking Jordan with me, I had sought refuge with my mother and sister in Auburn, Alabama. That night was the first time I'd gone out since my separation, and I'd come to Atlanta to see my long-time girlfriend, Dee Nelson.

All of a sudden, here came this man with neatly trimmed brownish hair and a beard and mustache, graying around the edges. He wore glasses, but they didn't have the effect of making him seem studious; in fact, my first impression was that he was something of a rogue. And it appeared that he had his eye on one of us, either Dee or me.

"Hello, ladies," he said in his deep, smoky Southern baritone. I didn't know who he was, but I figured out quickly he must be a prominent figure of some kind, because even though there were three or four people ahead of him, the bartender looked straight at him and said, "What'll it be, Mr. Grizzard?"

Now that rang a bell. I had once dated a guy who got extremely irate if he woke up in the morning and found that the *Constitution* did not have a column that day by a certain Lewis Grizzard. But I'd never read the column.

Lewis ordered a cocktail, and as he waited for it, he began to chat with us. By now it had become apparent that I was the intended target of his smooth talk, and was it ever smooth — as suave a set of lines as I'd heard from a man in a long, long time.

Only one thing was out of place. Any man attempting to pick up a woman in a bar (assuming it's not five minutes till closing and she's not desperate) knows he'd better take his time. Otherwise, it's likely she'll tell him to take a hike.

But this one was definitely in a hurry, and there turned out to be a good reason why: "Darlin'," he said in a low voice, leaning closer to me, "if you ever want me to wine and dine you on the French Riviera, you'd better write your phone number down real quick" — the bartender handed him a matchbook and a pen — "on this pack of matches, because my date's probably flushing right about now."

It was a daring move, and it could just as easily have turned me off — I wasn't at a phase in my life when I had a lot of patience with men pulling sneaky tricks — but I found myself being charmed.

And fortunately for him, his date lived up to all his observations about women immortalized in the 1987 book *When My Love Returns From the Ladies Room, Will I Be Too Old to Care?* I wrote down the phone number, and in one neat motion he slid it into his hip pocket as he fell in step with the woman, who had finally emerged.

That would become a private joke of ours for years to come. On *many*, and I do mean many, occasions when we were out by ourselves, I would scope the area before leaving him to go to the bathroom.

I stayed in Atlanta for a couple days, but when I returned to Auburn, I found that he'd left a message on my answering machine the morning after we met. Though he'd interested me enough to give him my number, I wasn't about to call back a man I'd just met. I wasn't just playing hard to get. It was a Southern thing, the "V" word (values) — at home I would get grounded if Daddy ever caught me calling a boy, because women don't call men.

But he called again and asked me to go out with him to Chops, this time as his date. (If I did, I sure didn't intend to drink a lot!) Not only did he invite me, he even sent a limo to pick me up in Auburn and bring me to Atlanta.

We hit it off instantly, and talked and talked and talked that night about everything from religion to grandmothers to the qualifications of being Southern. (He wanted to make sure I was before he committed himself to any more time with me.) And after being married to an Italian from the Bronx for more than two years, I found his Southern charm quite refreshing: It was nice to go out with a man you couldn't ever picture saying "Yo!"

I also remember three things he announced to me: first, that he was three months from bankruptcy; second, that he was due for open heart surgery to replace a faulty valve; and third, that he intended to play golf every day.

When it came to the golf part, he looked at me over his glasses and spoke in a very deep voice. I later learned that this was an imitation of his father, and he did it sometimes in fun and sometimes in earnest. Eventually he even told me that he'd practiced this little speech for some time beforehand.

He must have expected me to put up a fight, and I think he was astounded when in a very nonchalant way I said that was fine with me. But honestly, I had a child who needed all the love and attention I could give her. I was occupied.

As for the bankruptcy part, that was his business, quite literally. But the matter of the heart surgery — now, that was something to be concerned about. And yet we were too busy having fun to think about it often.

We spent five hours together talking nonstop that night, and from the beginning it was clear that we would be seeing a lot more of each other. Otherwise he wouldn't have bothered to issue all his disclaimers about golf and money, etc.

On the other hand, neither of us pried a lot into the details of people we'd been involved with before we met, nor did we ask too much about what went on during times we were apart. Auburn is a good two hours away down I-85 from Atlanta, and we continued to have separate lives — which included dating other people.

When I met Lewis, he already had a girlfriend — *not*, however, the woman who'd left to powder her nose at Chops. This was yet another one.

The way Lewis always told it afterwards, she stole his little black Mercedes. She didn't go hot-wire it out of a parking lot, but she kept it after he let her borrow it for the weekend, and when he demanded that she give it back, she threatened to embarrass him with malicious gossip. So Lewis just let her have the car, and made her sign a contract stating that she'd never attempt to contact him again.

With that phase of Lewis' life behind him, I became the new girlfriend, and in September I went through a major rite of passage: my first Georgia game with Lewis and his friends.

Now, to anybody who's ever even heard of Lewis Grizzard, saying that UGA football was an important part of his life is like pointing out that one element of Madonna's marketing technique is sex. It's so obvious that it's embarrassingeven to hear somebody remark on it.

Yes, Lewis was a devout worshipper at the Church of the Sacred Bulldog, a fact that was never more clear than in his last request on his deathbed. (I'll come to that later. No doubt, to him the idea of people playing soccer — *soccer!* — in Sanford Stadium at the 1996 Olympics would be a sacrilege.)

Anyway, when he invited me to go to the second or third game of the 1990 season, it was an awesome and terrifying thought. What would I wear? Should it be red and black? Would his friends like me? What should I talk about?

I decided to wear a nice linen shirt and a skirt (neither of them red or black), and not to talk about the Dawgs any more than I had to in order to keep from seeming like an idiot. That way, I couldn't get myself in trouble, and they wouldn't know they had a secret Tennessee fan in their midst.

We arrived on the morning of the game to find Athens, like any other American college town on a Saturday morning in the fall, decked out for the big event. Students, alumni, and fans all sported the UGA colors, and there were signs and banners everywhere. When we met up with Lewis' friends to tailgate before the game, they were all eager to see us. Well, they *were* interested to meet me, I'm sure, but the fact that we had the vodka also had something to do with it.

Very quickly I realized that I had underdressed for this momentous occasion: I mean to tell you, those wives and girl-friends had on Bulldog earrings, Bulldog pins that lit up, Bulldog shoes — and the men weren't a whole lot different. (Except for the earrings part.) Every bit of clothing was red and black. It was a sight.

Yet as the day wore on and the vodka continued to pour, I began to feel pretty comfortable with them. The women were much nicer to me than many Southern belles, who have a ten-dency to get a little catty at the sight of a newcomer. I soon found out *why* I got such good treatment: They saw me as a stabilizing influence on a man who had a habit of corrupting *their* men.

When we were all feeling a lot more sociable and friendly, one of Lewis' dearest friends, Betty Poss, took me over in the corner and said, "Do you like Lewis?" I said, "Yes, of course I do." She asked, "Will you be good to him?" Again I replied, "Yes. Why do you ask?"

Sounding very stern, Betty said, "Well, honey, you've got on a hell of a lot more clothes than the girl he had with him last week — and from the looks of you, I don't believe you'll be hop-ping up on the poker table after the game and taking your clothes off!"

It turned out that Lewis' female guest the week before had been a stripper (actually, the woman who later took his car), and Betty's husband was one of the men thus entertained at the card table. I think she was real happy to see him with somebody a little more — shall we say, *traditional* — but as for me, I was thinking, *What the hell have I gotten myself into?*

I had many a hurdle ahead of me.

One of these involved Lewis' friends, most of whom didn't like for him to have a steady: "It takes him away from his card-playing time at the Men's Grill," they'd say. (The Men's Grill, of course, was not so much a place as it was a state of mind.)

Now, I think those who were most sincerely his friends never wanted to dictate his choices in a companion, but there were some who, I guess, felt a little unsure of their relationship with Lewis, and they tried to drive away anyone they saw as a threat. Quite a few made little remarks like, "Yeah, I guess Lewis asked you to marry him and bear his first-born child, like he does every woman. How many Grizzards had he had when he said it?" (A Grizzard was his own special drink, the recipe for which he gave in *I Took a Lickin'*: double Stoli, tall glass, rocks, with orange juice neat on the side.)

The Men's Grill was not the He-Man Woman-Haters' Club. Oh, they *loved* women, but that's a different story. Lewis was bad about going off with his pals for the day and doing things I didn't approve of: About once every season, he'd hit the streets of Buckhead, and when he did, my phone would begin to ring off the hook. Word would soon get out — "Grizzard's on the hunt" — and I'd have to sort out the rumors and tall tales from the truth. In the beginning, that was my biggest challenge.

There was an adjustment period of about a year, a time when I had to get used to being associated with such a flamboyant character. Sometimes there would be some truth to the rumors, and that hurt, but learning to weigh through the exaggerating tendency of human storytelling was something I got better at over the years.

Don't think I didn't question him. I did. I just didn't stay angry at him as long as other women he'd known. Most of the time I just got even.

And it was true that he would, indeed, when he got enough vodka in him, carouse in the streets of Partytown and ask any woman who caught his fancy to marry him and bear his first child!

After he and I had been dating for about eight months, I was snooping around (as most women do), and I happened to find a Valentine's Day card from a certain "Lana" in his bedroom dresser drawer:

> Lewis,
> I really miss seeing you! If I am to be the one to bear your first-born child, we are going to have to start seeing each other more often. Please call me.
>
> — Lana

I was furious. He'd had the *same* conversation with me just the night before over six Grizzards and dinner at Chops. So maybe his Men's Grill colleagues were right: After six Grizzards, he'd ask *any* woman to become the mother of Little Lewis.

And then there was the Grizzard Groupie Gang, as I called the entourage of jealous women vying — and dying — to be in the presence of the great LMG. There was always a little jealousy brewing any time he had more than one woman with him. It didn't matter what the subject was, there would always be a disagreement, and I think it gratified his ego too much for him to put a stop to it.

I was far from being the "jealous wife." As I've said, we tried honestly to respect each other's individual identities, and it wasn't until May 1991 that we even began to date each other exclusively.

In that first year, we just had a lot of fun, and partied like crazy. I was getting over my divorce, and he was still very much in the mode of being the wild man of Buckhead, so we drank many a night away.

Not that I became just another pal; he wined and dined and wooed me like no man I have ever known, and Lewis had a real way of making a woman feel not merely like a lady, but like a princess. I know his golfing buddies (not to mention his three former wives!) might find this a little difficult to comprehend, but in spite of being a one-hundred percent, red-blooded "man's man," Lewis had a terribly romantic side to him. That first year was like a fairy tale, and he was my prince who'd swept me off my feet.

Just as some of Lewis' most hard-core chauvinist friends didn't like the idea of any woman getting so much of his attention, a lot of my feminist friends (I am not a feminist myself) never could understand my relationship with that famous Neanderthal, Lewis Grizzard. They loathed him.

He didn't think women should be pro football players or Navy SEALs, he believed in treating women with special respect, and the sight of a pretty girl could always turn his head. But that did not make him a sexist — at least, not any more so than some men who claim to be ardently pro-feminist.

When I met Lewis, I was still married to my husband, even though we were separated and no longer had any kind of relationship. I made it clear that for the sake of Jordan, as well as my own convictions about marriage, I could not consider having an intimate relationship with a man until I was no longer married. Not only did Lewis respect that, but he had as much to do with upholding the standard as I did.

A part of his restraint had nothing to do with high morals, though. He added together the fact that my ex-husband was Italian, lived in south Florida, and owned a restaurant up north, and it could only mean one thing: Lewis had seen *The Godfather*, one of his all-time favorite movies, too many times, and he was convinced that my ex was a mafia don. Therefore, if he so much as touched me — "a mobster's wife"! — he'd end up being dumped in the Chattahoochee River wearing a pair of cement shoes.

Even long after my divorce, I'd wake up in the middle of the night and find Lewis' feet moving under the covers. He would be sweating from head to toe, and he'd wake up breathless. It turned out he was running in his sleep, dreaming that Dean was chasing him. Lewis did not exactly have a "put 'em up, buddy" type physique, nor did he have the instincts of a fighter. I think he believed he'd wake up one day with a horse's head (or in his case, Catfish's head) between the sheets.

But aside from that, he really had matured in his attitudes

toward sex, and he loved to remind me how lucky I was to have been graced with his presence at the ripe old age of forty-three. "Darlin'," he'd say, looking over his glasses at me and speaking in that voice as though to say *I'm gonna tell you the straight scoop,* "I've been living on my reputation for the past fifteen years." He said he was too old to run the streets, and there were too many diseases out there — how romantic he could be in his choice of words sometimes!

I do believe I had him during his best years. Lewis had mellowed with age, and not only had he mellowed, he had learned. He had the wisdom of someone who's made quite a few mistakes, and sometimes he would tell me about the phases of his learning curve. With that competitive gleam still very much in his eye, he said, "I used to think I had to win every fight — always get in the last word — and I usually won because I was a real son of a bitch." He wouldn't go to bed after an argument, he said, unless he had a victory under his belt, and he would always know he'd "won" if "my wife wasn't speaking to me and I was sleeping on the couch." Vodka was the great soother of all pain in those situations, he told me, but in the end he always had to apologize anyway.

So, he said, "I simply learned it was better to listen." Now, that's not to say that by the time I met up with him, Lewis Grizzard had reformed all his rascally ways and begun work on his Doctor of Divinity degree — that should be clear from some of the stories that follow. But still, he was older and wiser.

Another thing about Lewis that doesn't fit with the picture most feminists have of him on their dart boards is that Lewis always listened to me. We disagreed on a number of things, but except on a few issues, he always heard me out and respected my opinion. Never did he make me feel guilty or wrong or inferior for something I said, though there were a few times when he ignored observations he didn't want to hear. He was, after all, still Lewis Grizzard, and stubbornness and hardheadedness are not exclusively female traits.

Traditional though Lewis and I may have been, I was hardly a poor defenseless woman in the relationship. The first major turning point came for us after ten months of going out, and when it did, it was because I was tired of his behavior.

At first being with him had been a blast, but he spoiled me by getting me so used to going out and painting the town. I started noticing how I'd show up at his house (or vice versa) with plans to go out together, whereas he'd be expecting us to spend a quiet evening at home — which meant me cooking for him and the two of us watching movies. That was nice, but I'd usually spent much of the week alone, and I wanted to do something fun. When Lewis didn't, I figured he'd used up all his energy partying; by the time I showed up, all he wanted to do was kick up his feet and let Mama Dedra attend to all his needs — including some needs that mamas don't attend to.

What I didn't realize was that his schedule was exhausting him. Not only did he have his work (newspaper, books, speaking) and the travel involved, as well as the many forms of play that in Lewis' case were as important as work because they constituted part of his mystique (golf, football, drinking, gin rummy), but there was that ride back and forth down I-85, not to mention me and my demands. By the time the Opelika exit sign appeared, he was ready to do nothing but play the couch potato.

Still, I didn't really understand this, and one night in May 1991 when he showed up with his usual plans in mind, I told him I didn't want to see him anymore. If these were the terms he wanted for our relationship, I said, I couldn't put up with it any longer.

Well, Lewis did not exactly take this calmly. More crushed than angry — though he was plenty angry, too — he tried to talk me out of it. "Maybe it would be easier if you lived with me," he said.

That was a *NO* — absolutely not! I would not have my daughter growing up with a mommy and a live-in boyfriend.

I was ready to call it quits. But I knew I loved Lewis, and that I probably would regret saying good-bye. And then he had a great idea: "Would it make things better if I moved you to Atlanta?" he asked, making sure I understood that he meant me having a place of my own.

I thought about it, and said yes. Soon afterward, Bulldog Movers (!) showed up in a truck to transport Jordan and me and our entire household from the isolated college town of Auburn to a high-rise in the big city of Atlanta. Lewis and I, without exactly planning to, yet both knowing in the backs of our minds that this was what we'd wanted all along, had become "serious."

I had no idea how much lay ahead for me in the next few years with Lewis Grizzard. But as I now recollect all that went on between us, I know that it was an experience of a lifetime — an adventure like no other I've ever had.

We went through a lot of different phases during the forty-four months we shared, and we became different people together. We grew a lot, and for both of us (but especially for me), it took some adjusting.

For one thing, I'm not sure Lewis or Jordan knew quite what to make of each other for a while. At first he didn't pay much attention to her — just about his only comment regarding her would typically be, "Can you get a babysitter?" — and she had just about as much interest in him. All that would change with time, but until she and I moved to Atlanta, the two of them were like foreign objects to one another.

However, my cockatoo, Bubba, hit it off instantly with Lewis. I guess it was the name, not to mention the fact that Bubba liked to crow and strut his stuff just like a certain Southern male I knew.

Every morning around 7:00, he'd get up on the fence and squawk — Bubba, that is, not Lewis — and he sounded just like a baby screaming. Lewis, wanting to be kind to his newfound love, dared not say anything about her wailing child. But after about the third weekend when he woke up in Auburn to this noise, he bounded down the stairs one morning and — this was one of the few times I ever heard him yell — hollered at the top of his lungs in his best "Major Grizzard" voice, "In God's name, Dedra, give that child a pacifier! And if that doesn't work, tell her I'll buy her a new red BMW for her sixteenth birthday —

but just let me get some sleep!"

He was completely embarrassed when he found out it was Bubba making all the racket (while Jordan slept soundly), especially because he realized he could have put an end to it weeks before.

Lewis, in case it hasn't already been made clear, didn't know much about children.

And there were other aspects of ordinary everyday life about which he didn't know much. Money, for instance.

On our first date, in the course of telling me about his impending bankruptcy, he told me he'd gone to his accountant the week before and asked him, "If I wanted to put all my cash in a brown paper bag and hop the next Greyhound bus out of town, how big would the bag be?" He didn't understand about liquidity and all that; he just wanted to know his net worth in paper bag terms, and he got irritated because he couldn't get a straight answer.

Lewis said his goal was never to be wealthy, and that was partly true. Besides brown paper bags, he measured wealth in golf club memberships. To him, being rich meant belonging to elite clubs such as Melrose on Daufuskie Island, South Carolina, or Lake Nona in Orlando, Florida.

But he never spent much money on clothes, and to be so macho in other areas, he wasn't as much into cars as one might think. He owned a red Jaguar convertible for a while, but he traded it in for a red Chevy Blazer. The Jag just didn't fit his style, he said; he'd just as soon have had a truck as anything else.

Lewis did have simple tastes, though they weren't always inexpensive ones. "As long as I have a warm bed and you, darlin'," he loved to say, "that's all I need." I knew that wasn't completely true, but it sure was nice to hear.

Though questions about money sometimes weighed heavily on his mind, they weren't enough of a burden for him to so much as learn how to balance his checkbook. He was a writer, a man with a God-given talent for storytelling which he'd used to make a lot of money — but *managing* that money was his downfall.

Because of his inability with dollar signs, he relied on others — a lot of times on the wrong people. I think it's a situation a lot of celebrities run into: It's a full-time job maintaining the persona they've created for themselves, and they don't have time to keep their own books. Many a time Lewis told me that his creativity left him no mental energy for the mundane affairs of life; he was too busy being "the Southern humorist and columnist," which took a lot of work. There were only twenty-four hours in a day, and he had to trust his higher finances to someone else.

When it came to his smaller sums (the kind he would wad up and shove in his pocket), he had a very reliable manager: me. That is, he could always rely on me to make good use of the money he left in his pockets.

Behind every genius is a person (usually their spouse or "significant other") who acts as a stabilizing influence, and I was definitely that for Lewis. In his world, things just magically happened: Food appeared on the table, dust and grime never took hold in the house no matter how sloppy he got, and clean underwear spontaneously generated in his chest-of-drawers.

I didn't mind doing these things. I loved Lewis, he took good care of me, and there was plenty of give-and-take in the relationship. Besides, some jobs had special fringe benefits — like taking his dry cleaning to the laundry.

Lewis had a bad habit of never letting his paper money see the inside of his wallet. It just went straight into his front pocket, where he put it after paying the bartender or covering his greens fees. Most of the time he would be in a tremendous hurry, frantically finishing up a column and screaming for his limo driver or car keys, and if he was on his way out to the golf course he'd simply dump all his money onto the dresser. But usually the "wad," its size determined by how wild the night before had been, never got any further than his pants pocket.

This was always to my advantage, because money he missed in his pockets became mine. The first few times I took his clothes to the laundry and went through the pockets, only to find portraits of Mr. Jackson, Mr. Grant, and Mr. Franklin, I promptly returned it all to Lewis. But he'd always smile and say I should buy something nice for myself. I thought this was rather generous of him, especially since I couldn't even get my first husband to ante up for grocery money.

After several times when he returned the cash to me, I decided it was fair game. From then on, the dry cleaning became my No. 1 favorite labor of love. In a week, I could bring in anywhere from $60 to $150 this way (depending on how often Lewis went out), and as a result of that he started to become a little more attentive to his cash.

Still, he didn't ever get *all that* attentive. It was kind of a little game between us, and I think we amused the girls at the dry cleaners. They would wait for me to show up, and nearly every time they'd see me come away a big winner in the Lewis Grizzard Lottery.

Clothing eventually became a major subject between us, and I had an extremely minor effect on changing his dress habits. Considering that we're talking about a man who was as stubborn as a goat's tooth, even such a tiny thing as getting him to wear Armani jeans seemed like quite an accomplishment.

I don't think it's possible to bring Lewis to your mind's eye without seeing him in what amounted to his uniform: Gucci loafers with no socks, khaki pants, golf shirt or button-down Oxford, and navy blue blazer. It's a clean, classic look — essential "Buckhead Boy" fashion — and in the beginning I didn't mind it. But after a year of his showing up in the same outfit (only changing the golf shirt), I became annoyed.

"I've been dressing like this all my life," he said, taking a defensive tone. "What is it you don't like?"

I came right to the point. "It's not that I don't like it, but there's no variety. All that changes is the color of your golf shirt. How would you like it if every time you picked me up for a date, I had on the same dress? You'd get bored awfully quick."

This struck a nerve. The flamboyant Mr. Grizzard would have rather been called a Communist (or a Tech fan) than boring. "Bored?" he said. "*Bored?! BORED!?!*" Clearly he was taking this personally. "How did we go from changing my wardrobe to being bored?"

I had already managed to aggravate his hostility earlier that day by using a little hairspray on him and brushing his hair back while he was talking to me. Lewis was known to use his fingers for a comb.

We were on our way out to dinner, and it was clear that things were escalating dramatically to the verge of open warfare. But Lewis managed to solve the problem. After I began to suggest specific items of clothing, he handed over his gold American Express card, and off to Atlanta's Lenox Square mall I went the following day.

It was at least as much fun to shop for Lewis as for myself, especially because I had a sense of a mission about it. I knew exactly what I wanted the *new* Lewis Grizzard to look like. I love Italian clothes, and most of the new wardrobe came from Italy: two very nice pairs of slacks, a black long-sleeve cotton shirt and various other shirts, some gorgeous leather suspenders, a new belt, and a nice pair of loafers from Bally's.

I brought the clothes home, and he seemed happy that I had so quickly attended to his fashion needs. But as he looked through the endless packages and reviewed the credit card bills, he demanded to know how a pair of "britches" could cost $280.

"They're Italian," I responded, taking a *Silly Rabbit — Trix are for kids* tone.

He folded his arms and said, "Well, I'm Southern." As he watched me hanging up the clothes, finally he said, "You expect me to wear all this?"

"Yes, honey," I said. "You'll look smashing."

"Yeah, but the collars don't have buttons," he pointed out grudgingly. Yet he promised to wear the new clothes happily.

We went out for dinner the following weekend, and I decided it was time to the showcase the new Grizzard.

I coaxed him into the pants, and he complained that they itched. I told him this was only on account of their being fine Italian wool. "Feels like a croker sack to me," he grumbled.

But I managed to get him to keep them on, and I hooked him into the suspenders and eased him into the shirt. Now that shirt

— *that* was something new. If it were a math problem, and you'd been asked to find the set S of all Lewis Grizzard's shirts that had both (a) more than three buttons and (b) no button-down collar, you would have come up with zero. But now there was something in that set.

Our entire conversation that evening revolved around how uncomfortable he was. It was like that song, "My Head Hurts, My Feet Stink, and I Don't Love Jesus": His legs had welts on them from those "croker sacks," his feet had blisters from the new shoes, and by the time we left the restaurant, he was hobbling. A miserable evening was had by all — but he sure did look good!

That was not the end of my trying to dress him up in what I considered stylish clothing for the '90s man. One day I very nearly caused a permanent rupture in our relationship by showing up at the house with a new green and burnt orange silk shirt to go with his khakis. My reasoning was that if he got to keep half of his old attire, maybe he'd let me change the other half.

To Lewis, it sounded like I was trying to cross Al Pacino with Jerry Clower. He ordered me to take back the shirt and report directly to H. Stockton in Lenox Square mall — do not pass Go, do not collect $200 — and ask for Frazier Dworet, his personal clothier of long standing.

At first I refused to do that, but then I thought, *OK, maybe I am taking this to an extreme. Somebody's got to be reasonable in this family.* I went to H. Stockton and, without asking for Frazier, walked around. Seeing nothing I liked, I went to Mark Shale instead. There I purchased another ensemble and brought it back to Lewis with the claim that I'd gotten it from the sacred H. Stockton.

Somehow I'd misplaced the receipt, I said — the one with the H. Stockton logo.

This new outfit was more preppie than the silk shirt, and therefore much more to Lewis' liking, but he still wasn't all that crazy about it. "Are you sure you went to H. Stockton?" he kept asking me. I stuck to my story, but the clothes stayed in his closet anyway.

My only real clothing victory with Lewis was the pair of Armani jeans I bought him. He loved them so much he even wrote a column about them. The first time he put them on, we made an amazing discovery: Lewis Grizzard had a butt! Well, actually he didn't, but those clever Italians made him look as if he did. I loved him in his new jeans, and, surprisingly, so did Lewis. If he liked something, it was hard to keep him from wearing it every day, so I bought him three pairs. That way, at least he'd change them once in awhile.

This was about as close as we ever came to seeing eye-to-eye on the matter of his clothing. During the Christmas season of 1993, I even went to H. Stockton and had Frazier help me pick out a new navy blazer, a camel-hair jacket, and five or six pairs of "Buckhead" khaki pants. I also got Lewis some Gucci shoes (for wearing without socks, naturally), and went to the Ansley Golf Club pro shop, where I purchased a couple new paisley and striped golf shirts. I had given up trying to change his style.

On the day we got married in Emory Hospital, he wore his Armani jeans and his H. Stockton sweater. I believe it was symbolic. He didn't let me change his wardrobe like I might have, but at least I got to spruce it up a little, and both of us ended up more or less pleased with the result.

As minor as my victories were on the clothing front, they look like the Gulf War compared to the efforts I made to change his taste in food. That was more like my Vietnam.

In the middle period of our relationship, when we'd begun to settle down together but had not really gotten used to each other's likes and dislikes, I cooked for him a lot and thought for sure that I was giving him exactly what he wanted. Naturally I was concerned about his heart, and I made the mistake a lot of other people did.

A few times when we were out and he was eating fried chicken or something, somebody would come up to him and get very irate that he was treating his body that way after all he'd been through. What they didn't know, and what I didn't know at first, was that eating had nothing to do with his heart condition, which he'd had from birth.

Drinking and smoking, of course, were a different matter, but even they weren't the cause: as for food, the doctors wanted him to eat all he could, regardless of whether it had the "heart-smart" seal on it or not. (They would have preferred heart-smart, of course, but cholesterol was not Lewis' problem.) Lewis was one of those fortunate souls on whom fatty foods didn't seem to have any effect except pleasure at the taste buds: no cholesterol worries, no high blood pressure and, unlike me and three-quarters of the United States, no gaining weight. The only problem was getting him to eat.

One day I overheard him talking to one of his Men's Grill friends on the phone. He said I was cooking, and it was likely to be some kind of "ini" food (linguini, fettucine, zucchini, etc.), which he said he couldn't bear.

I was crushed, then furious. Up until then he'd acted as though he enjoyed my cooking, and I felt terribly insulted — especially because I realized they were all laughing about it at the Men's Grill.

After he got off the phone, I lit into him. How dare he talk about my cooking to his buddies!

Well, that was like kicking an anthill. He wheeled around on me and began to list off all his food preferences, none of which I'd been satisfying up to that point: "Listen here, honey: I want my chicken fried, not grilled; I want my steak with gravy; I want my green beans cooked, not steamed; and I want my tomatoes raw. If you can learn to do that, I'll love you forever, darlin.'" I thought my lecture was over, but then he had one more thing to say: "Oh yeah, I want hamburger meat in my spaghetti sauce, not any of that dern ground turkey."

"All right," I said. "But let me ask you this: Will you still love me if I get fat?"

His reply was a classic case of a man wanting the best of both worlds: "I didn't say *you* had to eat it."

The truth was, I had no interest in eating all that fatty food, because I was always much more health-conscious than Lewis. But I made up my mind that day that if he wanted good ol' home cookin' with the grease breaking out all over it like sweat, that was what he'd have. I called Mamaw Kyle in Tennessee and began a course of instruction in classic Southern cuisine.

I learned to cook the best country fried steak you ever put in your mouth. I began putting evaporated milk in my mashed potatoes, and I never stewed another tomato. Nor did Lewis ever again say another bad word about my cooking.

And I've since learned a valuable lesson: If there is no one there to enjoy your cooking, then why waste your time preparing it? I wish he would walk in my kitchen right now and say, as he often used to do, "How 'bout a pot roast for Sunday lunch, Mama?" I'd trade all the "ini" food in the world for that.

It was important to decide that I would not try to control Lewis' habits. I had tried to change Jordan's father, and gotten nothing but a lot of disappointment for it. In Lewis' case, I don't believe he would have lived any longer if I'd had a different attitude about it; it would have just seemed like longer to him.

For the same reason, I never said anything to Lewis about his smoking except an occasional, "Would you mind blowing that over there?" Dr. Randy Martin, on the other hand, couldn't be so tolerant, and when Lewis took me to meet him in early 1991, Lewis tried to get me to cover for him.

He had built up Dr. Martin to me for some time, and I was thrilled to meet the man who had saved my honey from the scalpel in 1990. Lewis loved Randy, and of course he was excited for me to meet him, but on the way to the doctor's office I noticed that Lewis looked a little nervous. It was just a routine visit — why should he worry?

As we got closer and closer to the place, he began to make all kinds of unusual offers. It was like one of those things you get sometimes in the junk mail: "You May Have Already Won a Prize!" In my case, I was being offered a choice of either a large sum of money, a vacation in Jamaica, or a shopping spree in New York.

Why, pray tell? That was the catch — I had to pick one of the above *before* he told me what I had to do to earn it.

But I wouldn't pick until he told me why. We were getting awfully close to Dr. Martin's office, and suddenly Lewis began to regress years. He was pleading with me like a six-year-old, literally on the verge of tears.

By now I was starting to get mad. What was he keeping from me? Did he have some kind of incurable (and/or contagious) disease he hadn't told me about?

In the midst of my anger, sitting in the waiting room with him, I decided to choose the vacation in Jamaica. Mad as I was at the moment, I still wanted the one that afforded maximum time with Lewis.

And then he explained what he wanted me to do: "See, darlin'," he said in a whisper, "I told Randy I quit smoking, and all I need you to do is to back me up on that."

He was actually afraid, and he wanted me to lie to an M.D. I said sure, no problem — knowing full well that Dr. Martin could smell the smoke on his hands, breath, and clothes a mile away. As it turned out, Dr. Martin never asked. (He never had to.) I didn't squeal, and we enjoyed a lovely tropical vacation in Jamaica. Lewis smoked the whole time.

In my first marriage I had tried to change a man. My happiness had depended on his willingness to become what I wanted him to be. Needless to say, that turned into a disaster. So with Lewis I never made that mistake. I accepted him exactly as he was, and let him do as he pleased. He was a grown man, and it was his body — his lungs, his life. I chose to accept him, and I never regretted a minute of it.

There were things about him that could have used changing, things that did begin to change in the last year we spent together, but I knew I couldn't *make* him do anything he didn't want to do. He had to come to grips with change on his own terms. And he did.

Strange as it may sound, initially I had the idea that I could actually persuade Lewis Grizzard to leave town with me on a fall weekend and go into the mountains, miles away from the nearest football stadium, to "look at the leaves."

In particular, I had this fantasy about us going to Vermont and staying at a bed-and-breakfast in the hills. I imagined lazy mornings lying in bed together, long breakfasts in front of a picture window, days of driving and hiking, nights in each other's arms before a roaring fire....

Lewis, on the other hand, pictured being stuck in a state that, as far as I know, has no football to speak of; where the nearest pro team is the Patriots (as if anyone would bother); and where you can't find any decent college or professional action any closer than Pennsylvania. And that's not to mention the fact that he'd be surrounded by Yankees.

For three years in a row, we compared good leaf-turning weekends to the weekends when the Dawgs would be too far away; then finally I realized it was hopeless. I was involved with a man for whom there was no such thing as an unimportant UGA game. And there was no such thing as a UGA game that was too far away. As everybody knows, when the sun is in the fall equinox in the northern hemisphere, the center of the universe is located somewhere about 33° 56′ N, 83° 24′ W — or more specifically, on the fifty-yard line at Sanford Stadium, Athens, Georgia, USA. And when there's an away game, well, the center of the universe just shifts.

Therefore, Lewis and I never did anything romantic on any weekend from Labor Day to Thanksgiving. He always took me with him to away games, of course, and it was a good thing, because otherwise I might never have seen him on a Saturday until December 1.

Anybody not familiar with the whole Lewis Grizzard mystique might think I'm kidding when I talk about the lengths he would go to not to be separated from his beloved Dawgs, but I assure you I'm not.

I remember the time Lewis had a speech scheduled in Mississippi the night before the 1990 Auburn-Georgia game. I was still living in Auburn, and he planned to breeze into town on the milk run, and together we'd rush to the game. But he was late getting in, and by the third phone call it became apparent to me that he wasn't going to make it.

I was philosophical about it. No big deal — it's just a game, right?

Yeah, right.

Lewis violently cussed his business manager for booking a speech so far out of town that it made it almost impossible to arrive on time. This was a violation of Rule No. 1: "Do not create any situation that gets between me and my football."

I said he should calm down. After all, there would be another game next weekend. But this was not enough for Lewis Grizzard. Next thing I knew, the phone rang. It was him. He was at the Opelika airport a few miles down the road with Mike Matthews, one of his Albany buddies. They'd caught a ride on a single-engine plane with a dead body being sent back to Alabama for burial later that day. Lewis had packed all the essentials: football tickets and a gallon of vodka. There was no limit to the lengths he'd go to see his precious Dawgs play.

Many times, Lewis' affection for the Bulldogs superseded any other commitment, and that could include a commitment to being civil.

When my mother and stepfather invited us to join them in Columbia, South Carolina, for the inaugural game of the University of South Carolina as an SEC school — it just so happened they were playing Georgia — it seemed like a good idea. We'd be sitting on the Gamecocks' side, and that was a new thing because, of course, we always sat with the Dawgs. I had no idea what we were getting ourselves into, but I was sure Lewis could behave himself.

It never dawned on me that he wouldn't. But seating Lewis with a rival team's fans was like inviting a dyed-in-the-wool rural Southern Baptist to a Sunday afternoon wine-and-cheese party with the Episcopalians in Buckhead. Of course, football is only a game and shouldn't be spoken of in terms of religion. Ha! To Lewis, it was a faith and a way of life — yours against mine.

After a hot day of golfing at Reynolds' Plantation, we all jumped in Lewis' limo to go tailgating before the game. The vodka flowed, and I started to sense that he was getting cranked up in a way that might spell danger later that evening.

First he questioned my mother's directions to the stadium, insinuating that she didn't know what she was talking about and that he, Lewis, was more qualified to get us there. Then he turned on me and demanded to know where I had gone in Buckhead the previous Saturday night.

He was on a roll.

We entered the stadium (which was where Mother said it was), and waded through a sea of Lewis' admirers, who all wanted to shake his hand and say hello. I could practically see his ego starting to swell, and I knew that with all the different forms of intoxication he was under, he was likely to get out of control. It was almost as though there was a full moon, and the animal in Lewis was about to come out.

I was sitting on the other side of him from Mom, noticing how he was getting livelier and livelier. I tried to interest my stepfather in sitting next to Lewis and engaging in a little male bonding, but he declined, and I knew then that I was on my own. Mom and I exchanged meaningful glances.

Meanwhile, Lewis began to wonder aloud why USC had even been admitted to the SEC in the first place. What kind of a name was "Gamecocks" anyway? How dare they join the sacred Southeastern Conference?

And how dare they be beating the Dawgs?

All this, of course, was being said in the middle of major Gamecock territory. His words turned some heads; I wanted to bury mine. I do believe it was the only time I ever regretted being seen with Lewis McDonald Grizzard, Jr.

I began to sweat profusely. This was the Lewis I'd heard about but never witnessed, the man who had his identity so tied up with the Bulldogs that if they lost, he took it more than personally. To him it was a way of life.

Thank God, Georgia came from behind in the third quarter and went on to win the game. The upswing in the Dawgs' fortunes had the effect of mellowing Lewis. At the same time Mother had managed to cool down the crowd of angry Cock fans around us by passing around a napkin on which she'd written an expression of concern for the intoxicated Southern columnist.

We got out of the stadium unscathed, and all returned to normal on a drowsy trip home in the limo. He apologized later for his behavior. Lewis was still a hero to me, but I vowed never to go to another game with him if we couldn't sit well within the safe confines of Dawg territory.

That was not the worst experience I ever had with Lewis and football. One time he was going to be in Nashville for some sort of function — he attended so many, I can't remember the particular event. I'm an east Tennessee girl myself (Cleveland, to be exact), and I thought this would be an ideal opportunity for him to meet my grandmother, or Mamaw Kyle as we called her.

I was proud to be with him, and Mamaw could not have been more excited that *the* Lewis Grizzard, Jr. — the Southern humorist, the man who loved Jordan so dearly and had taken care of Mamaw's baby (me) — was finally coming to her home. To see her working around the house getting ready, you would never have known that this woman was eighty-eight years old.

She got the house ready, even going so far as washing the walls. She waxed each piece of paneling, and each knickknack was in the perfect place. By the time she was done — and all this wasn't easy at her age — the whole house gleamed.

She fried chicken, and she stewed chicken. She had green beans cooking on the stove for hours, smelling good enough to lift you right out of your chair, and she had plump fresh red tomatoes from the garden, which made your mouth water just seeing them sliced. From the garden too came mint for the iced tea of her honored guest.

Lewis was traveling in the limo, and we planned that he would leave Nashville at 9:30 Friday night and arrive in Cleveland at midnight. Mamaw would have dinner waiting for him, and she'd made up his bed; after a nice big breakfast in the morning, he had a tee time at the Cleveland Country Club with my brother, whom he'd never met. After that, he'd go to meet my high school sweetheart at his bar in town. Then back to Mamaw's house for her first real opportunity to visit with the man she'd heard so much about from her precious grandchild. This was to be one of the highlights of her life.

At 11:59, we were thinking he'd roll in at any minute. At 12:30, we figured he was running a little late. By 1:00 a.m., I didn't know whether to worry or get mad. We went to bed at 2:00, and I had a hard time sleeping.

At 8:00 in the morning, Mamaw was up and shuffling around in the kitchen, expecting a sleepy Lewis Grizzard to emerge from the guest bedroom at any moment. But the bed was just like she'd made it up the day before.

With all kinds of images in my mind of Lewis' limousine skidding off the road on a sharp mountain curve, I started calling his place in Atlanta. I left messages, hoping he'd check them — hoping somehow there had been a misunderstanding and he'd simply gone home.

And then I finally caught up with him. There hadn't been any misunderstanding at all. Lewis had simply decided to blow off Mamaw and had ordered his limo driver to take him and Steve Enoch, his business manager and buddy, back to Athens for the game the next day. He'd checked his messages, all right, but had simply decided to ignore my frantic calls because he didn't want anybody interfering with a day of football.

I had made two mistakes. First of all, never let Lewis Grizzard go off with a buddy and expect him to show up as promised, even when it's to meet your eighty-eight-year-old grandma who's the most precious person in your life. Lewis doesn't know her, and given the choice, he's likely to pick a weekend with the Dawgs. Mistake No. 2: Never plan anything on a weekend when Georgia is playing, even if he claims it's not going to be a good game and he'd rather be with you and your grandma. He doesn't really mean it.

Well, it doesn't take a whole lot of imagination to figure out that I had some rather strong opinions to share with Mr. Grizzard, to say the least. And even after I got off the phone, nowhere near forgiving him yet, I still had to deal with my family and friends. I was humiliated, and Mamaw's image of Lewis was shot.

But she loved me enough that she tried to console me in my embarrassment. I felt like it should have been the other way around: After all, she was the one who'd gone to all that trouble, and her eighty-eight years old.

That Thanksgiving Lewis came to dinner at Mamaw's, and all was forgiven. I, of course, had let go of it a long time before — though I never had such a hard time forgiving him for anything. But there was something about him that made you want to let him off the hook, even for the worst of his offenses.

All's Forgiven: Lewis makes up with Mamaw Kyle

I also understood the difference in our perspectives on the event. I don't believe he understood how important it was, because he had no family left except for his aunts, no such thing as family reunions and get-togethers to attend. Family was a memory to him, something he'd almost had and lost as a child; to me it was everything.

Whether it was football or drinking or his love for the ladies, the things that made Lewis amusing could also be the most upsetting. He was known to take a drink or two — or three or four. His chosen drink was vodka, and because he liked the taste of it better than that of orange juice, he developed his own variation on a screwdriver, the Grizzard, so that he could determine the vodka-to-O.J. ratio himself. It wasn't a hard drink to make, yet from time to time a waiter or bartender would screw it up — and woe unto them when they did, for they soon would inherit the wrath of Lewis.

Generally, when Lewis Grizzard took a drink a good time was had by all. He had more wit and charm than any man I have ever known, and he knew better than anyone how to enjoy himself and bring laughter to those around him. With Lewis in the room, there would always be glasses hoisted, and the stories would flow: side-splitting and sometimes misty-eyed tales of old loves and ones that got away, skirts chased and hearts broken.

Many times when he was heavy into the vodka, I learned a lot more than I wanted to. The unfortunate part about this was that we were usually with friends, and generally everyone was hearing the new story for the first time. He'd let something slip, I'd put two and two together, and I'd be steaming for the rest of the night until I could get him alone. But by the time we arrived home, he would either be too drunk, or would pretend to be too drunk, for an argument.

Then I would confront him the next day, and he would deny ever telling the story in the first place, or else he'd blame it on "group entertainment." He felt it was his duty to entertain his friends, he'd say.

Or else he'd just claim he didn't remember. Now that was a neat alibi, I thought. How could you stand accused of something you don't even remember doing? There was nothing to argue.

I'd ask him, "So where'd you go last night with your buddies?"

"Well, we started out at Longhorn," he'd say, "and then, uh, I know we went somewhere else, but I can't remember where." Then I'd point out the $1,600 receipt from the Cheetah on his dresser. (This is a strip club in Atlanta, and I'm not exaggerating about the amount.) He'd squint at it and say, "I don't know how I got that," or, better yet, "It was a donation to the American Heart Association."

Uh-huh, I'd say. I'll bet those girls had some nice hearts.

Other times he'd come in from a night out and in his pockets would be three or four napkins bearing phone numbers written in various flowery handwriting styles with sweet little messages like, "It was nice talking to you tonight — please call me." I would go into my overdrive jealousy mode and hold out the wad of napkins to him. His reply? "I don't remember." Sometimes he'd say something like, "Aw, that was just some ol' girl I met last night — she was uglier'n a bowling shoe." Then I *knew* she was beautiful.

Maybe he felt like he didn't owe me an explanation. After our first year together, I got used to his way of playing possum and realized it was his way of fighting — or rather, not fighting —

and I simply began throwing away the napkins whenever I'd find them. I knew he wouldn't have the gall to ask me for them if they were missing.

There was a little-boy quality to Lewis that made it hard to stay mad at him. I could *get* mad at him without any problem — he gave me plenty of help in that area — but once we'd made up, there was no desire to hold a grudge.

A couple times, he'd been known to get other people angry, people in the bread-and-butter department that he would have been wise not to irritate. By and large he had a remarkable work ethic, instilled by his mother, but on these two occasions he acted like a college freshman during Rush Week.

The first time, we had flown to Washington for an appearance on "Larry King Live." Lewis hated to fly, and he got heavily into the cocktails on the flight, by which I don't mean just one or two drinks: I mean half a dozen Grizzards in the lounge at Hartsfield, and another dozen or so on the plane. Years later, after he died, people writing reminiscences often referred to Lewis' supporters and detractors, and how he'd managed to anger some groups severely. Usually that meant militant gays, for some of his comments on their lifestyle; but there was another group who hated him even more than ACT UP did, and that was Delta stewardesses.

Lewis loved to joke about how he hated flying, quoting the Bible verse, "Lo, I am with you always," as proof that God didn't want us up in the air — "High, you're on your own." But, of course, he had to fly in order to crisscross the country the way he did, so his solution was to apply a major dose of local anesthetic. More than once, he actually drank up all the vodka on the plane, and a couple times he was nearly grounded before take-off because of being "too drunk to fly." (They might have had a point if someone had expected him to drive that sucker.) At any rate, though I don't remember any specific incident on that flight, I'm sure that by the time we got to Washington National Airport the stewardesses were saying, "Thank you, and have a nice stay in Washington," through gritted teeth.

We arrived at the Waverly Hotel around 4:00 p.m. and I,

knowing we had to be at the show by 10:00, became worried. I ordered coffee, and he ordered Dom. He insisted on taking me to a little boutique down the street, where he bought me some beautiful lingerie. That was all good and well, but I coaxed him back to the room, hoping I could make him take a nap. I ordered more coffee (which doesn't exactly go with napping, but also doesn't go with being drunk) and he ordered Tattinger.

I was losing the battle, and I had to think fast. I was terrified to have to call Steve Enoch in Atlanta and tell him Lewis was intoxicated; instead, I called the show and talked to the director. Lewis wasn't feeling well, I said. The director didn't want to hear it: It was much too late to get a replacement, he told me. "We'll just put on extra make-up," he said, and I thought, *You'll need a lot more than make-up.*

After I got off the phone, I began to get angry at Lewis. I screamed at him and started throwing things. He actually became scared at this "volatile" behavior, as he called it. He gave up, lay down, went to sleep, woke up, ordered coffee, and performed beautifully on the show. I, on the other hand, was exhausted. I should have thrown the fit hours earlier.

Then there was Las Vegas. Lewis was to be the opening act for Randy Travis at Bally's, his Vegas debut. He loved seeing his name on the marquee: It seemed to say that Lewis Grizzard of Moreland, Georgia, had finally hit the big time. When we drove by it, he smiled; later on he peered out at it from our bedroom window and said wistfully, "I wish Mama was here to see this." He looked like a little boy when he said that.

His boyhood friend, Dudley Stamps, had shown up for opening night along with Danny Thompson, another of the famous Newnan boys. Now, from the stories Lewis has penned about Dudley and the others, it should be clear what kind of danger it posed for them to be loose together in Las Vegas, especially when Lewis was due to open for Randy that night.

We all went to the bar for one cocktail before Lewis was to go up to our room for a nap. One turned into two, and two into ten. Stories flowed. I was having a ball — we all were — but then Steve Enoch, Lewis' manager, started to get a look of concern.

Here it was an hour till showtime — opening night, the big time, Randy Travis, Las Vegas — and Lewis Grizzard was knee-walking drunk. We finally got him up to the room, and he took a short nap, then we had him soak up some of that alcohol with dinner and tons of coffee.

Still, it was the worst performance I ever saw him give. I felt pretty sick myself from too much vodka, but I didn't have to perform.

Needless to say, Randy Travis was not a happy camper. Yet Lewis made it through the performance, and in spite of that weak start, he did great for the rest of his run on the Las Vegas stage.

Somehow he would always steer clear of trouble. He'd go right to the edge but pull back before he went too far. As flamboyant as he might have been on the outside, Lewis didn't much care to go to the principal's office and have his permanent record put in front of him.

Still, there remained a restlessness inside of him. Only in the latter part of our time together —after we'd adjusted to each other's ways and he learned he could trust me no matter what — did Lewis let me see his most secret fears and vulnerabilities.

In some ways, Lewis had the heart of the proverbial clown who cried in the alley. The nonstop party helped him to forget about things that hurt, and kept him from his pain. All this would build to a crescendo with his third heart surgery, and after that — in that extra year God gave me with Lewis — the layers were peeled back.

That final fling of his, the one leading up to his surgery in March 1993, lasted three whole months. He knew that afterward he'd have to give up the vodka: aside from the obvious reasons, as Randy Martin pointed out in a discussion that was more brother-to-brother than doctor-to-patient, he would be taking daily doses of the blood-thinner Coumadin, and it wasn't a good idea to mix hard liquor with that.

Lewis had always enjoyed his vodka, but in those final months of partying, he drank out of fear. I wondered if all the alcohol in his system would affect his surgery, and I think

Randy was worried too.

In the year that followed, I would be enormously impressed with the way Lewis put aside the vodka. He occasionally had a glass or two of red wine or a Heineken when we were out to dinner, but he never — not once — ever had another Grizzard. I considered this an amazing feat, one I honestly didn't think could be done.

I believe I am the only one who knew the anguish Lewis really went through in that last year. His struggle to live was immense, and he only hinted from time to time (as in the story about his finger in *I Took a Lickin'*) at the pain. It was like nothing I'd ever experienced, either within myself or with another person, and Lewis fought a courageous battle every step of the way.

With those thirty-one million extra seconds of life that he got, Lewis showed me — and everyone else who knew and loved him — what he was made of. Into his every waking moment he poured his strength and courage, the will to win which compelled him to write that great column, sink that twenty-foot putt, or for the first time in his life make that special relationship work.

There were a lot of bumps along the way for him. He tried his best to give up the cigarettes, and did for a while. But he had to keep at least one vice, and laying aside the Marlboros was more than he could handle. After all, they'd already taken not only his Stoli, but also his anti-depressant medicine.

Lewis had a hard time sleeping, and if he didn't take six Imipramine tables every night, he would toss and turn until dawn. Therefore it became my job to make sure he had his pills. (As in all areas of responsibility except his writing, Lewis relied on others to take care of him. This was, after all, a man who couldn't keep track of his own house key.)

At any one time, I must have had twenty six-pill stashes: in my purse, in the dash of the limo, under the doormat, and in each of Lewis' "most-likely-to-be-worn" blue blazers.

I had learned the hard way that I didn't want to be around Lewis when he hadn't had his Imipramine the night before. This was always judged to be my fault, not his, though a couple times he took it out on James Shannon, his chauffeur. On mornings like that, the monster in Lewis came out. It was an experience worth missing. I would have paid large amounts of money to vanish at those times.

There seems to be something about creative people, and Lewis was nothing if not creative. As history has shown, whether musician or painter or writer, theirs is a lonely and often troubled life. Even when someone like this takes on the apparent traits of an extrovert (as Lewis certainly did), if you go a little beneath the surface you'll almost always find that the bubbly outer self is floating on a deep pool of melancholy.

When not in the limelight, Lewis would often become depressed and quiet, and underneath the "plain ol' Georgia boy" persona was a complex and perplexing personality. Without his pills to help him sleep, depression weighed him down. I think it all went back to the disappointments of childhood, which he spoke of often.

I loved the stories Lewis told about his father, "the Major," more than just about any other of his many tales. Quite a few of these he immortalized in my favorite of his books, *My Daddy Was a Pistol and I'm a Son of a Gun*, but to sit down and talk about his daddy most often sent Lewis crying into his beer — or in his case, into his vodka.

Lewis dealt with what we would now call, in our psychologically correct language, "abandonment issues." The loss of his father to alcohol and his father's aimless wandering after the war haunted Lewis on a daily basis. That image, of the hard-drinking Major going from town to town, winning over church congregations and public school faculties before fleecing them of their money — it was classic American literary stuff, like the story of the King bamboozling a revival group in *Huckleberry Finn* or something straight out of Faulkner. Surely things like that in his background accounted for a part of Lewis' power as a spinner of tales, but the pains themselves were real. Lewis had learned to live with disappointment, and he talked many times about the image of a little boy with his nose pressed up against the glass waiting for Daddy — the daddy who never showed up.

Several times I tried to set an appointment for him with a psychologist, but never to any avail. He'd usually say something like this: "Dedra, there are two kinds of people in this world: Those who cope, and those who don't. I cope, and crying and talking to you about my daddy is my idea of therapy. Besides, you don't cost $200 an hour, and you don't hold me hostage either!" That was that: Shut up and listen, honey.

I was glad to be the one with whom he chose to share all those problems. As he returned to his childhood roots in his mind, reliving things that had happened to him thirty-five or forty years before, it drew me closer to him. I would listen intently, and on many occasions I cried with him. I missed my daddy too, and I had my own issues of abandonment to deal with, so I could relate to him without pretending.

As Lewis and I had gotten to know each other over the years and delved deeper into each other's souls, there had been many times of crying and talking. (But there was always more laughter than tears, even at the very end.) This intimacy between us, this baring of our innermost thoughts, accelerated after his third surgery. It was then that his physical condition forced him to sit still and, instead of doing anything, to just *be*.

We spent many a day on his couch, and when he got too angry at the freaks on daytime TV, we'd watch movies together, hundreds of them: new, classic, sleeper.... I think I rented nearly every one made.

In the evenings we'd sit out front watching the rollerbladers go by. One time he and James watched two gay men "get it on" in broad daylight in front of his house. (They were in a car, and that's about all the description I'm willing to provide.) Lewis had, of course, earned a lot of enemies among the gay population with his columns concerning their lifestyle, and there's no doubt those two showed up and put on their little act for spite. It did made a good story, and added some excitement around the Grizzard house during this lull in the life of the great storyteller.

More often Lewis would sit on his front porch and rock, looking back over his memories of boyhood, of his mama, of

Grandma Willie. Every once in a while he'd say, to someone who'd been with him longer than I (and who offered the advantage of not saying anything back), "Lordy, Lordy, Catfish, where have the years gone?" Then he would become tickled at himself. He knew he was beginning to sound more and more like someone's grandfather.

In those twilight days, he drew closer and closer to the people who had mattered most. Lewis had a problem with attracting hangers-on, people constantly coming around with lines like, "Lewis, I've run into some real bad luck, but if you could just spot me ten" — and that usually meant ten thousand — "I'd be back on my feet." He was like *Thidwick the Big-Hearted Moose* in the Dr. Seuss book, too kind to give any of these parasites the boot until the point when, like Thidwick, he could no longer carry them.

In his last year, he associated only with people I'd call "his equals," those who were friends for friendship's sake, and not out of any ulterior motive. More and more often, he talked of his old Moreland/Newnan friends, and on his birthday in 1993 (his last, as it turned out), I brought many of them together for a surprise party.

I had planned it at our favorite Italian restaurant, Nino's, where we had spent many a quiet evening talking and reminiscing. Dudley and Danny would be there, along with Camilla, and Lou Williams ("the red-headed cheerleader"), among others. Lewis always had a crush on Lou, even in his last years; she represented his youth to him.

They were all there, all waiting, but for a while on that October 20 it didn't look as though Lewis would be there. He *did not* want to go out that night, and I had to persuade him. First I attempted to give him a shower. Now, it was sometimes hard to get him under the water nozzle on a good day, let alone any time when he felt a little stubborn, like now. He wouldn't budge, so I tried to sweet-talk him into a romantic evening. No luck.

I finally resorted to throwing a fit, and I demanded we go out for his birthday. When all else failed, this was the way to get Lewis off dead center, because he didn't like to fight.

Reluctantly he went upstairs (without showering), and proceeded to get ready for what he thought was a quiet dinner with me. The way he moved, you'd have thought I was leading him off to the gallows.

Later that night, when we entered the restaurant and the Moreland clan appeared, his eyes misted over. He looked at me and thanked me. It was the first time in his life he'd ever been truly surprised, he said. And I believed him. I know in my heart this was one of the best nights he spent in 1993: an evening to remember, full of laughter and joy, with the people he loved — and the people who loved him.

As that last year went on, I could see Lewis slipping into another phase of his life. He worried about Jordan and how the world would be when she came of age. He wondered if he would be well enough to scare off the boys with ponytails and earrings who came to court her. He wanted to move her to the country before she realized that there existed such a place as a mall to hang out in, and before she had bunches of "hoodlums" for friends.

The world was evolving, turning into a place he didn't understand. Everything was changing, and Lewis didn't like change — yet he was changing too.

I had always loved the kind of man he was, and I loved even more the man he was becoming. As I've said, I was not then, nor will I ever be, a feminist. I don't mind staying home and taking care of my family, and I admired the chivalry of Southern gentlemen, a tradition Lewis personified. I liked the way he opened my door for me and treated me like a lady, how he always helped me out of the car and stood up whenever I returned to the table from the ladies' room. I respected his way of doing things, and the centuries of history behind it.

That had always been Lewis, and yet as the shadows began to fall on his life, he went far beyond the gallant beau to become something nobody (not even I) expected him to be: a family man.

It had often puzzled me that Lewis Grizzard, who rode around with a bumper sticker that said *Honk If You Were Married to Me*, never managed to sire any young 'uns, as he liked to say. Still, I wasn't complaining: Having a child myself made me thankful I didn't have to contend on a daily basis with an ex-wife/mommy.

"It takes a lot of responsibility to raise a child," he told me. "I've never felt stable enough for that." He was too busy being the child himself. But as time went on, we began to talk seriously about having — as he called our imagined offspring — a "little Lewis."

I asked him why he was so sure it would be a little Lewis and not a little Dedra, whereupon he would remind me about the kings of old who beheaded the queens who didn't bear male children. I would always retort that it was the male who determined the sex of the baby. He had a hard time getting around that one.

Although it was not to be, Lewis wanted very badly for us to have a child, especially after his brush with death made him aware of how much he wanted a legacy. Besides that, he'd made a promise to Jordan that he'd give her a little brother, and a promise to Jordan was a serious thing.

Time had built a bond between those two, the little girl whose father had gone away and the man without a child of his own. Because of the scars that ran deep within him, he was able to show me the importance of a child's love for her father. That may well be the most important lesson Lewis taught me in our relationship, and it definitely was the one I found most difficult to learn. His deep, undying love and respect for his father, in spite of everything the Major put him through, made it hard not to listen to his advice.

Jordan's father was a lot like Major Grizzard. He made plenty of promises, and in four short years Lewis saw Dean keep precious few of the ones he made to his little girl. Every time he would tell Jordan he was going to take her to Disney World, or on a vacation in Florida swimming with the dolphins, or whatever it happened to be at the time, she would always become ecstatic; but Lewis and I usually knew that as good as it sounded and as certain as it seemed that *this* time he wouldn't let her down, his promises would never come to be.

It was painful to watch her in all her excitement, anticipating the arrival of her father and knowing he wouldn't show. Then an hour or two or three after the time he was supposed to arrive, the phone would ring and it would be Dean with some lame story that would make me want to reach through the receiver and wring his neck.

She'd cry, because little children usually know the truth in spite of whatever adults may tell them, and we would pick up the pieces of her shattered little heart time after time. Lewis never complained about this; instead, he became Jordan's biggest ally when it came to her father. He'd even take up for the man, and where Dean's excuses left off, Lewis' excuses *for Dean* would begin. He could see how much Jordan loved her daddy, and he'd reassure her that her daddy loved her. He'd buy us plane tickets and encourage us to go visit her father. On birthdays and Father's Day, when I would have sent nothing at all, he'd make me send cards from Jordan and me.

As good as it sounded, none of this was an act on Lewis' part. He never tried to take Dean's place in any way, and any chance he had to put himself ahead of Dean in Jordan's eyes, he would always be pointing out to her how great her father was.

In the short run, it might have been easier for me if he'd taken my side in all this, because of course my view of Jordan's father and Jordan's view of her father were not exactly the same. But every time I'd get irate at Dean — or at Lewis for taking up for Dean — he would calm me down and say, "Dedra, whatever else he may have done, he is her father, and there's nothing you can to do to break that bond."

The funny thing was

Family Man: Lewis, Dedra and Jordan's first garden

that in the course of this Lewis became a father to Jordan, who never could quite rely on her own daddy, and Jordan became like a daughter to Lewis, who never had any children of his own. He loved us both, but she really stole his heart. It was she who put a twinkle in his eyes when she'd wake him up in the morning, and every time she crawled in his lap and called him "Daddy" anyone present could feel the strong bond of love between the two of them.

Some of my fondest memories of Lewis now are when I picture him trying to type a column with Jordan in his lap. I think she eventually broke every typewriter he had, and I know for sure that she broke his concentration every single morning.

And it was Jordan, not me, that he asked to marry him. It was February 1993, and we were on our regular winter retreat to Orlando. (Naturally, Lewis had to go wherever the golf was, like those two surfers in *The Endless Summer* who traveled the world in pursuit of "the perfect wave.")

For close to a year before that time, he'd been going around introducing me as his fiancée. I loved hearing that title applied to me by him, but there was nothing formal about it: no getting down on bended knee and popping the question, no date set for a wedding, no ring.

One evening we were out to dinner with friends, and we happened to be joined by one extremely handsome man. Not only that, he also just happened to be Italian, and this — along with the fact that he took a liking to me — got Lewis' attention. When Lewis first met me, he thought I was Italian. (I'm not — there weren't too many immigrants from the Old Country who settled in east Tennessee.) But I forever more had a reputation with Lewis for liking things Italian — clothes, food, ex-husband. And now there was this particular Italian at our table. We started to flirt, and I could tell Lewis was getting bothered. The two of us had a little game of making each other jealous, but clearly this situation was getting to him. In the middle of the conversation he switched from calling me Dedra, and started throwing in the phrase "my fiancée" every chance he got.

The gentleman, however, was too cool for that. He looked at

Lewis with a raised eyebrow, glanced down at my hand, and said, "Ah, but she doesn't wear your ring?"

Clearly this steamed Lewis, but he didn't do anything about it for several days. Then on February 14, he called a conference of his running buddies at the country club, and they all loaded up for a Valentine's Day party.

Now, what business a bunch of straight guys had going out together on Valentine's Day, I didn't know. All I knew was that we had plans for that evening, and he was late getting home.

Hours passed. I was furious. Finally Lewis called, sounding half-intoxicated, and said he'd be home shortly. He claimed he was out buying me a Valentine's Day surprise, but I could easily picture him huddled over a pay phone in the men's locker room, a gridlocked gin game going on behind him. I recognized this behavior: He was "buying time."

It was 9:00 by now. I practically had steam coming out of my ears. I thought, *This better be more than chocolates and a silk nightie.*

By the time Lewis arrived, I had sent the babysitter home and was past the point of screaming at him. He had a package under his arm, and he asked Jordan to come sit with him. She said, "Lewis, you're in the doghouse. Mommy's real mad."

"Not for long, darlin'," he said. He took her little hand and knelt down so he could look into her eyes. His face was glowing.

All of a sudden I knew what was happening, and all my anger subsided in one big rush of emotion that made my heart beat faster and brought tears welling to my eyes.

"I love you, Jordan," he said, "and you know I love your mama." He went on to pledge his allegiance to us both, and promised to be the best "stepdaddy" a child could ever have. At that point Jordan interrupted him, saying she didn't like the word "step-" because it reminded her of the mean stepmother in *Cinderella*. Therefore, they agreed that Lewis would become her "second daddy."

With that out of the way, the crying began. I'd already gotten a head start, but then Lewis joined in and so did Jordan. Then he opened one of the boxes he was carrying in his little

Valentine's bag, took out a ring, and placed it on her finger.

She looked up at me and said, "Mommy, I think he wants to marry us."

We planned the wedding for May and we would have gotten married then, but after his heart surgery it seemed better to wait a while.

Soon it was Valentine's Day again — our last. He took me out to an elegant restaurant, and when I jokingly demanded my present, he said quite seriously, "Darlin', my being here is your present." Then he gave me the dearest card I've received:

Dear Dedra,

You have done for me what I thought nobody could — made me realize that *one* is a lonely number and *three* is a perfect one. (Maybe even four.) All my love for the one who has stood by and waited through an awful year. The ones to come *will* be better!

All my love,

Lewis

And soon, as the calendar kept moving through our last year, it was time for the annual refuge in Orlando. Lewis had by now recovered enough from the 1993 surgery that he could go back to his beloved golf, and was I ever glad. Every winter we had spent together in Orlando had been a wonderful refuge for both of us, but the proximity to Disney World and Sea World made it an even bigger deal to Jordan. She was growing up, though, and in the fall of '93 she entered kindergarten. Therefore, when winter rolled around, we could plan to be there for only part of the time.

Well, when I say that our time in Orlando was a bigger deal to Jordan, I'm of course not taking into account the fact that Lewis Grizzard, Jr., could be more like a child than any child. "What will I do without you?" he asked me over and over again. "How will I live? What will I eat?"

Jordan seemed downright self-sufficient by comparison. Lewis had a gift for making you feel sorry for him, and for days

250

beforehand the caretaker in me worried that he wouldn't be all right. I knew for sure he wasn't going to get a good night's rest; ever since they'd taken him off his Imipramine, he couldn't sleep unless I were beside him.

But what was I to do? Jordan had to go to kindergarten. "It's the law, honey," I told him.

During this time, Lewis called me every day in Atlanta and preached to me about the benefits of home-schooling for Jordan. It was a must, he said, what with all the crime and drugs and irreverence children were being taught behind the doors of the public schools. I didn't pay too much attention to this new crusade; I knew he was just lonely and needed me.

But when he sent Jordan and me tickets to Orlando, I decided that a couple days' worth of hooky couldn't be all that harmful to a little girl's future. After all, it *was* kindergarten, and she could learn more from Mickey Mouse — or from a famous writer — than she could back in finger painting class with the other kids.

Jordan and I arrived in the middle of a thundershower, and Lewis (who had promised sunshine if his two favorite ladies came to central Florida) was quite upset.

"Don't even unpack your suitcase," he said in a half-gruff, half-sweet voice when we got to the house. "Let's just throw your and Jordan's things into the car — I promised you sunshine, and we're gonna go get some."

I couldn't believe my ears. Lewis Grizzard was actually being spontaneous for the first time in a year. I began to get nervous.

I told James, the chauffeur, to get ready for a trip, but Lewis said no, it would just be the three of us. "Daddy's driving," he announced, "and we're going south."

I wanted to say, "Lewis, honey, don't tell me you've been disobeying Randy and drinking!"

This was a man who never drove anywhere, not even to the store to buy a pack of cigarettes. Actually, he did drive from his house to the golf course back home, but that was practically across the street — and that was for something even more important than cigarettes. Most other times, Lewis opted to let someone else drive him, whether it be in a boat, a plane, or a limo. He might get white knuckles, especially in the air, but it was still a better risk than waking up to headlines reading, "Lewis Grizzard, Famous Southern Columnist, Jailed For DUI."

But there we were, packing up the car, and when we were done Lewis climbed into the driver's seat. "Everybody buckle up," he said, looking over his glasses in the rearview mirror at Jordan, who did as she was told. I marveled. I could have been sitting next to Ozzie Nelson or Ward Cleaver.

Off we went to Daytona Beach, Lewis and Jordan singing, "This old man, he played one / He played knickknack on his thumb." We stopped and ate donuts until we were sick, then we went to a seafood restaurant and watched the rain fall on the ocean.

Wow, I thought. *I should have made him spend a month alone years ago.* This was great! I was falling in love with him all over again. Hope began to arise in me as I felt our lives returning to normal once more.

For the fourth time in our relationship, during that week in Daytona (actually, it was Ormond Beach), we planned our wedding.

Since there hadn't been much conventionality about our relationship, we didn't want to get married in the conventional style either. First we discussed Mamaw Kyle's backyard as a possible venue. It was to be just a small affair, which in my mind meant ten people on the list, but Lewis couldn't get his below sixty. I didn't figure Mamaw could handle that kind of crowd, not at ninety years old.

Besides, Lewis wanted to have a golf tournament at Cleveland Country Club on the *day* of our wedding, an idea which I quickly vetoed. We also talked about getting married at Great Waters/Reynolds Plantation, where he had a second home. Again, Lewis wanted to turn it into a golf tournament and get married on the eighteenth green; again I said no.

Then I remembered that two of our friends had gotten married in a bar, and I said why not get married at the place we met? At the very place where we first laid eyes on one another, where the first words passed between us — there we would exchange our vows. So after checking available weekends in April with Don Harp, my pastor at Peachtree Road Methodist, I called the manager of Chops to arrange to rent the place. We made a guest list, and of course Jordan would be the flower girl.

As for the honeymoon, we would ask Randy Martin and his wife to join us in Italy. Lewis wanted to give something back to Randy for all his special attention, and that way he would also have his doctor with him in case of emergency. Italy wasn't the U.S.S.R., but after his awful toothache experience in Moscow almost ten years before, he wasn't about to risk getting ill in a foreign country.

We had come a long way since the times when Lewis would whisk me away from my house in Auburn and expect me to find a babysitter for Jordan while he and I painted the town. On this trip, we mostly stayed at home, and I cooked dinner while Lewis taught Jordan how to play gin rummy.

On the fourth time she beat him. "I have it," she said.

"Have what?" Lewis asked her, even though he knew.

"You know, Lewis," she said. "Jomeo rose." She couldn't quite pronounce it.

"Jomeo rose? You mean gin rummy."

She gave him her cards, and Lewis cheered. Jordan did indeed have "jomeo rose," and Lewis had a card-player in the family. It may well have been his proudest moment with her. They did a "high-nothing" and he reshuffled the deck.

After far too short a time, I had to get back to Atlanta so Jordan wouldn't miss too much school. It had been a perfect little vacation, and I couldn't remember when the three of us had spent such wonderful hours together.

At the time I had no idea that this would also be our last trip. One night when we were out in a restaurant in Daytona, Lewis held Jordan in his arms and rocked her to sleep. Several onlookers stopped to ask if she were his granddaughter.

As I relive it all now, I see how frail he looked, even though I didn't realize it at the time. I remember, too, that his right foot was terribly swollen. He told me he thought he had been bitten by a spider, and I prayed that what he said was true; still, looking at his legs, I feared the worst. I wonder now if he somehow knew the end might be drawing near.

Jordan and I flew back to Atlanta on Tuesday. At about 8:00 p.m. on Friday, February 25, 1994, I was sitting at my kitchen table with a friend when the phone rang. It was Ernie Cain, Lewis' best friend.   He was calling from the emergency room of Florida Regional Hospital, he said. That day, as though making up for all the time lost in his year of recovery, Lewis had played twenty-seven holes of golf. It had quite literally "put him to bed."

I'll never forget the panic in Ernie's voice. He told me to come quickly: "It's serious."

After we hung up, I tried immediately to dial up Lewis in the emergency room, but they wouldn't let anyone through except a member of the family. I tried to explain to the orderly that I was his fiancée, but that wasn't enough.

I kept calling throughout the night. He had thrown a blood clot to his kidneys, and doctors had him stabilized and under observation in the ICU.

Oh God, I prayed. *Is this it? Please don't let him die.*

After arranging to leave Jordan with my sister, I took the 6:00 a.m. flight out the next morning.

When I got to the ICU at Florida Regional, I found Lewis in a tremendous amount of pain. "I thought you'd never get here," he said, and he began to cry. I held him and rubbed his back for as long as the nurse would let me, but we were not at Emory and this was not home. It wasn't long before she made me leave.

Wherever Lewis went, even in the worst of times, there was always laughter, and I know this would have made it into a column had things gone differently: The hospital was run by Mormons, and you couldn't get a Coke or coffee because of the caffeine, but they gave him his own *morphine* pump with which he could dose himself every six minutes for pain.

As everyone knows, the presence of other people brought out the born entertainer in Lewis, and that didn't go away when death began to knock on his door. Even flat on his back, he was on his toes, and his humor kept all his friends and most of the doctors in stitches. It calmed our — and his — fears.

I wanted to get him home, to Emory, where people knew him and had treated him before. I got on the phone and started making calls; through the grapevine, I got the message that Jim Kennedy, CEO of Cox Enterprises, which owns the *Journal-Constitution*, had offered the use of his private plane.

So the arrangements were made, and on Thursday, March 3, we rode together in an ambulance from Florida Regional to the small airport in Orlando. I would give anything for a photograph of Lewis on that ride: strapped in on the stretcher fully clothed, enjoying a much-anticipated Coca-Cola with the aid of a straw, and grinning from ear to ear. He looked like a commercial — if he'd had a Braves cap on, they could have called it "Three Atlanta Favorites."

Lewis looked good, and he even remarked that he expected to be back on the golf course by Saturday, he felt so well. I believed it — he honestly sounded like he would be.

He was back home, and I was glad of that for several reasons, not least because of Jordan. In the past year of Lewis' recovery, she'd suffered immensely because of being switched between relatives and babysitters. During that time I seemed to always feel guilty, because if I was paying attention to one of the two most important people in my life, usually it was at the expense of the other.

Gabby, the nurse from Emory, and a doctor had flown down and come back up with us. When we got to Atlanta, Lewis was registered in the hospital under the name Weyman C. Wannamaker, Jr., a tactic he often used to avoid publicity and overworked phone lines for the poor nurses and the public relations department.

The day after we got to Emory, Friday, March 4, Dr. Martin walked in Lewis' room with a concerned look on his face.

Randy had not been like an ordinary physician, but more like a member of our family — the brother Lewis had never had, a best friend, a confidante. He'd cancelled several vacations to stay with Lewis when he needed him, and on the previous New

Year's Eve he'd given me a much-needed night off and told me to go out with my girlfriends while he sat up with Lewis. It was Randy who pushed Lewis around in a wheelchair among the tulips at Emory on Easter Sunday 1993, Randy who rubbed his feet when they were swollen, Randy who helped him out when the "bloodsuckers" could no longer find a vein. It was a love and compassion that went far beyond what mere duty required.

And now Randy had to deliver the worst possible news to Lewis: a fungus had attached itself to the Dacron patch on his heart. They would administer antibiotics, but because the patch was a foreign object, there wasn't a lot of hope of killing the parasitic growth.

Randy and Lewis cried together.

'Why Me? Why Now?' No Answer

Steve Enoch is president of Atlanta-based Enoch Entertainment, which provides management and financial planning for artists and entertainers.

This was the worst possible news Lewis could have received. Medication would not be able to control the infection that was attacking his artificial heart valve.

After Dr. Martin delivered the news and tried to comfort Lewis, he left the room. Just the two of us remained. Out of our silence, Lewis asked me if I had ever seen the movie "The Avengers." I wasn't sure, but I nodded yes anyway. In the movie, he explained, Karl Malden played a Chicago cop who had a wife and child. He got sick, was hospitalized for a while, and then went home to find that his wife had moved out and left him. He was devastated and moped around for several months trying to get his life back together. Finally he met a girl who was good to him and cared for him. One day soon after meeting this girl, he answered a call about a domestic violence situation. When he arrived at the couple's house, a man opened the door and shot him point-blank in the chest. After tumbling down a long flight of stairs, the character, lying on his back and looking up at the sky, says, "Why me? Why now?"

"That's how I feel," said Lewis. "Why me? Why now?"

I said nothing.

A few minutes later Lewis said, "Ron Gant can't hit in the World Series."

"Huh?" I asked, dumbfounded.

"In the Georgia-Florida game last fall," he continued, "the damned Florida official saw the Georgia receiver call time-out with only four seconds left, and Georgia ended up scoring on the play. The official said the play was no good because time-out had been called, so they come back and run the play again, but this time Georgia doesn't score and Florida wins the game. The official saw the receiver call time out right before the ball was snapped, so they couldn't get a break. I can't get a break, and today's the day I needed one. Ron Gant can't hit in the World Series and I can't get a break."

A Reason To Fight Even Harder

BY DEDRA GRIZZARD WITH JUDSON KNIGHT

Dedra Grizzard is the widow of Lewis Grizzard. She lives in Atlanta and is partner with Steve Enoch in Bad Boot Productions, which controls the intellectual properties of Lewis Grizzard.

As soon as I heard the terrible news, I called my minister, Don Harp, again — this time not to plan a wedding but to pray for Lewis.

How we got from one Friday to the next is a blur. I put Jordan in therapy dealing with death, just in case. By Friday, March 11, it had become clear that the fungus wouldn't go away; it was the beginning of the end, and now we knew it. There were decisions to be made, specialists to be called, friends to be told, and prayers to be prayed. We needed just one more miracle, and I believed with all my heart that we had one left.

Randy didn't let us maintain any illusions about the operation: it was a long shot, he said, at best a fifty-fifty chance. That was when Lewis, with tears in his eyes, asked me to marry him. "I want you to have my name if something should happen to me," he said: it would be a source of strength for him, and getting married before the surgery would give him a reason to fight all the harder. It would be the edge he needed to survive.

Sometimes when the nurses weren't looking, he'd get me to

go with him into the bathroom of his hospital room, which was his "secret" place to go smoke. (Of course it was about as secret as a billboard, but as long as he smoked only in there, the hospital staff looked the other way.) One afternoon near the end, we went in there and he made me promise I would never leave him. I promised. He must have said "no matter what" a hundred times, and just as many times, I promised that no matter what, I would never leave him.

I meant it. Lewis was my everything: my friend, my lover, my confidante, my teacher, my parent, my child. He was now to be my husband, too, and a father to my daughter.

We planned the wedding for Wednesday, March 16. The planning gave us something positive to focus on, and it lightened both our hearts at a time when we felt enormous fear and dread.

We at first intended to have the ceremony in the hospital chapel, but Lewis' guest list ballooned from ten to fifty in just twenty-four hours, and that number of people added to my own family and friends would have been too much for that little chapel. Someone suggested the new Carlos Museum on the Emory campus, but Randy didn't favor letting Lewis go even that far from the hospital itself. We ended up without too many options, so we decided on a room in the cafeteria with enough space for seventy people.

Lewis got himself into a terrible predicament by asking two of his closest friends, Ernie Cain and Tim Jarvis, each to be his best man. He soon became more worried over that than the surgery, thinking surely the one who got left out would feel slighted. How can you have two "best men"? It's not even a term that's made to be pluralized.

Then on Wednesday, the day of the wedding, I left him for a few minutes to get a blood test (an easy thing to do, given our location). When I returned I found him looking awfully chipper. "I've got it, Mama!" he announced. Ernie, he explained, could give me away, and Tim could stand beside Lewis at the altar. *Voila!* Two best men.

My choices weren't as complicated: my sister Shelley was my maid/matron of honor, and as we'd planned from the begin-

The Wedding Party: (L-R) Dedra's mother Gail Hill Vann, Ernie Cain, Shelley Kyle, Dedra, and Tim Jarvis with Jordan and Lewis

ning, Jordan was our flower girl.

On Wednesday night, our wedding guests — including doctors, nurses, and PR people — all gathered in the cafeteria. Along with them came the media, who had sniffed out the story and arrived in droves with cameras and notebooks at the ready. Dick Feller and Timmy Tappan, the musicians who traveled with Lewis on his concert tours, came in from Nashville to sing a special song for us. Lewis' Aunt Una and his stepfather, H.B. Atkinson, drove up from Moreland, and my mom came from Columbia, South Carolina.

This was not a traditional wedding in terms of dress or location or anything else, including the part about the bride and groom arriving separately. Randy led Lewis and me the back way to the cafeteria, through the kitchen to avoid the newspeople. Lewis made cracks the whole way.

Just before the wedding, he told Don Harp something that pretty well summed up how much he'd learned about marriage from his years of experience: "When she tells me to sit down and shut up, I understand those words." (Actually, he inserted a litte salty terminology between "shut" and "up" — and in front of the preacher!) "I've finally figured it out," he continued. "A relationship isn't about winning — it's about listening."

That really touched me, even though he hadn't really become as docile as he made it sound. I don't think I would have liked it if he had, but he'd certainly gotten a lot more used to give-and-take.

Then the music began to play, and I was walking down the aisle on Ernie's arm. There sat Lewis in his wheelchair, crying. We said our vows, and again he made me promise never, ever to leave him — "in sickness and in health" — and I felt those words more strongly than I have felt anything I've ever spoken in my life.

Lewis put the ring on my finger, and I did the same for him. Then he did something unusual and unforgettable: he leaned over and placed a ruby and diamond ring on Jordan's finger. They both cried. Don Harp said he had married hundreds of couples, but never had he seen anything like what Lewis did — truly we were all three married now.

Afterward, Lewis had two-and-a-half pieces of wedding cake, which was

Double Ceremony: A ring and a kiss for Jordan

strawberry and freshly made by my caterer. Then he posed for pictures with his friends, relatives, and golfing buddies, with my family — and, of course, with the blushing bride.

The next day, Thursday, March 17, the day before his surgery, Lewis again sat me down for a talk, this time at the foot of his bed. I was reluctant to listen because I knew he wanted to discuss the possibility of his death, but I listened anyway.

First of all he thanked me for Jordan, and said he'd truly loved her as if she were his own flesh and blood. He looked at me and said, "I don't want you to be sad if I don't make it. Jordan is going to need a *father*, and I want you to get on with your life."

He drew me closer and I thought he was going to whisper something desperately romantic that I would carry with me forever. But instead he looked at me over the top of his glasses and said, "But if he has a ponytail and an earring, I swear I'll come back to haunt you every day that you live."

He told me he missed his Mama, and he spoke of things she'd done for him, how she and he had saved pennies in a shoe box for his

Tears of joy and fear mixed for Lewis and Dedra

college education. Tears came rolling down his cheeks as he promised me I would never have to do that with Jordan. Part of me wondered if she would appreciate her education as Lewis had his — I doubted it.

He pleaded with me to not be sad if he should die. He'd lived a full life, he said, and had done more in forty-seven years than most people did in a lifetime. I knew that was true.

He told me he loved me more than I would ever know.

The next morning, Friday, March 18, they rolled him out of his hospital room. It was the most helpless moment I have ever known on this earth.

I suddenly wanted to be alone with him to reassure him, to tell him all of the thousand things that had just occurred to me in that instant when we said good-bye.

But the orderlies kept going, wheeling him away. I ran alongside of him and kissed him. I told him how much I loved him and that he had to live — for us, for Jordan and me. I wanted to scream it to him: "You have to live!" But I didn't.

The orderlies kept moving, pushing him toward his destination. I had never loved him as much as I did in that moment when I knew he was slipping away from me. I went to my knees, crying hysterically. Everything was completely out of my control.

The operation took nine hours, and when it was done the doctors and nurses seemed to think that it had gone well. I wanted to believe them, but an uneasiness kept creeping up on me. *There's something wrong here,* I said to myself, unable quite to put my finger on it. One of Lewis' favorite expressions came to me: *This is a ho-ax,* a hoax. It played over and over in my mind. Everything had gone just a little too smoothly.

At some point on Saturday morning, I remember thinking that he looked at Jordan and me sitting beside his bed — or at least that he flinched when he heard our voices. It may have been merely a figment of my imagination, but in my heart I want to believe it was so, because it would have been his last acknowledgement, his last gesture of love.

It was now March 19, and I had spent virtually the entire time since February 25 — twenty-two days, around the clock — with Lewis in the hospital, first at Florida Regional and then at Emory. I was exhausted, and the doctors told me I should get some rest.

They assured me Lewis would need me more later than now, and this time around I understood what that meant: Once he woke up and got that tube out of his mouth, I wouldn't get another moment's rest for at least sixty days. He'd most likely have complications, which would mean a long recovery, and he'd be a bear to live with. But by football season, I assumed, he'd likely be back to normal.

Then we could take our honeymoon in Italy. Then we could play house. Then we could begin to make the baby he so desperately wanted. It would be the beginning of a whole new life for all of us. Happy thoughts raced through my mind.

And so I let them talk me into going home for a while. I picked up Jordan and took her with me to Piedmont Park, where we spread a blanket and lay beneath a peaceful afternoon sun.

Without my noticing it, living for the past month indoors with only fluorescent light above me, the world had passed from winter into spring. The dogwoods had bloomed, and the sight of them and the smell of perfume in the air had brought all of the city outdoors to experience the richness of the season. If there's ever any time and any place to believe in hope, it is Atlanta in the last weeks of March and first weeks of April.

But at 3:00 p.m. on the afternoon of Saturday, March 19, I didn't feel that way. As I lay on the blanket, I had the sensation of something passing by me, something I couldn't see but could only feel. It was like a slight wind brushing my face, a breeze that was not physical; then the most overwhelming fear and horror filled my body, and I felt sick at my stomach. Nausea swept over me, and I wanted to throw up whatever food I'd managed to put down in the past twenty-four hours. *Lewis,* I thought. *Something is wrong with Lewis!* I raced back home and called the ICU.

No one could seem to tell me anything. A doctor would call me back, they said. So I hung up and waited. Ten minutes passed. I called again. "The doctor will call you back." No one would tell me that Lewis was *not* OK, but I knew....

I jumped in the car and rushed to the hospital, just five minutes away. By the time I got there, they had taken Lewis down for an emergency CAT-scan.

I waited, and it was like sitting on a chair made of nails. Finally the doctors came down the hall, pushing Lewis on a gurney. From their expressions, I knew that they brought with them the worst possible news.

In particular, I will never forget the look on Mary German's face. She had held Lewis' hand through three separate hospital stays, and like Randy, she was more a member of the family than just a nurse at the hospital.

With words she finished telling me what her eyes had already said. Lewis had suffered a massive stroke, possibly as a result of debris floating around in his body after the operation, and as she described it, "his brain was squashed" by the stroke. Both sides were completely blocked, and they gave him no hope at all.

His left pupil had dilated at 3:00 p.m., and his right twenty minutes later; soon after that, his brain had died. Three p.m. — had it been his spirit stopping off to tell me he was on his way home, or only the connection we shared because of our love and all we'd been through together?

As for what I felt and how I reacted in the hours that followed, it's hard to explain it in rational terms, because we don't experience the death of someone we love in a rational way. I went around and around in a cycle of disbelief, helplessness, hopelessness, and anger. Emotions ran rampant in my soul.

First of all I couldn't believe that this was really happening, and I kept praying that I would wake from my nightmare. And after I didn't, there was nothing left to do but cry. When the pain became too great, I drifted in and out of consciousness.

Lewis was gone, and with him all our dreams together, all our laughter, all our hopes. I tried to be thankful for the time we'd been able to share, but sadness overwhelmed me. After all the promises we'd made to one another, the vows we'd exchanged for a life together that stretched on into the distant future, I was left alone. My faith was battered. What could God be teaching me now? I'd had to learn so many lessons in the last four years — what good could Lewis' death serve?

As I continued to think these thoughts through the long hours as the shadows fell on Saturday, Lewis Grizzard remained technically alive. They had him on a respirator, which breathed for him, and ironically enough, his heart was beating just fine.

We all agreed Lewis was stubborn, a fighter in everything he did in life. He would also be stubborn in death. Dr. Martin told me his blood pressure was dropping and the body would surely pass once they turned off the machine. Still Lewis, or at least the shell that had housed him, hung on. As though he were still somehow there, I talked to him and prayed with him. I called Gilbert Steadham, his preacher, and he came and we prayed.

I think that over the course of that long, murky Saturday

night, many friends came and said their good-byes. Lewis' aunts, Una and Jessie, came. My sister Shelley was there, helping me through. Many others passed through his room, but I have no recollection of who. God has a way of relieving some of our grief with a loss of memory.

Dr. Martin talked to me about using Lewis' heart for research. I said I thought he would want that. Unbeknownst to me, Lewis had signed a living will, and I was thankful when I learned that, because I couldn't believe Lewis would want to artificially sustain his life after *he* had departed his body.

On Sunday morning, March 20, Lewis was still with us. Randy had suggested we turn off the respirator, and so at 10:44 a.m., just a quarter of an hour before church services would begin all over the city, we did.

Before our eyes, Lewis' body was beginning to turn blue due to lack of oxygen. But I wasn't looking at the physical object before me; in my mind's eye I was seeing our whole life together, from our first meeting to the last time I remembered him smiling at me. I thought of him at our wedding and the doctors wheeling him away from me before that last surgery.

Then suddenly that vision was blocked, and instead I saw Lewis in a black tuxedo, standing before a train in a station. He looked handsome and very healthy, not at all like I'd seen him in the past year. His face was content and solemn, and there was no pain in his eyes. He was well; he was whole.

I could hear the engine roaring, and billowing clouds of white smoke filled the air. In a moment it would pull out of the station, going — where? He wore a top hat, which he tipped to me as if to say farewell. He gazed straight into my eyes, saying good-bye, and then he turned and boarded that train and rode away.

Afterward, in the physical world of his hospital room, I held his body and cried, and the nurses in the ICU cried with me. I sat with him for a very long time.

Over and over, in a whisper like a prayer, I said the words of the Twenty-Third Psalm. Years before, I'd sat beside my dying father in a Birmingham hospital and recited the same verses; what more can you say at a time like that?

Finally I gathered my composure and left Lewis lying in that sterile hospital room. Just the day before, all my hopes and thoughts and prayers had been tied up in that place, and now it was only a room, an empty space. It was over.

I walked out of the ICU and into a firestorm of flashing cameras and TV lights, an explosion of questions and microphones and reporters' faces. For the first time in at least twenty-four hours, I felt an emotion that didn't have anything directly to do with Lewis and me and my grief: anger at this distasteful journalistic ritual. I understood that these people had a job to do, but what about the job of being human?

As I drove away from Emory, I noticed that the wisteria was in bloom. People passed me on their way to church, others out jogging or simply driving around and enjoying a beautiful day. Most of them would soon pick up their newspapers or turn on their radios and learn that Lewis Grizzard, last reported to be in stable condition, had died; and at that news, many of them would shake their heads and say how sad it was to lose such a hometown favorite.

There would be much sadness throughout the Southland when the word went out that he had died, but for me the entire world had come to a standstill.

A year before, I'd prayed that God would give him one more year, and He had — almost to the day. *I only asked for a year,* I thought, and the tears began to roll down my cheeks. *Why couldn't I have been brave enough to ask for ten? Twenty?*

But maybe things had turned out as they were meant to be. We'd gotten our miracle after all: it had been that final year together, that year that had changed everything for Lewis and me.

Beating The Odds – Again And Again

By Dr. Randy Martin

Randolph P. Martin, M.D., is the Director of Noninvasive Cardiology and a professor of medicine in the Division of Cardiology at Emory University School of Medicine. He resides in Atlanta.

I quoted Lewis Grizzard long before I met him. His book about his first heart surgery in 1982, *They Tore Out My Heart and Stomped That Sucker Flat*, included some of the funniest things ever written about the medical profession, and I often used his lines in lectures I gave around the country. But when I finally got to meet him, the circumstances were anything but humorous.

Lewis was born with a defective heart valve that gradually calcified and narrowed, leading to his first heart operation — a replacement of his defective aortic valve. Shortly after the new valve was implanted, an abscessed tooth seeded his blood stream and a serious infection developed around the prosthetic aortic valve.

His second heart operation took place in the midst of this rip-roaring abscess, an infection that should have killed him. Miraculously he survived this operation, but putting a new artificial valve into the middle of an abscess pocket often leads to further complications, as it did in Lewis' case. With infection eroding the aorta, the second valve developed a significant leak.

Over time, this leak was causing both the destruction of Lewis' red blood cells, so that he was constantly anemic, and the enlargement and consequent decrease in the pumping action of his heart.

That's when I was asked by Dr. Thorne Winter, Lewis' long-time physician, to perform a special diagnostic ultrasound test-called transesophageal echocardiography. This is a procedure where a tube with an ultrasound crystal is passed down the esophagus, or food pipe, to a position behind the heart from where outstanding pictures of the heart can be obtained.

I had heard horror stories about how much Lewis hated doctors, and I was prepared for the worst when I met him in the emergency room for the procedure. However, we seemed to hit it off immediately and began a long relationship that was focused on keeping him alive.

It took me a long time to convince Lewis to have his third heart operation. But his heart was being ravaged by the effects of endocarditis, a significant infection of a heart valve or the lining of the heart, and he desperately needed the surgery. In classic Grizzard form, Lewis always said, "I wish I'd had 'outside carditis.'" He finally relented.

Once again, Lewis should not have survived his heart surgery. Not only did we discover extensive heart damage, but his heart refused to start following the surgery; he had to be maintained for five days with both a left and right ventricular assist device — something that few people have ever walked away from without a heart transplant. I'll never forget the words of Dr. Mark Connolly, the cardiac surgeon, as he removed the heart assist devices from Lewis: "Nobody will ever enter this chest again." But Lewis' heart started, and even more remark-ably, he then survived a life-threatening fungal infection that developed while he was in a coma for nearly ten days.

Shortly after he came out of the coma, I rolled him in a wheelchair outside Emory Hospital, thinking that the fresh April air would do him more good than any of the medicines we were pumping into his body. I pushed him across a portion of the campus where a professor had taken his class outside.

Despite his very frail condition, Lewis took one look at the professor and said, "He reminds me of Foster Brooks doing one of his impressions." This event crystallized in my mind how deep Lewis' intellect was, and how he saw humor in everything around him. He would need that sense of humor in the year ahead, the final year of his life.

That last year, although it was surely a gift, was one of incredible pain and suffering for Lewis...and for me, as his friend and physician. I believe it is only when you have the chance to watch an individual endure that sort of challenge that you get a true picture of the mettle of the person. I have physically seen Lewis' heart in the operating room three times, and I've seen it with tubes and pumps coming out of it, and I've seen infected valves being surgically removed from it. But witnessing his last year told me more about the man and his fiber than any microscope ever could have told me.

Lewis Grizzard was an incredibly strong individual. None of us can know the depth of his suffering that last year. It ranged from painful surgical repair of an infected abscess on his abdominal wall; to having a piece of his spleen die; to having an artery in his liver rupture, spilling nearly two pints of blood into his liver on the night after Christmas; to having an infected clot basically kill his right kidney. Any of these events would have taken a devastating toll on any of us, but Lewis survived each of them. His incredible will to survive and his enduring sense of humor gave him the power to go on. As one of my colleagues, Dr. Kamal Mansour, told Lewis once during the surgical cleaning of an open wound on his abdomen, "Lewis, you are strong — like a lion." Lewis loved that quote, and I think it described him perfectly.

In late February of 1994, I was in the Atlanta airport headed for a medical meeting in San Francisco when I received an emergency page. My office was calling to tell me that a cardiologist friend in Orlando, Dr. Bobby Boswell, had called to report that Lewis had been hospitalized with a renal infarct — a clot of material had gone to his right kidney and killed a portion of it. That started the two-week saga that ended with Lewis' last operation.

Jim Kennedy of Cox Enterprises, owner of the *Atlanta Journal-Constitution*, sent the company plane to Orlando to bring Lewis back to Emory. Shortly after his arrival, we did another in a series of transseophageal echocardiographic exams; as Lewis said to me, "I wouldn't expect anything less of you than the garden hose treatment."

I will never forget the minute during the procedure that I looked at Lewis' artificial aortic wall and valve; I saw a large, infected fungal mass, and I had the sinking feeling that I had just seen the probable cause of Lewis Grizzard's death. During the next two weeks we tried everything we could to forestall the inevitable — a fourth heart operation. We consulted not only with my outstanding colleagues but also with three internationally known cardiac surgeons in North America. The unanimous opinion was that if Lewis were going to survive, he needed another operation.

All of us knew that this operation carried incredible risk — no more than a 50/50 chance of survival for Lewis. The night he made the decision to go ahead with the surgery, the two of us

A Common Goal: Lewis and Dr. Randy Martin with their wives, Dedra (L) and Anne (R)

cried and hugged each other as he begged me to help him get through the surgery. As I told him then, and as I feel now, I would have done anything to lift that burden from him, though we both knew that this was his only chance.

On March 18, 1994, Lewis underwent eight hours of surgery. Through the skill of Dr. Robert Guyton, it looked like he was going to survive the operation that no one expected him to. At a news conference that evening we were cautiously optimistic.

Through Friday night and into early Saturday morning, however, a gnawing sense of dread in my mind became a reality as Lewis failed to wake up. Moving a patient who is hooked up to all sorts of life support systems for a head CAT scan is a real *tour de force*, but we felt we had no choice. The CAT scan confirmed our tragic belief — that Lewis had suffered irreversible brain damage and would not survive.

Lewis, in his wisdom, had filled out a living will which empowered me, as his physician, to determine that if he had no chance for survival he would not be kept alive by unnecessary means. From Saturday afternoon and on into the night, we allowed Lewis' new wife, Dedra, and his family and close friends to visit Lewis at his bedside and come to grips with the inevitable.

Early Sunday morning, March 20, 1994, we went in to visit him one last time. James Shannon, Lewis' driver and dear friend, came out of the Intensive Care Unit and said to me, "He looks just like the Fish did before he died." James was referring to the peaceful look on Lewis' face, the same peaceful look James had seen on Lewis' beloved black Lab, Catfish, before he died on Thanksgiving 1993. Through tears we all tried to laugh.

Shortly thereafer we withdrew life support systems from Lewis. I'll never forget sitting in the 4-A ICU looking at the consoles that showed me his heart rate and EKG, watching the slow, steady spiral down toward a flat line. The living Lewis had left us.

So what did I learn during those final two years that I was Lewis' friend and physician? I learned that the grieving process is a real event which *all* of us must go through when we lose a loved one. I had truly come to love Lewis as a brother and as a patient. I had come to love his incredible strength, his boundless humor, his towering intellect, and his love for family, friends, and life.

We are all better for having known and read him. I did not truly understand how many thousands of lives this man touched until I saw the incredible outpouring of prayers and love for Lewis during his operations of 1993 and '94. Whether you agreed with his point of view or not, you couldn't help being touched by his sensitivity and his commitment to the things he believed in, and being impressed by his deep talent as a writer. He leaves an emptiness that won't soon be filled.

His Way Was The Right Way

BY JIM MINTER

Jim Minter, former editor of the Atlanta Journal & Constitution, is one of the country's most respected newsmen. He writes a weekly column from his home in Fayetteville, Georgia.

Up close, Lewis Grizzard was a very private person. Not everyone knows about his countless acts of kindness to friends and strangers: his work for the Heart Fund: bringing a young fan from Louisiana to Emory Hospital, where specialists tried to restore his sight.

Melissa Segars was a young woman, twenty-five years old, who had a dream. She wanted to go to college, become a veterinarian, take a cruise, get married and have a family. She wanted to be able to go places without being tubed to an oxygen tank.

Like Lewis, she had a congenital heart problem. Her only hope was an experimental operation in a St. Louis Hospital. The operation would cost more than a million dollars. Friends and neighbors in Fayetteville, a small town south of Atlanta, set out to raise the money. Lewis wanted to help. Melissa, who had won the hearts of everyone with her courageous and cheerful attitude, wanted to meet Lewis. Neither could have been naive about their personal odds.

Furman Bisher's wife, Lynda, arranged a luncheon. I drove

Lewis to the Bishers. He had been in bed all morning with a post-operative infection that made it painful for him to sit up, but he didn't let the pain show when he met Melissa. They hit it off.

They shared stories about their many experiences in surgery. Lewis deftly maneuvered to bolster her courage for the dangerous heart-lung transplant she was soon to undergo in St. Louis.

"They just give me a shot," he told her. "I never feel any pain or fear. Then I wake up." He didn't say three weeks later, after doctors finally got his heart beating again.

Melissa smiled. "That's the way it'll be with me," she said. She was so excited she couldn't wait to go to St. Louis. Soldiers have won medals with less bravery.

As we drove away, Lewis didn't speak for a long time. There was a deep sadness in his eyes. Then he spoke. "She's such a pretty little thing. So young. At least I'm forty-six years old and ugly."

A few weeks later Melissa died from complications following her transplant in St. Louis. Lewis developed more complications of his own. Miracles were running out.

Other than doctors at Emory, especially Dr. Randy Martin, his cardiologist and friend, nobody realized how sick Lewis was in his last years and months, or the pain he endured. James Shannon might have known. His dog Catfish might have. Dee Matthews, his guardian angel from Albany, Georgia, and Gerrie Ferris, his secretary at the newspaper, might have known. He was good at hiding pain. When he had to leave a party early, he'd make it look as if he had downed a couple of vodkas too many. The truth was he was hurting, or the abscess in his stomach had started bleeding.

Lewis first hired James to chauffeur him to speaking engagements. At the end, James was probably Lewis' best friend. He moved in with Lewis. In that long last summer, when Lewis was too sick to go out of the house, he sat with James and Catfish, watching practically every televised pitch of the baseball season.

Each morning James brought Lewis his *Constitution*, folded to the crossword puzzle, where Lewis began his day after looking over the front and sports pages. On especially bad nights, when he was hurting so much even pills wouldn't let him sleep, he would get out of bed to sit for a while on his front porch. Almost before he settled in his rocker, James would be there, not saying anything. Just there.

The day before his last operation, Lewis worried about what would happen to James if things didn't come out right. When they didn't, James told me he had lost his best two friends, Catfish, who had died a few months earlier, and now Lewis. Then James left town. He said he could never work for anyone else.

How Lewis continued to write his column, make speeches, play golf, and carry on a reasonably normal life for as long as he did is a mystery. How he kept his sense of humor is a larger mystery.

Capt. Lewis M. Grizzard, Sr., United States Infantry, war hero, would have been proud. Lewis wondered if he had the courage to do the things his daddy did. He answered his own question. He did.

In his last days, facing an operation and knowing the odds were slim to none, needing powerful painkillers to endure the long nights, he entertained a stream of friends and family with hilarious stories about growing up in Moreland, about Chicago, about characters in the old *Journal* sports department.

Every day he planned to resume his column. He had James bring his typewriter to his hospital room, but he was too weak to get past the first paragraph. When company came, he climbed back on stage, playing his comedian's role.

A nurse asked how he was feeling. "Did you see 'Schindler's List' (the movie about Nazi concentration camp survivors)? I'm third from the left."

When Dudley Stamps and David Boyd brought a barbecue sandwich from Sprayberry's in Newnan, he pushed away the half dozen tubes stuck into his various parts, ordered a large Coke, and dined with relish.

When Myrna and Loran Smith, old friends from Athens, dropped in on a particularly bad day, he griped about the food, the needles, nurses and doctors who had cold hands, interns who woke him in the middle of the night.

Loran and Myrna said they had to leave. "Before we go," Loran said, "there's something I want to tell you, so you won't you hear it from someone else. I've been diagnosed with leukemia."

"I felt like the all-time jerk," Lewis said later. "Here I am whining about my aches and pains, and Loran has leukemia!"

He said as soon as he got out of the hospital he was going to write a book about dogs. He said he was going to buy Furman Bisher, who had moved to the country, the most expensive riding lawn mower he could find — thanks for having Jim Kennedy fetch him from Orlando in the company jet.

He read the newspaper every day, complained about errors, second-guessed editors, and agonized over the sorry state of journalism. He thought of a thousand things they ought to be doing down at the newspaper. He was an editor to the end, as God might have intended.

Some folks at the newspapers didn't appreciate Lewis and his mostly World War II values. Many of the young turks who had come aboard were children of the '60s, either wet-behind-the-ears northern kids or natives feeling guilty about being born south of Cincinnati. Lewis didn't go out of his way to make himself loved.

Not all women appreciated his humor. Wives of new newspaper executives who had moved with their husbands to Atlanta were incensed when he wrote that northern women don't shave their legs.

In 1982, my wife and I traveled with the *Journal-Constitution*'s new publisher, David Easterly, and his wife to New Orleans to see Georgia play in the Sugar Bowl. On New Year's Eve we were having dinner at Antoine's. The conversation got around to Lewis, as conversations often did.

Julie Easterly, a charming young woman who before marriage had been a reporter in Ohio, said something to the effect that Lewis' claim about northern women not shaving their legs was libelous, defamatory, mean-spirited, and why did we permit such lies in our newspaper?

David, once a reporter and editor himself (later president of Cox Enterprises, which owns the whole works), is a Texan with a good sense of humor and a tolerance for employees who write daily columns. When I remarked that Lewis was also dining in Antoine's that evening, David set out to find him and bring him to our table. "I'm going to have him feel your calf," he told Julie, "so he will know northern women really *do* shave their legs."

Julie protested. David ignored her and was off searching Antoine's cubby-hole dining rooms. "I could kill David," Julie confided. "I forgot to shave my legs this morning!"

David came back with Lewis, who never got around to testing his theory on Julie's legs. He stayed for a long time entertaining us with his stock of newspaper stories. When he left, he had another fan.

One of the things Lewis planned to do, if he survived his last operation, was to patch up a relationship with *Journal-Constitution* management that had gone sour. His editors killed some of his columns, toned some of them down, and called him off some his favorite targets: militant feminists, pompous civil rights leaders, and men who wore rings in their ears.

Stars can be difficult to manage. Lewis was a star. But on my watch at the newspapers, I never had anyone more anxious to get the job done right, to please the bosses, or more appreciative of breaks that came his way. When he wrote a questionable paragraph, all I had to say was, "Lewis, do you really want to say this?" He'd grumble and say, "Aw hell, I guess you're right." Many times he'd drop by the next day to say thanks.

That's not to say he didn't cause some grief. For example, there was his column about the young lady who wore tight-fitting jeans to a laundromat in Birmingham and then sued because she got pinched on the fanny. The women in the newsroom, including his own secretary, signed a petition demanding that I do something about his sexist column.

Because he punctured colored balloons as well as white ballons, he was accused of being racist. He wasn't, any more than most of us, of whatever hue we happen to be. Anyone who claims to be absolutely free of racism needs to ask some questions: Where do I live? Where did I go to school? Where do I go to church? Who did I date, and who did I marry? Who did I invite to dinner last night? Part of Lewis' role was to prick egos and underscore stupidity, two items on which no one race holds a monopoly.

They make a living on "Saturday Night Live" by asking such questions. Mike Royko does it all the time in Chicago, but he wasn't born in Moreland, nor did he attend the University of Georgia. He may not even own a country music album.

If a strident edge crept into some of Lewis' later columns, it was probably because he felt so rotten, and because when offended liberatti took potshots, he was inclined to shoot back.

He was never healthy after a wisdom tooth went bad on a trip to Russia. By the time he got back to London, he was desperately ill. They gave him a shot and shipped him home to Atlanta on Delta, to one of the suburban hospitals where the staff didn't know much about his case. This was before Dr. Randy Martin came on the scene.

When I saw him in the hospital, he had a raging fever and was talking out of his head. He looked like he might not make it through the afternoon. I went into the hall, called his doctor at Emory, and told him Lewis was going to die. I'm no doctor, but I think my diagnosis was right. Within hours he was at Emory, being readied for surgery and a second pig valve. He barely made it.

Perhaps if he had gotten that wisdom tooth pulled before he went to Russia, he would be alive and well and writing his column today. Why didn't he understand that with a pig valve inside your chest an infection from a bad tooth can be fatal? Why didn't the doctors make him understand?

Although his doctors knew better, he knew better, and I knew better, I never really expected Lewis to die. I thought Randy Martin and the Emory surgeons could raise the dead. They had done it once.

For a long time, I'd almost pick up the phone when I read something in the newspaper I wanted to talk about. I expected his call on Sunday morning to analyze the Georgia football game and point out how the paper didn't cover it worth a damn.

I thought I understood, more than most, how really good he

was. I knew he had a huge following. But I didn't have a clue, until after his death and the massive outpouring of love and grief. The letters still come, from all over the country, saying how much he was loved, how much he is missed. A surprising number of them begin, "I'm a Yankee but...."

A letter in the *Jacksonville* (FL) *Times-Union* was signed by somebody named Roderick Bryant.

"I used to feel that all southern white men were in the Ku Klux Klan, or at least sympathized with it. Then I started reading Lewis Grizzard's column about ten years ago. He displayed a sensibility that his peers lacked, along with a distinctly lyrical style of writing that could only be acquired south of the Mason-Dixon Line. Grizzard's columns expressed his viewpoint without having to humiliate anyone to do it. I am a young, black, and somewhat militant man, but I truly would have loved to have had a conversation with Grizzard. We could have talked about Georgia football or Florida fishing, or just shot the breeze. Grizzard evoked memories of warm evenings spent on the porch, sipping iced tea with your dog at your feet. The only downside to that is you have to go inside sometime. Take it easy, Lewis, I'll talk to you later."

Roderick Bryant pretty well summed up the life and times of Lewis Grizzard.

Some evenings I sit on my front porch and wonder: What would have been his impact on Atlanta and Georgia if he had stuck to local subjects and never been syndicated? Why did his editors (mainly this one) insist on making him write five columns a week? (Try one a week and see how fast the sack empties!) What would have happened if he had become top editor on a large newspaper? What if he had been given, or taken, the time to write novels? What would he have said about the O.J. Simpson trial and the baseball strike? And the biggest what if of all: What if he hadn't come down with that bad wisdom tooth in Russia?

I wonder about those things, but I don't worry about them. Like Sinatra, Lewis did it his way, and when the box score is totaled, he did it right.

Memories Keep The Spirit Alive

By Dedra Grizzard with Judson Knight

Dedra Grizzard is the widow of Lewis Grizzard. She lives in Atlanta and is partner with Steve Enoch in Bad Boot Productions, which controls the intellectual properties of Lewis Grizzard.

As I write this, Jordan is six years old, and thank God she's a happy child, stable and strong and full of life. Whenever she says "Daddy," it's Lewis she means. Oftentimes she'll bound down the stairs of our house and say, "Mommy, wouldn't it be nice to see Daddy sitting in his chair, typing on his typewriter?"

And when she says this, sometimes it's hard to reply. Even now, I can hear

Mother and daughter and an empty space

those keys clicking in the sunlit breakfast room, smell that cigarette burning in the ashtray as he rubs his forehead and struggles for a word, and hear that sweet voice calling into the kitchen, "Mama, another cup of coffee, please!"

It's been hard to bury him, and I mean that literally at least as much as I do figuratively.

For a long time before his death, Lewis had discussed with me the things he wanted done when he died, and we'd made a list. Drunk, sober, before operations and after, one thing had never changed: He wanted to be cremated and sprinkled on the fifty-yard line at Sanford Stadium in Athens.

Neither of Lewis' aunts, his mother's sisters Jessie and Una, liked the part about cremation or the fact that I intended to honor his wishes. Aunt Jessie insisted that we have a traditional service for Lewis, and bury his body beside his mother's. Aunt Una went along with the cremation plan, honoring Lewis but still not quite understanding.

I tried desperately to hit a happy medium. I certainly hoped to please Una and Jessie, who had been very important in Lewis' life. Being the "new" wife, I wanted more than anything to do the right thing.

But my first duty was to Lewis, who had often expressed his fears of closed coffins and deep dark holes. He would be scared just *knowing* that he was in a box six feet under the ground, he said; that knowledge might be God's way of making him pay for the sins of his younger years.

I ended up agreeing to have an open casket ceremony for friends and family. I didn't think Lewis would have approved, but I did it for Aunt Jessie and Aunt Una.

As it turned out, Jordan was the main person to benefit from this. Dr. Martin and the Emory staff had fixed everything that had ailed Lewis in the last year, and she'd been convinced that if we took Lewis back to Randy one more time, he would give him a new heart. She needed closure.

To the funeral home Jordan took a troll doll that she wanted to put in Lewis' casket. She also wrote him a letter by herself, only asking me to spell the words:

I love my Lewis. I will be with Lewis forever.
Jordan

She walked in and saw Lewis lying there. She touched him and he was cold. There was no movement. She didn't like the smell of his body, she said, but I knew when I saw her beautiful green eyes welling up with tears that she finally understood.

We cremated Lewis with the doll that Jordan had put in his casket, and to make everyone happy, we buried half of his ashes beside his mother in Moreland. I secretly sprinkled some on his father's grave in Snellville, Georgia. The rest I kept with me until just the right time.

Meanwhile, there was much to be done in the aftermath of Lewis' death. As "the widow Grizzard," I had my own place in the limelight, and though the vast majority of people were very kind, there were a couple of bad apples who wrote cruel things, trying to make me appear as a golddigger. One reporter even had the audacity to question my choice of clothing for Lewis' funeral.

If Lewis had seen those types of stories, he probably would have rubbed his hands together and laughed. Lewis *loved* controversy and thrived on his hate mail, so he likely would have said, "Ain't it great just to have someone writing something about you?"

But I didn't have quite his stomach for it. It shocked me to see firsthand just how much damage the printed word could do to a real flesh-and-blood person. I wondered how any decent human being could write that sort of stuff about someone in mourning, a person with a child who will grow up and read those stories and perhaps wonder if they're true. In Lewis' stand-up comedy routine, he would always say, "You people write to me and ask me why we can't be more truthful and accurate in the newspapers. What do you want for a quarter — the truth?"

Fortunately, I had other things to keep me occupied. To protect us from getting broken into by Grizzard souvenir thieves, I put all of his stuff in his office. This was the inventory: five typewriters, a set of golf clubs, his clothes, a few pair of worn-out Gucci shoes, a leather jacket, photographs, golf trophies. He had many awards and keys to different cities he had gathered along the way. He had his railroad memorabilia and his hole-in-one golf club, ball, and score card framed. He had several pieces of crystal from playing in the Crosby Golf Tournament. He had a clock I'd given him for his birthday. He had an old bicycle I never saw him ride, and a tennis racquet I never saw him use.

And that was all that remained, in a physical sense, of Lewis Grizzard — that and the remainder of his ashes, which I kept in my bedroom for two and a half months.

At first it was frightening to have such a thing so near. But on several occasions I felt his presence, and it was a calming and peaceful feeling once I got used to it.

On June 16, 1994, I decided the time had come to fulfill his dying wish. I was now working with Steve Enoch on a daily basis, and after we left the office, we headed for my house and retrieved Lewis' ashes. Placing them between us in the car, we headed out of Atlanta down U.S. 78 toward Athens.

It was a gorgeous day, and along the way Steve and I got very sentimental over the man we'd both loved dearly. As we rode on that stretch which so often had led to a Georgia game in the past, we reminisced about Lewis, recalling our favorite Grizzard stories.

We talked mainly about the wild man, the character, the immortal LMG. That was a man who belonged to everybody. But I had memories more specifically my own, of the Lewis I knew in intimate moments — especially when we traveled together.

There was the time in San Francisco in May of 1992 when we stayed at the Ritz-Carlton on Nob Hill. I fell in love with the place. We'd driven north to see the redwoods, eaten a romantic lunch in Sausalito, even seen Alcatraz (Lewis' idea, of course). That was all in a day and a half, and then he had to leave for a speaking engagement.

To say good-bye to San Francisco after just thirty-six hours would have broken my heart, and he knew that, so even as I was packing my bags, he called the front desk.

"I'd like to reserve this room for Ms. Kyle," he said, looking at me, "for as long as she would like to stay." Then he summoned the bell captain to our room and handed him a $100 bill. "My lovely young fiancée," he announced, "will be staying in this fair city and hotel of yours indefinitely. I'd like to ask you to watch over her and make sure she has everything she needs."

It felt like something out of *Pretty Woman*. What a man!

Going back a little further, I remembered my thirty-first birthday in 1991, when he took me to Europe. First we went to Paris — dinner at Maxim's and La Sayers under the stars, the Lido and the Louvre — and then we caught the Orient Express to Vienna.

We were on the train for twenty-four hours. Lewis wore his tuxedo, and I a black gown from a vintage clothing store. There we were on Lewis' favorite form of transportation, recreating his favorite period in history, the 1940s. It was as if we had traveled back in time, and I could feel his passion for that simpler, more romantic era.

I was on the Orient Express with Lewis Grizzard! I had to pinch myself several times to make sure I wasn't dreaming. We spent most of the evening in the bar car, where Lewis asked the pianist to play our special song, "As Time Goes By."

In Vienna he showed me some place where Hitler had made an important speech. History was his thing, not mine — I couldn't have said for certain if Hitler was part of World War I or II. (I'm not joking.) We also saw a castle that had belonged to the dictator, we went to the opera, and we stayed at the wonderful Imperial Hotel.

From Vienna we traveled to London, planning to recuperate from our jour-

A Rare Sight: Lewis wearing a tie in Vienna

ney in the Dorchester Hotel. But then we noticed that there were people milling around, and it turned out that Pavarotti was giving a special concert in honor of Princess Di in Hyde Park.

This may have been the most spontaneous thing Lewis ever did with me. It was pouring down rain, but he purchased an umbrella from the concierge and ordered a bottle of Dom Perignon. Taking my hand, he led me toward Hyde Park, and there we hopped the park fence and, with eight thousand people watching, made our way to the front.

It was magical. We kissed and laughed and held each other until we were soaked to the bone. Then we returned to the hotel only to find that the performance was airing live on HBO. We watched the rest of the concert in front of the fire and ordered room service.

Still further back, I had a memory on the borderline between sweet and bittersweet. It was December 1990, and I'd finalized my divorce; to celebrate, Lewis and I went to Jamaica with Ron Hudspeth and Ron's girlfriend. We rented a house on the beach and oh, how the stories flowed between Lewis and his old running buddy Ron. I found out more about him that week than I wanted to know: He'd never intimidated me before then, but the stories I heard made it easy to understand why his past three marriages hadn't worked.

It was here that I began to ask questions both of Lewis and of myself. It was too late for me to give up on him or to walk away, for I had fallen in love.

I remember dancing on New Year's Eve on the cliffs in Ocho Rios under a full moon with "As Time Goes By" playing — that was before it became our song. He sang into my ear, and for the first time ever he whispered that he loved me. He held me in that old-fashioned way my daddy had done many years before, not like a '90s man but like a true gentleman.

He promised to make a difference in my life and vowed that "as long as it is good for both of us," he'd always stay. Those were the words I wanted to hear.

I remember feeling a little sick to my stomach that night. I loved him so much, and he'd said all the right things, but I was afraid he would break my heart. Still, I surrendered. *This is it,* I told myself. *He's the one for me.* God had smiled on us both, and together we would be happy.

As all those memories flooded through me on that drive to Athens, it seemed awfully hard to recollect anything that I hadn't liked about Lewis. But there were plenty of things I could remember that I'd loved:

I loved the way he opened the door for me and called me "darlin.'" I loved the way he peeked over his glasses at me and gave me fatherly advice. I loved the way he respected — maybe "worshipped" would be the word — his mother. I loved the way he understood me and always listened, and never criticized me for anything I ever did. I loved the way he loved my daughter and praised me as a good mother to her, my proudest accomplishment in the world.

A peek over the glasses meant fatherly advice.

I loved the way he laughed when he got really tickled, and I loved the way he told stories. I loved his voice and the way he looked in his Armani jeans. I loved to watch him win at a game of cards or a round of golf. I loved his stubbornness and his refusal to change. I loved his traditionalism and his longing for older, simpler times. I loved the fact that he could not sleep without me.

And now there Steve and I were on that gorgeous day, riding to Athens to take Lewis' ashes to their final place of rest. He had died a day before spring began, and today was almost the end of the season; it seemed like the right time to close that chapter.

He had told me that if it became a chore for me to do this, "Call Dudley — he's always dying to do something illegal." But this was something I wanted to do myself. I suppose we could have called the Dawgs' office, and they would happily have put together a special ceremony for the man who had so often praised their team in print, but again, I wanted to keep it simple.

Steve and I stopped for a six-pack of Bud somewhere along the way. We visited Lewis' father's grave at Zoar Baptist Church in Snellville, then continued on to Athens.

We rolled into town and found Sanford Stadium. It was empty, and it felt spooky in the way that places that often hold large and noisy crowds, but are for the moment completely silent, can feel. The somber mood over the vast building could not have been more appropriate for the occasion.

All the gates were locked. Steve scaled the fence, and I carefully handed the ashes, safe in a plastic bag, to him before climbing over; then we ran toward the fifty-yard line. We were sure we wouldn't be shot for sprinkling Lewis Grizzard's ashes on the field, but arrest was a possibility. That only added to the thrill.

We ran as hard as we could, and when we got to the middle of the football field, I realized that the yardage lines were not marked.

"What do we do?" I asked Steve in a panic.

"For God's sake, Dedra," he said, "just toss them. Lewis knows where the fifty is!"

So I dug into the bag, feeling for one strange, tingling moment the last remains of the man I loved; then I lifted a handful of ashes and tossed them into the air. They glinted in the sun, no longer gray and dead but turned to gold, as they drifted slowly earthward to the ground Lewis had cherished in life.